SWIPE THERAPY

MIRA SUMANTI

Copyright © 2025 by Mira Sumanti

All rights reserved.

No part of this book may be reproduced in any form or by any electronic or mechanical means, including information storage and retrieval systems, without written permission from the author, except for the use of brief quotations in a book review.

Disclaimer: The stories in this guide reflect the author's recollection of events. Some names, locations and identifying characteristics have been changed to protect the privacy of those depicted. Dialogue has been re-created from memory.

ISBN: 978-1-968339-00-5 (ebook)

ISBN: 978-1-968339-01-2 (paperback)

ISBN: 978-1-968339-02-9 (hardcover)

"The wound is the place where the Light enters you."

- RUMI

ADVANCE PRAISE FOR SWIPE THERAPY

"Mira Sumanti's story is a bold, bizarre deep dive into love, heartbreak, and self-discovery. Equal parts curious and chaotic, she treats life like a live experiment — tracking every twist, high, and emotional crash in search of something real. Love might be the mission, but unlocking herself is the true endgame.

A striking debut from a truly remarkable voice."

- IBTISAM OMER
a global marketing executive, also best friend and maid of honor (wildly unqualified to write this, deeply biased, fully complicit in several of her poor life choices — and yet, here we are)

TO ANYONE WHO'S EVER FOUND THEMSELVES SWIPING MINDLESSLY ON THE TOILET.

YOU ARE NOT ALONE.

CH. 01   P. 13

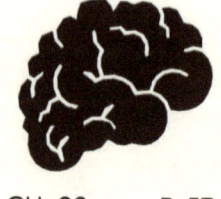

CH. 02   P. 53

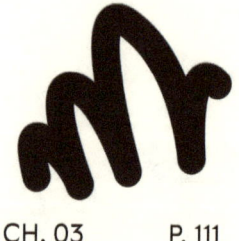

CH. 03   P. 111

CH. 04   P. 159

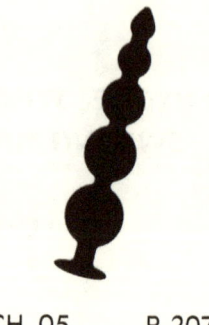

CH. 05   P. 207

CH. 06   P. 249

9	**PROLOGUE**
13	**CHAPTER 1: THE BREAKUP**
53	**CHAPTER 2: THE NEUROSCIENTIST**
111	**CHAPTER 3: THE REBOUND**
159	**CHAPTER 4: THE MISTAKE**
207	**CHAPTER 5: THE PORNSTAR**
249	**CHAPTER 6: THE WEDDING**
279	**CHAPTER 7: THE ONE**
339	**CHAPTER 8: THE PRAGMATIC ROMANTIC**
351	**APPENDIX** GUIDE: HOW TO SURVIVE A BREAKUP UP IN YOUR 30S
357	**ACKNOWLEDGEMENTS**
360	**ABOUT THE AUTHOR**
362	**ABOUT THE PUBLISHER**

CH. 07   P. 279

CH. 08   P. 339

PROLOGUE

"Please hit me," implored one of the highly intoxicated Japanese men at the bar. His speech was slurred and pleading. I was wearing a low-cut, cropped, studded leather vest and low-rise, belted shorts. I looked him in the eye, half of my butt cheek on display.

"Hit me," he repeated, the words thick with a Japanese accent, his breath reeking of one too many highballs. I regarded him with a mix of disbelief and dismay. He managed to straighten his body, close his eyes and respectfully bow his head, earnestly begging, "Please."

I ignored his request and maneuvered around him, making my way back to my seat in the narrow, red-lit, ten-seater bar. I sat at the far end of that space, with my chair positioned next to the stage and its metal (human) cage.

Absorbing the madness around me, two leather-clad Japanese ladies dashed towards me with wild enthusiasm. "Sugoi! Kawaii!" they exclaimed, clapping their hands and forming circles with their thumb and index fingers as a sign of approval. Their actions reminded me of characters from a Japanese manga—a surreal touch to the already bizarre setting.

I felt utterly wired thanks to the adrenaline rush from embracing my dominatrix persona in a Tokyo bondage bar mixed with the buzz from the drinks I'd consumed earlier. It was like the music in my head had been turned up a notch, transforming my heartbeat from minimal techno to full-on dubstep at 140 BPM—thunderous and syncopated. Shaking with a mix of fear and excitement, I settled back into my seat, palms together in gratitude, and smiled at the animated ladies before turning my attention back to the man I'd come here with.

"Wow...," Satoshi's jaw dropped. "You...look...a-ma-zing!" He looked like a kid given unlimited screen time, fixated on my transformed appearance. Meeting his drooling, inebriated gaze, I sensed a shift, a realization setting in. Our "relationship," if you could call it that, was about to take an irreversible turn.

"Alright then." I raised my glass, taking a large gulp of my vodka ginger beer. "Give me your arms." I began pouring the red, burning candle onto Satoshi's already blotchy skin. His fists clenched at the initial touch of the hot wax on his wrist, and he let out a moan, shutting his eyes as I continued the slow ascent of the candle up his arm, allowing the wax to accumulate. I paused at the bend of his elbow, letting the molten wax build up, drip by drip, over his pronounced veins.

His arms tensed up, trembling. He dug his nails into the palms of his hands, clenched his jaw and ground his teeth to stay quiet. And then, as one more heavy drip of wax brushed the sensitive inner fold of his arm, our eyes locked and he let out a scream—deep and orgasmic, blending pain with pleasure. My thoughts went haywire.

You know, I should have been married.
Uff...What the hell am I doing?
I didn't plan any of this!
How the hell did I end up here?
This trip should have been a part of our Japan honeymoon.
Maybe we would have been making babies now.
But here I am, in Tokyo with Satoshi doing...this.

You're probably wondering about that Satoshi dude, still moaning with pleasure from the pain I had inflicted on him. Nope. He was not my boyfriend. We'd actually just met again that night

after several years of not seeing one another and things kind of just...happened.
   So how did I get there?
   Alright, let's rewind...

Chapter 1

THE BREAKUP

IMAGE 1: *A text exchange, five weeks before our wedding date.*

I sat dumbfounded, staring blankly into my phone, alone in the empty Google Jakarta office on a Friday night. The building had an eco-friendly automated lighting system, which meant that I had to keep getting up to wave my arms every 30 minutes just to keep the lights from plunging me into darkness. My laptop screen stayed on, in hibernation mode, even though I wasn't working on anything at the moment. I caught a glimpse of my reflection on the black screen: a messy top-bun, mascara smudged under tired eyes. *Sigh*. Friday night, 8 pm and there I was, the lone occupant of the office.

I was waiting. I wasn't waiting for Jakarta's infamous Friday night traffic to clear, nor for a social invitation to officially kick off the weekend. I was waiting for him to leave. I refused to come home until I could confirm that my fiancé had departed our apartment and was en route to the airport, bound for Amsterdam.

The clock seemed to mock me as it ticked away—8:12 pm. Disappointment and anger took over as I reflected on the lines he had crossed, calling my mother names and abandoning our shared life just five weeks before our wedding. He had chosen to leave instead of getting his act together.

Finally, a text came through: "I'm in the cab to the airport." Great. It was time to pack my bag and leave. Home awaited, and I needed a drink. No, I needed *many* drinks.

Then came another text. "Oh, and I also took the 10 million cash at home because that's the only way I can leave this shit hole tonight."

I couldn't respond. I couldn't even breathe. His abrupt departure, coupled with the revelation that a significant amount of money—equivalent to $1,000—was missing, felt like the final blow. That's it. The end. In that moment, I knew deep down that any dreams of a wedding were shattered. There would be no postponement, no reconsideration. Nothing. Because there was no way any couple could come back from *that* low to "I do" in five weeks.

***

I got home that night and made myself a drink: vodka with soda water. I was still on my months-long wedding diet, so *fucking* soda water was the only mixer I had at home. Zero calories versus 124 per can of tonic water.

He had left the place in a mess. Traces of his escape were strewn all over our "shit hole" of a place, or I guess *my* shit hole. His drawers were empty and ajar, like gaping wooden mouths. His suitcases were nowhere to be found. The bathroom was stripped clean of his things save for one Gillette razor and his electric toothbrush charger. It didn't take a forensic scientist to conclude that someone *really* wanted to get the fuck out of there.

Oh, shit. And the money?

I headed towards the wooden drawer in the center of the bedroom—the repository of the refunded cash from my canceled Berlin bachelorette trip.

Please still be there. Please still be there. Please don't let it be...gone.

Stunned, I stood there, unmoving, I waited for the rage, sadness, mourning—*something*—to set in. But it didn't. It was as though this was happening to somebody else. I was a numb observer to my own life.

I...

FEEL...

NOTHING...

FUCK. When I feel nothing, it means that things are bad. Like *real* bad. My body switches to autopilot survival mode, activating my coping mechanism for when shit hits the fan: heart off, logic on—thank me later.

No.

No, no, no. Not this time.

My heart can't be off right now. I need to feel this. I need to freaking feel this. My fiancé just left the country, and I feel...nothing?!

I craved the release of a good cry, an exit from this numbness.

A song.

I need a song.

I need a song that can help me feel all these emotions.
Okay, Spotify.
I scanned the room to find my laptop. *Where the hell is it?*
Oh, there it is. Thank God.
And like fate, my frantic scrolling fingers stopped at Florence & Machine's "What Kind of Man." I hit play.

My whole heart screamed with Florence Welch's soulful voice: "What kind of man loves like this? / What kind of man?"
Why did he leave?
Was it all my fault?
How could I not see this coming?
As the soundtrack of the mournful night repeated in the background, I tortured myself with the same set of questions over and over and over again. By the end of the song's third replay, my heart finally switched on. Tears streamed down my cheeks, each one heavy. I collapsed onto the floor. Now the floodgates were open. At 29, my world was crumbling and my whole body ached with the knowledge that this was only the beginning of the end.

***

I woke up the next morning to a skull-maddening, vomit-inducing hangover—a delightful reminder of the copious amounts of vodka (and utterly useless soda water) from the night before. I glanced at myself in the mirror and found dark circles and puffy eyes accenting my #iwokeuplikethis look. Definitely not a moment for the Gram.

I reached for my phone, and a sense of dread settled in when I realized my fiancé hadn't bothered to make any contact while I was passed out throughout the night. *Sigh.* The only notification waiting for me was a reminder from my Google calendar about a flight I was supposed to take in about 12 hours.

Fuck. How on earth could I have almost forgotten about this trip?!

That day, I had a work trip lined up—a long-haul flight to Google's head office in San Francisco. The reason? My team, WorkBuddy, had clinched the runner-up spot in an internal Global Hackathon. We'd poured our brains into developing a smart job-finding app for blue-collar workers in emerging markets, specifically Indonesia. After weeks of virtual collaboration across borders, this trip was the golden opportunity to finally meet my team members face-to-face and present our winning plan together at the Tech Talk in front of various global Product VPs.

There's no way I'm ready for the presentation in front of the global leaderships!

Am I allowed to cancel this trip and call in sick for emotional distress?

Packing is the last thing I want to do right now.

At 1 pm and still no word from my missing fiancé. By that time, he probably had his feet firmly planted back in Amsterdam. Despite leaving him a barrage of voicemails, the only response I got was a text from his mother, coolly stating, "He is not ready to talk."

He's the one who bailed, leaving me stranded in this excruciating relationship limbo and *he* gets to decide when we talk? *Arrgghhhh.*

A decision needed to be made, and it needed to be made fast: wait around until he was ready to talk (in six hours? 24 hours? A week? God knows when) or just hop on a plane to San Francisco? With the processing power of my brain severely limited after a night of emotional outburst, I resorted to a pros and cons table:

	PRO	CONS
Stay in Jakarta	I don't need to pack	Waiting at home until I hear from him would KILL me
	I can go back to bed and continue to cry	I will need to explain to my boss why I am no longer going on the work trip
Go to San Francisco	No one there knows what's going on with me, I wont need to talk about it!	What if I have a mental breakdown when I'm there on my own?
	The Tech Talk presentation will be a good distraction	
	The long haul flight will give me time to think (and make him wait)	
	I actually like SF	

IMAGE 2: *The "Should I stay or should I go?" contemplation table*

My brain concluded that the benefits of going on The Trip far outweighed the convenience of staying put in Jakarta. Almost 24 hours of flying and blissfully being offline meant that, in case he tried to reach me, he'd be the one twiddling his thumbs in anticipation. Ha! Also, no one in San Francisco knew I'd just been dumped. Decision made.

***

I've always loved solo long-haul flights. There's this undeniable comfort and liberation in being alone, surrounded by a sea of other travel-bound strangers, officially cut off from the entire world.

The joy of not having any social obligation to chat with your seatmate (especially when stuck in economy) or the luxury of just lounging in your own private bubble for hours (a sweet bonus when work is footing the bill for a business class ticket) is something you don't encounter much on the ground. Despite my extroverted tendencies, I relish the chance to be completely antisocial on a flight. Phone off, hoodie up, headphones in—total serenity. No one can (or should) disturb me.

Now, seriously, why would the modern highflier world want to ruin one of the last sacred places on earth where you can genuinely disconnect from the digital world by having free Wi-Fi onboard?

So, here's my proposal: If you're on board with the idea of preserving this haven of digital detox in the sky, please sign my petition. Let's improve everyone's well-being in the air!

https://www.change.org/p/keep-wifi-off-flights

The other thing I love long-haul flights for is the precious time it affords me to pause and reflect. Ah, the bliss of reflecting without being incessantly interrupted by annoying notifications every couple of minutes. *Yes, Cita, your baby is adorable. No, Teguh, I don't need a play-by-play of your bubur Senopati breakfast. And Mario, please spare the high school WhatsApp group from your clickbait links!*

The quietness of the cabin when the lights dim and half the passengers are in dreamland creates the perfect backdrop for gazing back at the chapters of my life. They say because of the lower-than-normal air pressure in the cabin you're more emotional up there, making flying the moment I can connect better with my emotions—something I often need a little help doing. As a deliberate choice, I often pick the sappiest movie from the in-flight entertainment to let my tears flow freely in the sky. But this was no normal occasion.

Today's impending, dreadful flight to San Francisco filled me with the same sense of doom I had before my last emotional long-haul journey—my move from Amsterdam to Jakarta—just over a year and a half ago.

It wasn't just about moving back to the city I had called home until I turned 18; it also marked the start of a nine-month long-distance relationship with my fiancé. Boarding that "goodbye-for-now" flight felt like being forced, by strict Asian parents, to break up with your high school musician boyfriend. You knew it was the right decision for your future, but that didn't make it any less painful.

I did not want to get on that plane. But I did it anyway. And I couldn't help but feel sorry for my seatmate, a middle-aged Dutch man who watched with mild concern as I cried my eyes out for most of the flight. Strangely enough, despite all the initial fears and uncertainties, our relationship actually managed to weather the long-distance struggle until he made the move to Jakarta. And, well, that's when things started to nosedive.

At first, we were euphoric, relieved to finally be in the same city, no longer counting time zones or scheduling video calls. But reality quickly set in. He struggled to find his footing in Jakarta—the city felt chaotic, overwhelming, nothing like the carefree life he was used to in Amsterdam. Job hunting became a soul-crushing cycle of rejections, and when he eventually lost the startup gig he had been relying on, the stress only multiplied.

Meanwhile, we were knee-deep in wedding planning, an exhausting process made worse by cultural clashes, family expectations and a dwindling sense of stability. Every discussion turned into an argument; every small disagreement spiraled into something bigger. Love was still there, but it was buried under resentment, frustration and the creeping realization that maybe we weren't as indestructible as we thought.

***

That flight to San Francisco easily claimed the throne as my most unforgettable long-haul journey. Right up until the last boarding call, my fiancé remained unreachable. I had no clue whether we were still a couple, if we were just going to hit pause on the wedding plans or, for that matter, if he was even still alive. When were we supposed to have that talk? I had absolutely no freaking idea.

I should've been laser-focused on preparing for my Tech Talk presentation. Crafting a solid script, rehearsing until it was flawless—it was a golden opportunity to represent my country in front of the global team and shine in front of our Product VPs! But in that very moment, I seriously couldn't care less. *Screw it, I'm just going to wing it.* As the plane hit its 40,000-foot cruising altitude, more negative thoughts started sneaking in.

Was it all my fault?
Did I drive him mad?
Will we ever talk again? We have to. But when?
Could we ever get back together?

My head was spinning with these tormenting questions. I desperately needed a solid distraction before I spiraled into madness.

Just pick a movie, Mira.

But then, on second thought, I doubted my ability to commit to a two-hour-long movie in that state of mine.

Okay, TV shows then. Anything to divert my mind from the emotional tornado inside my head.

As I skimmed through the TV show list, *Jane the Virgin* caught my attention. *Hmm...interesting title.* The trailer hinted at an over-the-top romantic telenovela-style show. Perfect. A silly and funny show where I didn't need to use my brain was exactly what I needed. Let the brainless binge-watching commence!

Three hours and four episodes later, a strangely fitting episode unfolded with a wedding cancellation scene. Like a cosmic coincidence, Jane, the heartbroken and naive protagonist, voiced the very question echoing in my own mind: *How could two people go from wanting to marry each other to hating one another?*

And just like that, my eyes started to well up. Nothing resonated more than those words. The intense, hollow grief rushed back. I tried to control my tears, but it was futile. Well, I suppose this was the ability to feel that I had hoped for. I sobbed and sniffled into the sleeve of my trusted Y-3 sweatshirt, waiting for our descent.

Damn you, thin air up in the sky, for making me all emotional again!

***

The initial 48 hours in San Francisco felt like an eternity; I was holed up inside the trendy Clift Hotel downtown, trapped in an infuriating relationship and jet lag limbo.

All I could manage was to lie in bed, gaze at my phone and desperately hope that my fiancé would finally respond to my many messages (Hello? Are you alive? I miss you, babe. Pick up, damn it!).

I resorted to ordering room service whenever hunger struck, which mainly happened late at night since my belly was still operating on Jakarta time. The routine was simple: eat, pee, return to bed, cry and then rinse and repeat that pathetic cycle every couple of hours.

By the third day, I began to surrender the little remaining hope I clung to that he would eventually get back to me that week or perhaps *ever*. Was this how it was all going to end? Our three-and-a-half-year relationship concluded with my fiancé running away and ghosting me. *Brutal.*

As I prepared to cocoon myself in bed again that morning (I had craftily informed my colleagues that I'd be working from the hotel that day), a glimmer of hope flickered. I finally caught a glimpse of his status on WhatsApp: He was online at last. So, for what felt like the 273rd time, I summoned the courage to press the call button. To my surprise...he picked up.

"Hey..." I attempted to sound calm.

"Hi..." came his reply.

"Are you back in Amsterdam?"

"I'm in Utrecht..." His tone was cold and muted. "At my mom's place." It was like the warmth had been completely sucked out of him.

"I see..." I mulled over whether we should dive into the conversation then or wait like mature adults for an in-person discussion. However, the fear that he might disappear on me again pushed me to a decision. I can't let him leave me in another limbo for days. This needs to be sorted once and for all! And so, I cut to the chase.

"I guess there's no wedding, right?"

"No, I don't think so."

My stomach twisted. Deep down I knew that was an eventual possibility. But part of me had been hoping that the days of separation would bring him to his senses—that I would hear his warm voice, an apology, an admission that his departure was a mistake and a convincing plea to try again. We would make up and simply resume planning our dream wedding.

But no, none of that. Any chance of reconciliation was too late. Too many lines had been crossed. It was as if I was standing on the dance floor of a club after the music had stopped and the lights had come on. I wasn't supposed to be here.

NO WEDDING.

We will draft the cancellation email for the guests tomorrow.

We will figure out the finances later.

Oh, and it was also the end of our relationship.

When we both came around to saying it out loud—*no wedding*—we broke into tears. Separated by miles of distance, we shared a moment of sorrow, painfully agreeing to the one thing we knew would bring us unimaginable pain in the days, months and years ahead.

Memories of our relationship up until that day came flashing back: our first trip to Bali, the countless party nights and lazy Sunday sleep-ins, the New Year's Eve when he proposed to me. But as we ended our relationship, it felt as if someone had executed a right-click-and-move-to-trash maneuver on everything we had built. Three-and-a-half years of shared memories, laughter and tears—over.

The pain was undeniable, a sharp pang in my chest. But, even in the heartache, there was an unspoken understanding that perhaps this was the right course of action for both of us.

***

I had heard it a thousand times from those who had braved the wedding planning battleground—*it's never a walk in the park*. Still, as a starry-eyed bride-to-be, I dove headfirst into planning my dream wedding, fully aware that the road ahead would be bumpy. I expected the process to be stressful, frustrating even. And I wasn't wrong.

I could still picture it vividly—my fiancé's custom-made wedding pants, the ones he had been so excited about, finally arrived from the tailor. Only, instead of the perfectly tailored fit he had envisioned, they looked like they had been accidentally shrunk in the wash—too short, way too tight and completely unwearable. Cue the panic-induced tears.

There were also heated arguments with our wedding catering vendor, who, at the last minute, informed us that the menu tasting—something I had meticulously scheduled—could no longer happen on the planned day. The frustration, the scrambling to find solutions, the sheer exhaustion of it all—it was a never-ending cycle of mini-disasters.

Then there's the bureaucratic nightmare of dealing with Indonesian government officials for the pre-marital paperwork (who knew you needed a marriage recommendation letter and a health certificate from your RT [neighborhood association] and local community health center?!). It was a headache I never saw coming—a logistical labyrinth that made wedding planning even more stressful than it already was.

Navigating the maze of wedding preparations had its fair share of frustrations, but the vision of our perfect wedding day kept us moving forward. That dream, that promise of a celebration that reflected *us*, was what made it all worth it.

Our idea of a perfect wedding was a two-day love extravaganza on the enchanting island of Bali. We had imagined 150 of our closest friends and family flying in from all corners of the world, coming together for a celebration unlike any other. The soundtrack to our love story? It would be curated by none other than Optimo, our favorite DJ duo from Scotland—the same DJs who had energized countless dance floors where we had lost ourselves together. It was supposed to be magic. It was supposed to be unforgettable.

But marriage wasn't just about the wedding; it was about building a future together. I imagined us raising two adorable, bilingual, *hapa* Indonesian-Dutch kids, navigating the blend of our cultures with ease. After several years of our adventures in Asia, I pictured us eventually returning to Amsterdam, settling into the familiar rhythm of life there. I saw myself still immersed in the tech world, maybe at Google or some cutting-edge startup, while he embarked on his entrepreneurial journey, chasing the dreams he always talked about.

Once a year, our little ones would jet off to Jakarta to visit my mom and sister, connecting with their Indonesian roots. They'd also spend summers in Malaysia, where my brother, Uncle Dody, would put them through a rigorous quiz of math and physics—his own personal form of tough love that would probably leave them mildly traumatized.

Meanwhile, while the kids were off on their summer adventures, my partner and I would finally have the house to ourselves. I imagined us lounging in our Amsterdam apartment, indulging in a shared bottle of wine, laughing about the chaotic beauty of parenthood and the rare liberation of having a quiet moment together. The night would stretch on with easy conversation, lazy kisses and the kind of intimacy that only deepened with time.

We'd ride a mild buzz, wrapped up in each other, grateful for the life we had built. It was such a beautiful future. And for the longest time, I truly believed it was ours to have.

But then we said to each other: "*No wedding!*"

Just like that, years of dreaming, months of planning and countless wedding spreadsheets and Pinterest boards disappeared into thin air. The carefully crafted wedding we had envisioned—the one that had kept us going through all the chaos—was not to be.

No more enchanting first dance to "I Feel Love" by Donna Summer, with Optimo at the decks, setting the perfect rhythm for our celebration. No more exchanging heartfelt vows under the golden glow of a Canggu sunset, surrounded by the people we loved most in the world. No more epic wedding after-party by the villa's pool, fueled by music, laughter and the kind of love that makes you feel invincible.

Our dreamy autumn honeymoon in Kyoto vanished, too, the crisp scent of falling leaves, the soft rustling of kimonos as we wandered through ancient temples, the quiet mornings in a traditional ryokan, sipping matcha and marveling at how lucky we were. All of it—every meticulously laid plan, every shared excitement about the future—swept away in an instant.

Right-click. Move to trash. Gone forever.

The depth of the emptiness that followed was staggering. The logistical nightmare of unraveling everything we had built, canceling vendors, telling our families, answering the inevitable "what happened?"—it was suffocating. The crushing weight of anxiety pressed against my chest, tightening with every breath, threatening to consume me entirely.

And so, as you might have guessed, I went numb again. It was the only way to survive it all.

After I hung up from that phone call, everything else—the upcoming workday, the *big* Tech Talk presentation I had been preparing for weeks—suddenly felt inconsequential. Just background noise in the wake of something far greater crumbling around me.

A part of me shut down completely. My brain registered the motions—I knew I had tasks to complete, meetings to attend, responsibilities to uphold—but none of it mattered. My world had just collapsed, and yet, somehow, life expected me to carry on as if I hadn't just lost everything I had been building toward.

All I could think about was avoiding solitude in San Francisco for the next couple of days. I couldn't bear to be alone. I needed to call someone.

***

"Amir, can I crash at your place this week? I'm fine to sleep on your sofa." My voice reeked of desperation.

"Hey, is everything okay? I thought you're here for work. What happened to the work accommodation?" he asked, clearly puzzled.

"It's a long story...But basically I just broke up with my fiancé. There's no more wedding. I hope you can still cancel your Bali ticket."

"Oh no. So sorry to hear. Did this just happen? Are you okay?"

"No, not really. And I just don't want to be by myself at this hotel."

"Of course. You shouldn't be alone now." He sounded worried. "Come over. You can take our guest room, I'll just let my roommates know."

"Thank you."

"Are you still going to the office tomorrow? You told me you have that big presentation."

"I really don't feel like it but yeah, I still need to do that."

"Don't worry about it. We can go and take the shuttle together tomorrow."

"I think that would be good." I breathed a sigh of relief. "So when can I come over?"

"I should be home in about two hours. Let me text you my address."

"Okay, let me know later when you're home and I'll make my way there."

"Sounds good. You hang in there! I'll see you later and you'll tell me all about it, okay?"

"Thanks Amir, I really appreciate it." I hung up the phone and curled up under the bed duvet once again.

I first crossed paths with Amir through a work project at Google. This 30-something German with Persian roots was part of the Waze division, based in San Francisco. Waze was that lifesaver of a GPS navigation app, especially in traffic-filled cities like Jakarta and Kuala Lumpur—the one Google bought up a few years back. Amir, the Business Development guy of the app, jetted off to Asia frequently for his gig. Our worlds collided during one of his Jakarta visits, coinciding with a speaking engagement at a Google Indonesia event. Our introduction was instant, sparked by a shared love for techno beats, a penchant for good food and our mutual status as frequent flyers to Amsterdam.

After sharing the recent turn of events with someone trusted and securing a place to crash for the rest of the week, I swiftly packed my suitcase. My brain, devoid of emotional turbulence for now, methodically planned how I would make my way to Amir's place. I was acutely aware that the sooner I surrounded myself with other people, the better it would be for my mental state. But before I headed over to his place, there was still one last crucial thing I needed to do.

***

"I'm here to pick up my wedding dress," I informed the lady seated at the reception as I stepped into the enchanting world of Sarah Seven's bridal boutique in San Francisco.

Sarah Seven's boutique felt like your perfect living room: romantic, contemporary and oh-so-cute millennial twee. The real showstopper, though, was the grand full-body mirror positioned right in the middle of the room—and the beautiful bridal gowns elegantly displayed on a rack by the side of the room. Nestled between a hair salon and a psychic reader, the boutique had an unassuming charm that could easily be missed if you didn't know it existed on the second floor.

My mission? To retrieve my Sarah Seven "Practically Perfect" wedding dress in off-white. Yes, the wedding had just been called off, but that wasn't going to stop me from bringing the dress home. I found myself pondering potential futures for it—perhaps I could wear it on a different occasion, get it cut and tailored into a stylish cocktail dress, or simply donate it? Or maybe burn it? I wasn't entirely sure what I was going to do with the dress. What I did know was that I wanted to take it home. Besides, I had already paid half for it, so why not?

This visit to the bridal boutique marked what would have been my final fitting before the wedding. Call it curiosity, but I couldn't resist the urge to know how it would feel to put on my wedding dress just one more time.

I spent the entire Uber ride contemplating my decision. My mind was racing.

Mira, what kind of emotional torture are you putting yourself through this time?!

Why don't you just leave the dress behind?

What if you break down in tears when you put it on?

To all those discouraging thoughts, I simply said, "Shut the fuck up."

Going for the final wedding dress fitting was actually my second reason for being in San Francisco. I opted to pick up the dress in person rather than relying on the boutique to ship it internationally. Given Indonesia's reputation for shady officials and unclear regulations, trusting my country's customs process wasn't a chance I was willing to take. I didn't want to risk the dress getting stuck—or worse, lost—in shipment.

My backup plan was to have a US-based colleague who was traveling to Southeast Asia carry it for me. However, when the Tech Talk coincidentally got scheduled for the same week, it felt like a sign that I had to go in person.

As I settled onto the boutique's lounge sofa, I had déjà vu. The last time I was here was nine months ago. Back then, as an eager-to-get-hitched version of myself, I faced the challenge of finding an elegant yet minimalistic wedding dress in Jakarta that would suit our tropical Bali wedding plans. Jakarta's wedding dress scene offered either grand ballroom princess gowns, fitting for a Chindo (Chinese Indonesian) going for a Western-style celebration at a lavish hotel, or intricately hand-sewn designer *kebaya* for those opting for a more 'traditional' Indonesian wedding with over two thousand guests. I wasn't drawn to either option. My fiancé and I envisioned a more intimate and relaxed celebration away from the city, and I needed a dress that matched that vibe.

After scouring through countless boards and spending many hours on Pinterest, I stumbled upon Sarah Seven's contemporary bridalwear and instantly fell in love. Their beautiful low-key style dresses, crafted with the finest fabrics and paired with the most adorable names, captured my heart. Who wouldn't want to get married in a "Prosecco"? Or a "Kate"? The search was over.

Luckily, during that time, I discovered that Sarah Seven had a boutique in San Francisco. So, when my colleague Denise from the Manila office and I were sent for a Marketing 101 training at our headquarters, I seized the opportunity. I convinced Denise to extend her stay, and together, we embarked on a long weekend of wedding dress hunting that culminated in me ordering Sarah Seven's "Practically Perfect" dress from their boutique.

They say when you find the right wedding dress, you just know it. And for me, that certainly rang true. From the lightness of its draped chiffon material to the elegant shoulder-exposing heart-shaped neckline, the moment I slipped into the dress, I just knew it was the one. I could envision myself at the end of my wedding night, tipsy, dancing barefoot on the grass, holding up the back trail of the dress as I stumbled my way back to my room, with my new husband walking beside me, holding my arm with one hand and carrying my heels with the other. Plus, with a price tag of less than $2,000, the dress was simply, practically perfect.

I yearned to feel the chiffon gently grazing against my skin, holding onto that last thread of a dream wedding that was slipping away. If it wasn't going to happen, I thought, I might as well savor whatever was left of it. As the Sarah Seven lady skillfully pulled up the back zipper, I glimpsed in the gold-framed, larger-than-life-sized mirror just how breathtakingly perfect the dress appeared. Absolutely perfect. That is, until she zipped me up completely and asked me to turn around. That's when I noticed…it wasn't. More precisely, it wasn't perfect on me.

It seemed like I had lost too much weight. The heart-shaped bustier cup, which used to snugly fit my breasts, now displayed a noticeable gap. My boobs had downsized and I found myself constantly pulling up and readjusting the strapless dress, afraid it might slip down and lead to an unintended nipple-gate. *Sigh*. Even though I wasn't telling the Sarah Seven lady that anything was wrong, my body sure was.

It looked like the combination of the wedding diet followed by weeks of relationship limbo could take a great chunk off my weight and take a toll on my boobs. I made a note of that.

IMAGE 3: *A note to self*

In the end, I handed over the remaining deposit and left the boutique, Sarah Seven's "Practically Perfect" securely in my possession. I made it out swiftly before they realized that I was a sham bride. My mind went into overdrive attempting to convince myself that I had made the right, most rational choice. After all, why let a gorgeous dress go to waste just because the wedding was canceled? *It only made sense to take it home, right?!*

Despite my logical arguments, deep down in my heart, I couldn't deny the truth. I brought the dress home because I still clung to hope. A tiny, flickering hope that maybe, just maybe, with some divine intervention, we could still work things out—someday.

***

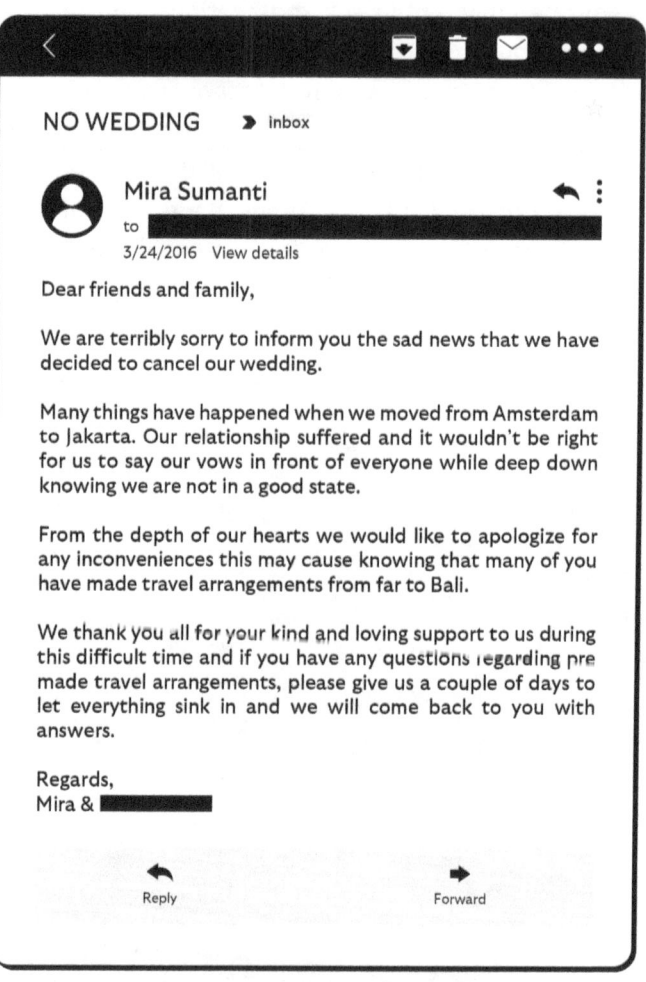

IMAGE 4: *The wedding cancellation email*

"Are you guys ready?" I glanced at my WorkBuddy teammates, a motley crew brought together by the shared ambition to make a mark at the Tech Talk: Simon, the brains from Google Play, Jim, the UX maestro from Maps, Nolan, our Business Development wizard and me, the marketing enthusiast. We were an unlikely quartet formed during the Hackathon—individuals who initially had no team but ended up creating something remarkable. Simon's idea for a job search app targeting blue-collar workers set the foundation. When I suggested focusing on the emerging market in Indonesia, drawing from my extensive product marketing research, Jim and Nolan jumped on board and WorkBuddy was born.

As we stood backstage, none of my teammates had a clue about the emotional turmoil I was grappling with after canceling my wedding just days before. But in the grand scheme of things, personal matters took a back seat to our collective mission: presenting WorkBuddy, the app that had clinched the runner-up spot at the global Next Billion Users Hackathon.

We were about to face our global product VP and some Engineering leadership from the Next Billion Users product area. Despite the chaos inside me, there was no room for breakdowns. I needed to gather my composure, push aside the recent upheaval and focus on our presentation.

For those intense hours leading up to the Tech Talk, the pressure and excitement served as a shield, momentarily making me forget the weight of the canceled wedding. Work became my refuge, a mental distraction that allowed me to temporarily escape the raw emotions and focus on the professional task at hand. The breakup, the canceled wedding—these personal tribulations momentarily faded into the background as the spotlight shifted to our team and the app we had crafted. High-pressure work, it seemed, was the unexpected remedy I needed to navigate what was left of my personal life.

"Let's do this!" Simon's enthusiastic shout echoed as we stepped onto the stage. He kicked off our Tech Talk with zeal, presenting WorkBuddy as "LinkedIn for blue-collar jobs," emphasizing the app's unique features such as job listings, learning and on-demand training opportunities for skill enhancement.

I chimed in, sharing crucial user insights about Indonesia, our country of focus. "The blue-collar job market in Indonesia is incredibly fragmented. People rely on social media, word of mouth or off-line methods like flyers for job searches. There's no centralized source of information," I explained. "Despite this, Android has a high penetration, making our audience highly accessible through mobile."

In the expansive auditorium at Google headquarters in Mountain View, I tried to summon the enthusiasm required for the presentation. The spotlight was on us, but as I glanced over the sea of faces, a sudden hollowness engulfed me. The Tech Talk, an achievement that should have filled me with joy and accomplishment, now felt like bitter irony. I just wanted it to be over.

"We have a working prototype ready for you to try," Jim informed the audience. "It's designed to be lightweight, ensuring seamless loading even in 3G, with minimal data usage, even on lower-end Android devices."

Despite the sincere applause from the audience and our collective smiles, I couldn't shake the feeling of being an impostor. The Tech Talk, an incredible opportunity, served as a stark reminder of my recent personal failure.

On that stage, I realized what truly mattered to me. It felt like none of the professional achievements mattered when my personal life was in shambles. At that very moment, I couldn't help but ponder how life would have turned out if I hadn't taken the Google job back in Jakarta. I was the one who wanted to join the company, and my (now ex) fiancé supported me by joining the cross-continental move. However, the city didn't work out for him, and things went south from there. Should I also blame Google for the failure of our relationship? Or maybe it was simply a case of an unhappy trailing spouse? The questions lingered.

***

After concluding the Tech Talk, the rest of my week was spent in a cocoon of solitude on Amir's couch. The desire to do anything had evaporated; I felt paralyzed. Following the email announcing the wedding cancellation, my inbox transformed into a constant stream of concerned messages: "Are you okay?" "What the hell happened?" "I'm here if you need to talk!" The well-intentioned flood of sympathy from friends and family only added to my burden.

Responding to these messages felt like an insurmountable task, a chore I had to fulfill but was not inclined to tackle just yet. With zero mental capacity for such conversations, I chose the path of least resistance: I turned off my Gmail notifications and responded to the flood of inquiries with resounding silence. It became my way of navigating the torrent of condolences.

The truth was, I didn't know what to say. The gut-wrenching heartbreak mingled with a sense of shame and disappointment created a cocktail that felt impossible to stomach. I felt like I'd taken a shot and missed the mark entirely.

"More tea?" Amir's voice broke through my thoughts as he presented a freshly brewed pot of green tea. Grateful for anything that could provide solace to my shattered heart, I welcomed the gesture, battling the combined effects of jet lag and insomnia. "How are you holding up?" he asked.

"I'm not sure," I confessed. "I think I'm okay?"

"Have you been able to sleep?" he pressed further.

"No, not really..." Each lingering question, every replay of "Where did it go wrong?" echoed relentlessly in my head, leaving me sleep-deprived for days.

"And how is *he*?"

"I don't know, to be honest. We haven't spoken a word since we sent that cancellation email."

"Aww, hang in there." Amir offered a comforting, friendly hug. The embrace felt warm and fluffy, like being held by a real-life teddy bear.

The tea, Amir's company, the fleeting escape—it all felt like a necessity. The idea of returning to Jakarta haunted me because I knew that the minute I flew back, I would forever be branded as the girl with a canceled wedding. And in the unforgiving eyes of Indonesian society, that carried a weight of its own. If you haven't settled down by 30, there must be something wrong with you, right? I wasn't prepared to face the judgment.

I dreaded the notion of returning home, anticipating the relentless questioning from extended family members. Their voices echoed in my mind: "What did you do?" "Where is he now?" "Is it really canceled?" "You need to be married. You're not that young anymore." I yearned to escape from it all. All I wanted was an extended time-out from life.

"What time is your flight again?" Amir refilled my cup.

"Uhm…I'm not sure. Midnight, I think. Sometime around that." I hesitantly reached for my phone. "Yeah, 12:15 tonight," my boarding pass confirmed.

"Do you want me to drive you to the airport?" asked Amir.

"No," I paused. "It's okay. I'll just get an Uber after dinner." I didn't want to be any more of a bother.

"Okay." Amir nodded his head. "Are you all packed?"

"Nope." I slouched back on the sofa and went silent for a while. "Maybe we don't have to break up?" My mind wandered from the present into a possibility I had with my (ex) fiancé. "Maybe we just canceled the wedding, but we can still be together?" I looked at Amir, hoping he would agree.

"Well, I don't know," Amir responded. "But from what you told me, I think it's hard to come back from that."

He was right. It all felt like one terrible nightmare, only to realize that when I woke up, it wasn't a dream after all.

"Amir…"

"Yes?" he replied gently.

"I-I don't want to go home." My eyes started to water. I wasn't ready.

He looked at me and sounded a deep sympathetic sigh. "Well...then don't," he suggested. "Stay a couple more days."

"I can?"

"You can stay as long as you need," he assured me. "Maybe... you want to join me at this party tonight?"

"Oh..." I contemplated. "Where is it?"

"It's at Public Works," he said.

"I've never been there." It piqued my curiosity.

"You'll love the DJ," Amir tried to convince me. "And I think we both know you could use a good night out. Dance it all out..."

He was not wrong. Maybe that's exactly what I needed: music. I needed to move my body to it. I needed movement to release all these stagnant emotions in me. "Okay, I'm in," it didn't take long for me to agree.

"Well done."

I grabbed my phone and dialed ANA to sort out a last-minute flight change. I tossed aside any concern for the pesky $150 change fee because, at that moment, I had made a firm decision: I was going to stay another day, and I was going to dance my sorrows away.

***

Public Works brought back memories of the now closed Studio 80 in Amsterdam, but on a grander scale. The venue boasted a minimalistic, slightly industrial aesthetic. The expansive main room featured an exposed ceiling, a pair of Funktion-One speakers (always a good sign in a club) and an oversized disco ball that cast its shimmering light over a bustling dance floor. The crowd was a familiar mix of intoxicated individuals—half hipster, half druggy techno enthusiasts, perhaps leaning towards yuppy hippies. This was San Francisco, so they were tech bros and not-so-starving artists.

I ordered my go-to party drink—vodka with Coke—and strolled to a dimly lit corner of the room. Standing there, on the brink of the crowd, I felt totally and completely alone. I observed the dance floor, gauging the right time to immerse myself in the lively crowd. Unsure about hitting the dance floor as a newly single woman, I took a few gulps of my liquid courage (vodka) to calm my nerves.

"Don't worry," Amir said, sensing my trepidation, "I'll take care of you."

I took a deep breath. "Okay," I said, grabbing his arm. "Let's dance," and followed him straight into the fiery dance floor.

The music, a Berlin-style atmospheric minimalist techno, blared through the speakers. A distinct blend of a skunky weed aroma and the tang of alcohol hung in the air. The lights, reflecting off the disco ball, rhythmically flashed to the beat, casting a warm glow on my face as I gradually danced deeper into the crowd. The familiar sights and sounds of a vibrant dance floor surrounded me, and I found myself vibing well with the place. I was genuinely grateful Amir had convinced me to stay.

In the past, on dance floors like this, now would be precisely the moment I'd seek out my ex. We'd intertwine our hands, finding comfort and safety as we surrendered to the music together. But now I was alone. *Well*, not completely.

I spotted Amir standing right beside me, nodding his head to the rhythmic beat. I approached him, "Can I get a hug?"

"Of course," he smiled and enveloped me. His arms felt like a heated plush blanket, so comforting again. I desperately needed that transfer of positive energy from him to calm my nerves down. And it worked. As I let go of his hug, I was finally ready to let the music take over completely.

My body jolted as soon as I heard that familiar growing synth sound that opens Donna Summer's "I Feel Love." I raised my hand up in the air, reaching for the red lasers beaming across the room. *I just want to dance.* The music reverberated through every inch of my body, a rhythmic pulse connecting me to the energy of the crowd. I swayed my hips steadily to the hypnotizing beats. *I just want to feel the love.*

The bass throbbed beneath my feet, and I surrendered to the intoxicating rhythm. I let the music wash over me, drowning out the echoes of heartbreak and disappointment. Each note became a lifeline, pulling me deeper into the blissful oblivion of the dance floor.

As the pulsating lights enveloped me, I rested my hands on top of my head and closed my eyes. *I don't want to go home.* No. It wasn't time for that yet. I wanted to stay in my little dancing bubble. It was safe there because no one could hurt me. *For tonight, let it be just me...and the music.*

Throughout the night, Amir was my dance partner and guardian. He danced right beside or behind me, seamlessly moving in sync with the rhythm. Like an autopilot system on high alert, the moment a male figure dared to encroach upon my space, Amir intervened. With a subtle yet authoritative gesture—raising his right hand, palm facing the intruder and shaking his head—he sent a clear message: "Don't you dare come closer." It was an unspoken warning, a protective shield around my sacred dancing bubble.

Amir's vigilant presence shielded me from unwanted advances, allowing me to lose myself in the music without the intrusion of the outside world. He played the role of a *stay-off-this-devastated-bride* warden with remarkable effectiveness. That is, until he decided to take a trip to the bathroom.

One moment, my eyes closed, lost in the music, feeling the rhythmic unity of my body and the beat. The next, I sensed a body creeping up behind me, dancing uncomfortably close. It was as if someone had decided to initiate a spontaneous spoon-dance session. *Damn.* I needed to extricate myself from this situation pronto, before things escalated into an unwelcome grind.

Swiftly, I turned around to face the guy responsible for invading my personal space. I struggled to focus my eyes in the dimly lit room (a near-impossible feat), attempting to discern his features. Yet, at that point, summoning the energy to care or shoo him away seemed beyond the capacity of my intoxicated self.

The guy introduced himself, "I'm Matt."

Under the pulsating strobe lights, his face came into view—cute and, illuminated by another flash, a nice smile adorned it. My gaze naturally descended, as if on autopilot, to scrutinize his outfit (a bad habit, perhaps). His sneakers were pretty bad. Bulky, overly designed, the kind that looked like they belonged to someone who hadn't quite figured out their sense of style.

I shook my head and waved my hand in front of my mouth, signaling that I couldn't (or wouldn't) talk. He seemed to get it and continued the spoon-dance routine.

Amir returned from the bathroom, catching the tail end of the shenanigans. I could read his expression as if he were mouthing, "Are you okay?"

I nodded in response to Amir's unspoken question, deciding to let this persistent fellow remain entangled in my dance space.

As the night progressed, Matt persisted in his attempts at a more sustained conversation. He threw in occasional questions like, "Where are you from?" and made offers for drinks, all while maintaining the spoon-dance routine. I couldn't care less about his origin, although I think he mentioned being from Massachusetts.

The following morning, just before my flight, a twinge of guilt crept in for abruptly leaving the club without bidding Matt farewell. In an attempt to clear my conscience, I penned a short tribute message to Matt on my blog. I genuinely hoped he understood my actions from that night and had since found someone more willing to engage in conversation on the dance floor.

***

Dear Matt from Massachusetts (if I remember your name correctly)

Posted on April 4, 2016 by Mira Sumanti | Leave a comment | edit

I'm sorry I just left you in the club without saying goodbye or leaving you my name (so you can stalk me later).

You seemed like a nice guy (with questionable choice of footwear), but a couple of days before that night I JUST called off my wedding that was supposed to happen in 5 weeks.
So as how you would imagine a devastated bride-to-be would be, I was nowhere near in the mood for a one night stand, make out session or even a kiss.

Yes, we were spoon dancing all night long but it wasn't really because I wanted to, but more because I was just WAY too damn drunk to even talk (and tell you to go away).
Also, you were pretty hot.
So whatever.

IMAGE 5: *The blog post for Matt*

It was a Tuesday morning when I stepped into Jakarta's Soekarno-Hatta Airport. Choosing to head straight to work instead of succumbing to the temptation of a nap at home, I convinced myself that powering through the day was a more prudent strategy to combat jet lag, so I made a beeline to the office, arriving just in time for lunch.

Being at work turned out to be a surprisingly effective therapy. I embarked on a mission to achieve the elusive inbox zero—tackling the 372 emails I had neglected during last week's emotional breakdown—and offered scripted reassurances to concerned colleagues who knew about the wedding cancellation (the default reply was "I'm fine. It was all for the best."). I found solace in the rhythm of daily tasks. The breakup catastrophe, which had consumed my thoughts just a week ago, now felt like a distant memory. It was over, done, dusted—the ship had sailed. Dwelling on it would serve no purpose. I had to move forward.

The week sped by in a blur. The breakup seemed to have little impact on my cognitive abilities, except for the persistent insomnia—likely a side effect of lingering jet lag—that kept me awake for hours each night. Still, functioning on an average of four hours of sleep, I felt surprisingly fine. The aftermath of the breakup wasn't as bad after all. I had survived! I was checking this off my to-do list! And when the weekend came, it was time to reward myself for enduring the storm.

***

I arrived at Irwan Team salon in Grand Indonesia mall early. The salon buzzed with the typical Saturday afternoon crowd—Jakarta ladies preparing to attend weddings of a thousand guests or more, most likely for a distant cousin or a not-so-close high school friend.

Luckily, I didn't have a wedding to attend because, after canceling my own "I do" ceremony, witnessing another couple happily tying the knot was enough to make me want to exit the room and throw up. Besides, as I looked around the salon at the women getting ready for the weddings of their friends and family, I felt disgusted by the huge amount of money and time that went into the preparation. No thanks.

Just like those ladies, the whole process of attending an Indonesian wedding involves hours of preparation. First, there's the 45-minute taxi round trip to and from the salon (about Indonesian Rupiah [IDR] 150,000). Then, an hour is dedicated to getting your hair styled—typically a modern updo or a wavy blowout (around IDR 350,000). Add another hour for fake lashes and makeup, rarely achieving a natural look (approximately IDR 500,000). Finally, invest an additional 30 minutes in a cab to reach the venue (another IDR 150,000). That sums up to a minimum of three hours and more than a million rupiahs[1], which is the baseline cost for attending the wedding of someone you don't know that well.

Now, imagine if you know the couple well, and the bride invites you to be part of her 25-person bridesmaid crew. Double all your initial expenses (because you can't settle for the basic hair and makeup package anymore) and factor in the cost of tailoring your bridesmaid outfit yourself (around IDR 1,500,000 or more). The financial commitment just keeps growing.

And then comes the actual wedding routine: You line up with the other thousands of attendees (which can take a good 30 minutes) to congratulate the couple (done in two minutes), hastily grab some dinner from the buffet (standing, no alcohol, wrapped up in 15 minutes if you skip dessert) and make a swift exit from the overcrowded ballroom (also, your heels are usually killing you by then). Occasionally, you might attempt a second round of kambing guling, those delectable fire-grilled lamb pieces bathed in sweet and spicy soy sauce, but they're often devoured by the time you reach for seconds.

---

[1] Since salaries in Jakarta are one-third of what you might make in international big cities like New York, London, or Singapore, this comes out to about $300-$400 to get done up for the event.

There's rarely an after-party featuring alcohol, except perhaps at a non-Muslim Chindo wedding, where you can try to consume enough gin and tonic to compensate for your initial investment. So, all in all, attending a Jakarta wedding typically results in a negative ROI.

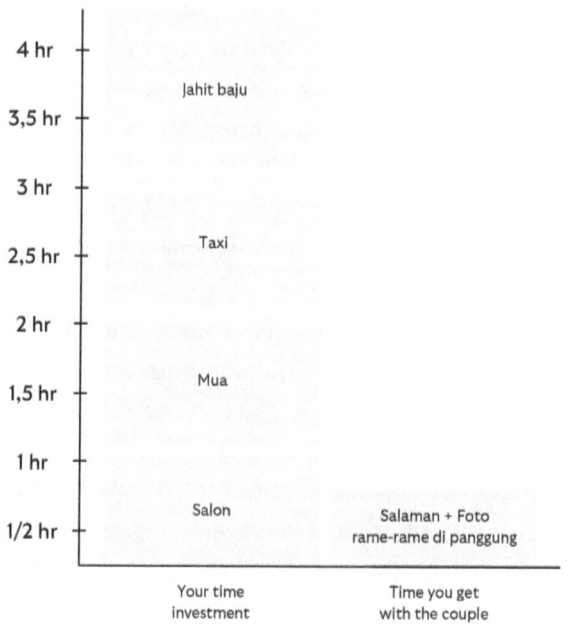

IMAGE 6: *Jakarta wedding ROI chart*

"Mira?" One of the salon assistants, holding her notepad and pen, came looking for me at the waiting area.

"Yes, that's me," I responded with enthusiasm. I couldn't wait any longer for my well-deserved reward after surviving a dreadful breakup: a two-and-a-half-hour Kérastase hair spa treatment that included a back and foot massage.

The salon lady, Karen, as her name tag indicated, guided me to the treatment room at the back, exclusively dedicated to Kérastase hair spa clients. No way was I going to do my treatment on the loud and bustling common salon floor. I craved a full rest and relaxation experience in a special room.

With only four chairs, the dimly lit Kérastase treatment room exuded privacy, cosiness and the scent of a mini escape to Bali, providing complete restfulness for the mind and body the moment you entered.

Inside, I stored my belongings in the locker, changed into the branded Kérastase tube dress and robe and made my way to the washbasin—the starting point of the seven-step treatment: wash, scalp management, steam, wash, hair management, another steam, wash again and then the optional blow dry. All the while, a massage therapist would soothe my achy back and legs with a gentle hot stone massage. Bliss.

I could feel the warm water trickling down my head. I rested my legs straight on the chair and relaxed my neck on the soft neck-rest of the washbasin, trusting the therapist to drench my hair and scalp with vitamin-packed shampoo. As he began to stroke my scalp as part of the cleaning process, I looked up to the grey ceiling and let my mind wander. With every gentle stroke came a thought.

Relax Mira, you deserve this.
One stroke.
That was nice. More.
Two strokes.
Yes, that's exactly where I have some itch on my scalp.
Three strokes.
Let's think about what just happened: The canceled wedding.
Four strokes.
I've cried, I've partied and now I'm fine. There's nothing else that would come after this, right?
Five strokes.
The wedding dress. So pretty. I'm glad I took it home.
Six strokes.

Jane the Virgin. Yeah, how could two people go from wanting to spend the rest of their lives together one day to completely hating each other the next?

Seven strokes.

My ex. How dare he?

Eight strokes.

The canceled wedding.

Nine strokes.

I'm all alone now.

Ten strokes.

MY...CANCELED...WEDDING.

My hands shook as I tried to grab onto the arm of the chair. I felt nauseous. I couldn't breathe. My evil brain played tricks on me. The very second I let my mind and body relax, anxiety, having lurked quietly around the corner, came straight in from the front door with her whole extended family of heartbreak, pain and suffering.

As the Kérastase treatment continued, each stroke felt like a countdown, not to relaxation, but to an impending emotional outburst. My thoughts raced, and the soothing spa environment turned into a battleground for my emotions. I tried to anchor myself, repeating in my head, *you're strong, Mira. You can handle this.*

But there was no escaping. The canceled wedding, the unspoken questions, the loneliness—they all converged into a perfect storm. The numbing effect of the party in San Francisco had worn off, and the reality of the situation hit me with a new level of intensity.

For the next few minutes—minutes that felt like an eternity—of hair washing, I was physically compromised. I tried so hard to hold back the tears welling at the edge of my eyes. It dawned on me then that there was still so much about the breakup that I hadn't figured out: unexplored, gut-wrenching emotions. I felt pinned to the chair by the weight of that realization. *How long would it take me to heal?*

It wasn't until the therapist lifted my hair onto my head, wrapped a towel around it and pushed me back up that I was able to get off the wash basin chair. I returned to my original seating in the treatment room and spent the rest of the hair spa day not saying a single word.

***

The next few days were a nightmare. Ever since that anxiety attack episode at the salon, it felt like the floodgates of emotional outbursts had opened wide. Insomnia kept me up until the late hours of the night. And every time I managed to fall asleep, agonizing night terrors haunted my dreams. It felt like I was being drowned alive in a dark, open sea. Petroleum-like black, thick water filled my lungs, suffocating me to the point of desperation. Panic crippled my body, cramped my hands and feet, drowning me deeper into the bottomless pit. Any attempt to scream for help was met with the unsettling realization that no sound was coming out of my mouth, as if the whole scene was muted and the nightmare happened in eerie silence.

Like another evil trick played by my brain, all the pent-up painful emotions I tried really hard to distract myself from during waking hours came haunting me in the subconsciousness of my sleep. It woke me up every one-and-a-half hours, trying to catch my breath, in uncontrollable tears. Once the tears subsided and I calmed down, I would fall asleep. But the moment I fell asleep again, the night terrors would promptly restart over and over again, until suddenly it was morning and I had gone through the night without a single minute of rest.

This vicious cycle repeated itself for the whole weekend. Come Monday morning, I was emotionally and physically drained. With my eyes puffed up, I wasn't able to get myself to move from my bed, let alone have the mental capacity to deal with even a single work email. I needed a break. I needed help. Because if the terrors and the sleepless nights were to continue, I knew my work would—sooner than later—suffer.

"Veronica, I'm so sorry. But I don't think I can come to work today. I haven't been sleeping for three days," read the WhatsApp message I sent to my boss on Monday morning. "I think I need to get some help."

"Are you okay?" she was concerned.

"Not really," I admitted. "I'm going to call in sick today."

"Of course. Don't worry about work. Let me know if I can help in any way."

"Thank you."

Veronica's response, filled with genuine concern, softened the edges of my anxiety. Taking a sick day felt like a small act of self-compassion, acknowledging that my emotional well-being deserved as much attention as my physical health.

That ex of mine might have actually had the upper hand—the luxury of being unemployed during such an emotionally wrecking time. Before the breakup, he had lost his job in Jakarta, just a few months before our wedding. While it had added to the financial strain between us, I now realized that maybe *not* having a job during a breakup was a kind of twisted privilege. He could cry at home all day if he wanted to, sink into his sadness without worrying about meetings or deadlines.

But me? I didn't have that option.

I had a full-time commitment to a company that paid my salary every month. There were projects in motion, deadlines looming, responsibilities I couldn't just abandon. Life didn't pause for heartbreak. I couldn't ask for a time-out, no matter how much I wanted one.

The breakup had already crushed so much—my future plans, my sense of stability, my ability to sleep through the night. But if there was one thing I refused to let it shatter, it was my work. My career was the *one* thing still holding me together. So I needed to get help before it was too late.

***

The clinic reception informed me that there were three other patients ahead of me, so I was asked to settle into the waiting area outside of Dr. Kandoe's office.

"Sure," I responded, taking a seat. I wasn't exactly sure what kind of help I needed—did I need a shrink, a support group, a psychologist, a lobotomy? All I knew was that Dr. Kandoe, a psychiatrist with a practice just a ten-minute walk away from my apartment, was available that morning. So that seemed like a good place to start.

Shortly after, a nurse holding a folder file emerged and called a name. Not mine. A late twenties couple on the far end of the waiting room stood up and made their way into the doctor's office. The guy looked tired and the lady looked scared, holding onto his arm tightly. *What's their story?* I wondered.

The arm clock fixed right above Dr. Kandoe's door became the sole focus of my attention. The small hand and the bigger hand ticked away for almost two hours until two more patients left, and finally, I was called in by the same folder-holding nurse.

I stepped into the bright room, a contrast to the dimly lit waiting area. Dr. Kandoe was in her seventies wearing oval-shaped glasses and a white doctor's coat. She seemed legit. She looked like your favorite, smart-yet-kind grandma who just likes to hear about your day.

"Have a seat," she motioned to the regular padded wooden chair in front of her desk—no fancy therapy sofa like in the movies. "So, what can I do for you...Mira?"

"Well..." I began, taking my seat. "Where do I start?"

My one-and-a-half-hour-long story—the canceled wedding, the panic attacks, the insomnia, the night terrors—resulted in an outburst of tears from my side and a prescription of clonazepam from Dr. Kandoe.

"They are anti-anxiety medications to help you sleep. Let's start you off with a full dose. Take it two times a day, one after lunch and one before bed," she explained, handing me the handwritten prescription. "And come see me again this Friday."

Feeling a bit lighter in my chest as I walked back home from the hospital, I knew my problems weren't exactly solved or that my entire set of emotions were properly managed. But having someone—a professional—hear my story made me feel validated. The fact that I had a medication that supposedly would at least help me sleep at night was reassuring. I felt hopeful that things would get better and that I would eventually be okay.

But as I got home, took my first dose of clonazepam with a glass of water, turned on my Out of Office (sick leave for the day) and curled up on my sofa, another thought dawned on me: *I am now single. Who do I call now when I have something on my mind?*

Am I eating dinner alone tonight?

Who is going to go to the cinema with me?

What should I do if I'm horny?

The breakup, compounded by what I would later learn was my rather anxious attachment style, exacerbated my worst fear of being forever alone.

And so, I downloaded Tinder.

Chapter 2

THE NEUROSCIENTIST

My initial experience on Tinder was like stepping onto a roller coaster for the first time—anxiety-inducing yet strangely exhilarating. I felt a blend of guilt for diving into the Tinder world so soon after the breakup, excitement at the prospect of the distraction that swiping could provide and nervousness simply because, well, I'd never done this before.

Who the hell are all these people?
What if I see someone that I know?
Am I going to get dick pics?
Who do I swipe right on?
What if no one likes me back?
Aaaaaa...
...And I haven't even started swiping yet.

My nearly four-year relationship with my ex kicked off just before Tinder became the go-to platform, turning swiping into the standard method for my generation's quest to find "The One" or, perhaps more realistically, the one good enough for an 11 pm booty call or on-demand cuddles. Until then, my only brush with a Tinder-like experience was a second-hand swiping escapade when my gay BFF, Jaka, let me take charge of his swipes on Grindr. Well, let me tell you, that was an interesting introduction to the world of app-based connections.

Swiping is brilliant because the simple right or left gesture turns the whole thing into a game. The uncertainty of when you'll get your next match creates a reward anticipation similar to a slot machine—*I want more...more...MORE!*—making the entire experience fun and addictive.

Swiping can also be dreadful when you realize that behind these "cards" in this game-like experience are actual people with genuine names, aspirations, and heartbreak stories. I was joining their single ranks, willingly adding myself to the stack of playing cards ready to be judged, kept or dismissed by hundreds of strangers—probably swiping absentmindedly while taking a dump.

At least I didn't start my Tinder journey on the toilet. It began rather respectably on my sofa after I had come to terms with the fact that I had officially become a heartbroken, lonely, almost 30, single lady and the time had finally come for me to no longer be a Tinder virgin. Plus, going on Tinder felt like I was sending a little "screw you, I'm moving on" kind of message to my ex. Ha!

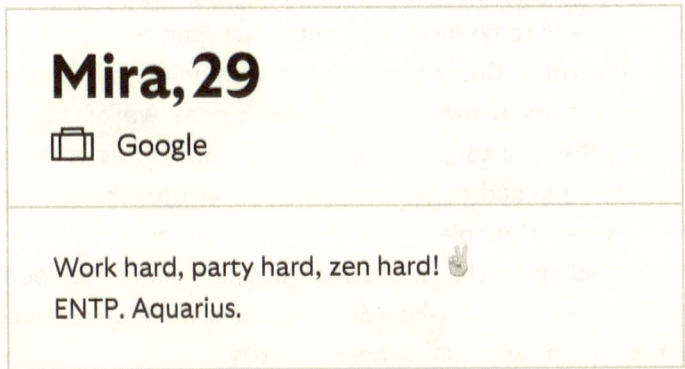

IMAGE 7: *My first Tinder bio*

I wasn't all that thrilled with my initial attempt at crafting a Tinder bio. I mean, let's be real, "work hard, play hard" was hardly the most original profile line. Nevertheless, I gave it a shot, attempting to inject a bit of zen flair to convey that I was all about that elusive concept of no balance in life. You know the drill: grind through the work hours, let loose and get a bit wild and then find solace in silent meditation. It was my attempt to encapsulate the essence of a well-rounded lifestyle, or at least that's what I thought at the time.

As for the rest of the bio, it was rather decent, right? Prospective matches got the basics: my name, the real deal on my age (no funny business there), where I clocked in my hours to prove I wasn't a slacker and of course, a glimpse into my Myers-Briggs personality type (yes, I'm one of those).

And then there was the pièce de résistance: my star sign. Gotta admit, I proudly flaunted it. Libra, Gemini, Aries—I'm sending a friendly wave your way. But Cancers? They were kindly told to steer clear. You know, astrology compatibility and all that jazz.

SWIPE THERAPY

Sure, my bio might not have been an award-winning literary masterpiece, but hey, I wasn't about to let that get me down. Being a marketer by trade, I couldn't help but apply some professional wisdom to my Tinder escapades.

Like in any marketing campaign, reaching the right audience is key. You want to connect with the exact kind of people you're looking to attract. Casting a wide net with universally appealing photos might seem like a good idea, but as we often say in marketing, if you're targeting "everyone," you end up resonating with no one. I aimed to craft my photos with precision, homing in on the type of people I wanted to swipe right on me. It's not about appealing to the masses; it's about making that perfect connection with those who had a better chance of connecting with me. My aim was quality over quantity.

Throughout my digital escapades, I've sworn by a cardinal rule that guided my online presence: My photos online need to look exactly like myself in the flesh. No more, no less—insert some millennial rant about the sacredness of authenticity. I mean, what's the point in dolling up your online self if it's miles away from the real deal?

Everything in life is about setting the right expectations. You expect to get a promotion, and you don't get it? Sucks. You expect Garbage, after several years of hiatus, to come up with a fresh new album and all you get is a "Best Of" album? Sucks. You expect your period to come next week, but surprise, it decides to make an early entrance—right when you've got a date lined up with plans for some "sexy time" afterward? Well, unless you're into period sex, it *FUCKING SUCKS*. So...Expectations, my friend. Set none of them, or at least set only realistic ones, and thou shalt never be disappointed. And the same golden rule applies to the world of online dating.

I get that on Tinder everyone is trying to "sell" themselves. The pressure to showcase your absolute best, FaceTuned and VSCO-edited photos to attract potential matches is off the charts. But here's the thing, wouldn't you rather have people be pleasantly surprised by how much hotter you are in person compared to your curated pics? That's the kind of impression that sticks.

Setting the bar too high with those picture-perfect shots can backfire. It's like signing up for a lifetime subscription to disappointment. Sure, you might catch someone's eye, but if you're not living up to the "promised" standards in real life, the first emotion your match feels is disappointment. And trust me, disappointment is not the vibe you want on a first date. You can practically bet that they'll be subtly swiping through other potential matches on their phone the moment you excuse yourself to the restroom.

So, here's a nugget of wisdom I picked up along the way: Set modest expectations and let people revel in the pleasant surprise when they finally meet you. It's like that golden piece of advice I got during one of my 360 performance reviews: under promise and overdeliver. *So, take it down a notch with all the photo filters, will ya?*

Armed with a well-crafted profile, I was ready to dive into the world of swiping. *This should be fun, right?* Well, at least I hoped so.

Before I knew it, there I was on Tinder, effortlessly navigating my way through the profiles of people in Jakarta, swiping at a speed of one per two seconds.

Nope
Nope
Nope
Nope
HELL NO!
Nope
Ha, I know this guy
Nope
Nope
Nope
Dude, seriously?
WTF?!
Nope

SWIPE THERAPY

Tech/startup guy. Hmm...why not?
Nope
Another Tech guy. Sure.
Oh, my friend is here
Nope
Right, you just practically blurred your face to get that smooth skin filter.
Nope
Hmm, he looks familiar.
Nope
You're a maybe
Seriously Tinder, you can do better than this right?

***

The Neuroscientist was my third match on Tinder. In the sea of globetrotters boasting about their 173 countries visited, the self-proclaimed foodies and those throwing in their height at a solid 185 cm because, apparently, that matters, I stumbled upon his profile, and it stood out like a gem:

"I work in the intersection of music, technology and neuroscience. If none of those interests you, then we probably won't get along."

The 43-year-old Neuroscientist hailing from Australia had more of an industrial band member vibe than your typical scientist. His hairstyle was straight out of the David Bowie playbook, trimmed on the sides, but on top, it was all about that sleek and stylish length. It was like encountering a scientist who moonlighted as a rockstar—hot.

The 14-year age gap between us didn't faze me one bit. I mean, my parents rocked an 18-year difference, so anything below their benchmark felt entirely reasonable to me. Besides, I'd already tested the waters with someone close to my age—the ex-fiancé saga—and well, lesson learned.

His profession as a neuroscientist added an extra layer of intrigue for me. I was already navigating the post-breakup roller coaster with the help of a therapist, but could a neuroscientist offer a scientific perspective on the whirlwind of post-breakup chaos swirling in my head? Maybe he had some insights into the intricacies of what went on in the brain during such anxiety-inducing turbulent times? It was a curiosity that blended the personal with the professional, and I couldn't help but wonder if his scientific know-how might shed some light on the emotional labyrinth I found myself in. And so we started chatting.

***

A cute & artsy frontal face pic. Something nice, clear but neutral enough on first position to avoid an immediate left swipe 😊

A speaking gig shot. Meant to show that I actually have both legs. Oh and also for a little work humble brag 😉

A Halloween picture, meant to 'culturally filter' people. Either they would think I'm a crazy one legged lady or they would recognize that's Cherry Darling! 🧟

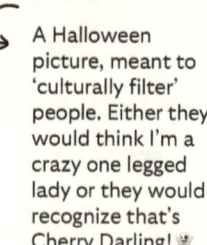

IMAGE 8: *My first Tinder pictures and their intended impression*

A Canggu shot meant to evoke "oh this chick seems chill" kind of vibe 🐻

Another Halloween picture as Mia Wallace because, well, I just really love Halloween ♥

"It's called MoSynth," he replied when I inquired about the avant-garde hand device wrapped around his hand in one of his pictures. "It's a motion synth." Aha! He just revealed important information. Now I had the name of a startup to search, which meant I could do some digging.

Lo and behold, his LinkedIn page materialized. A bachelor's degree in neuroscience from the University of Sydney? Smart. A PhD in computational neuroscience in Berlin? Oh, I absolutely adore Berlin and its crazy parties! Major plus point right there. Then there was the cherry on top—one of his published research papers, titled "The Temporal Code: A Prerequisite for Cortical Rewiring, Not a Correlational Hebbian Rule." I didn't understand a word of it, but damn, it sounded nerdy and irresistibly sexy (does this make me a sapiosexual?). I kept Googling.

His captivating TEDx talk, his startup's sleek website, the Apple iPhone ad that showcased his innovative motion synth device and a treasure trove of academic papers. It was an online feast, a buffet of information just waiting for me to review and consume. I was in digital stalking heaven!

The next few hours turned into a deep dive as I devoured every bit of content available about him. It was a bit surreal. Technically, this person was still a stranger, but with each photo, video and piece of writing, a strange sense of familiarity crept in.

I cooked up a whole bunch of assumptions about him in my head: the cool, young-at-heart scientist-turned-inventor with a penchant for interesting and obscure music. I mean, with that kind of haircut, how could he possibly have bad taste in music, right? I couldn't help it. I was more inclined to trust a stranger if their digital footprint at least looked promising.

Enter the Googleable scale, my go-to tool for assessing someone's online presence. Because let's be real, in this day and age, if your name doesn't yield any Google results you practically don't exist.

Now, here's the twist: the Googleable score isn't as straightforward as a simple "higher is better" rule. The correlation between someone's "Googleable score" and the "Trust" factor isn't a neat, straight line. Score under six? Too little unverifiable information. Could be they're playing hide and seek with the truth! Above eight? Probably a celebrity or someone with a carefully curated digital presence. Can you *really* trust that? The sweet spot? It's that green zone nestled between six and eight. Enough info to do a quick verification before diving into a real-life meeting.

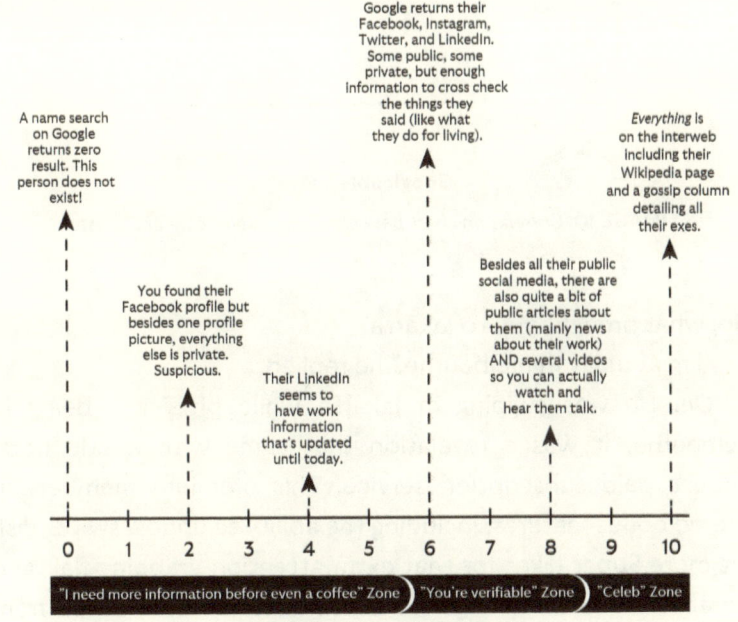

IMAGE 9: *The Googleable Scale*

So, back to the Neuroscientist. After my deep dive into his digital trails, the verdict was in—he was cool, proven not to be a catfish and securely nestled in the "okay to meet" green zone.

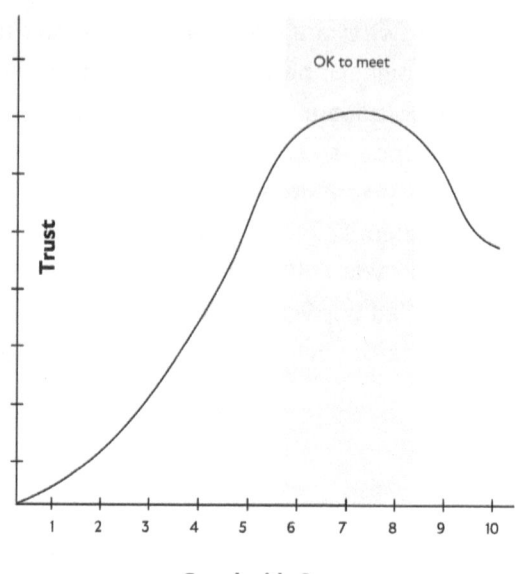

IMAGE 10: *Correlation chart between Googleable score and Trust*

***

"So, what brought you to Jakarta?"

"I'm actually in Melbourne," he replied.

Oh. He was swiping in Jakarta while physically being in Melbourne. It was a revelation that came with a side note: Tinder's paid subscription service. This premium membership offered bonus features, including the ability to undo a swipe, dish out more Super Likes for that extra attention-grabbing flair and the absolute game-changer—the power to remotely swipe from different locations.

"I plan to come to Indonesia at some point this year. I want to meet startups for potential project collaborations and maybe do a holiday in Bali."

"Cool!" I responded, but I was a little disappointed.

"Now, what's a smart young lady like you doing on Tinder?" he asked.

"Hmm...Good question," I paused and wondered if I should spill the unfiltered truth.

I don't know this guy.

Should I tell him what just happened?

No, Mira! That will freak him out!

Who talks about a canceled wedding in the first 15 minutes of a chat?

But...he's in Melbourne. I may never even meet him.

No, don't!

Fuck it. I got nothing to lose anyway.

What the hell am I doing on Tinder?

I mustered the courage. "I just called off my wedding two weeks ago. So, I'm here looking for...maybe a distraction?" I threw it out there and waited.

And then...silence.

Alright, that's it.

I've officially scared him off.

He is totally going to unmatch me now.

I really should have just shut up.

Oh well, I guess my Tinder adventure ends here.

Sigh...

But then those blinking dots appeared, signaling that he was typing. "That must have been really hard. How are you holding up?" his next message read.

He is still there! Phew.

"To be honest, I don't know," I pondered. "I think I'm okay, but I don't feel much these days."

"Which is understandable," he replied.

"Also, there are still a lot of things that need to be sorted. I realized that canceling a wedding is not that straightforward. We still have a lot of finances to balance out, logistics to cancel and more."

"Sounds like a lot of work for something that is no longer happening."

"Yeah, exactly. And it's really the last thing I want to be doing. The actual wedding date is in four weeks. It's supposed to be in Bali. All my friends are still going there for a holiday despite the cancellation. I also still have my ticket, and I don't even know what to do about it." It was surprisingly easy to be honest with this stranger.

"Seems like you've got a lot to think about."

"Yeah, I do."

"And Tinder is actually not a bad place to find a distraction." He added a wink emoji.

"Hehe, I guess so." At that moment, I was just happy and relieved that he still wanted to chat with me. A distraction was exactly what I needed. "So, when is your birthday?" I pivoted the conversation toward a lighter topic, attempting to gather another critical piece of information: his star sign.

"January 27th," he answered. "Why?"

"No way! You're an Aquarius too! Mine is January 29th!"

"Oh, how funny."

"Can I ask you some Aquarius questions?"

"Sure."

"Do people say you're cold sometimes? Like, maybe hard to read?" I inquired, drawing from my own personal experiences.

"Hmm...yes. I get that sometimes," he admitted. "That I'm not very emotional."

"Me too!" I responded. "All my exes think I'm a cold-hearted bitch. But I actually feel a lot. I just don't show it, I guess."

"I understand that," he said, before changing direction: "So what happened with the wedding? If you don't mind me asking…"

"Well, it's a bit of a long story," I said.

"It's okay. You don't need to share now. But whenever you want to talk, I'm here as a Tinder distraction!"

"Thank you!" I sent with an added smiley emoji.

***

I found myself wide awake at 4 am, haunted by the remnants of a dream featuring my ex-fiancé. Like Black Mirror's "Entire History of You" episode, the one where we're living in a time where you can replay and rewind any single scene from your life and project it on a screen, the scenes of my ex-fiancé's departure played out in a loop, turning the quiet hours of the night into an emotional battleground. It was like grappling with a trauma that pulled me from the depths of sleep, thrusting me into an unwelcome emotional outburst. And this ritual repeated itself every single night.

Even the anti-anxiety pill I took before bedtime seemed powerless against the emotional terrors that manifested in my dreams. Unable to slip back into the comforting embrace of sleep, I remained wide-eyed.

Desperate for an escape from the relentless grip of my own mind, I dropped the Neuroscientist a text, hoping that he was up already in his time zone.

"How do you erase bad memories from your mind?" I threw the question out into the digital abyss.

Unexpectedly, the Neuroscientist responded promptly to my dilemma. "What do you mean?" he inquired.

"Have you seen that movie *Eternal Sunshine*?" I questioned, referencing the film starring Kate Winslet and Jim Carrey.

"Yes, I have. Beautiful movie!"

"So yeah, something like that maybe. I really would like to erase the memory of my ex."

"Well, I'm not sure if we have something like that already, but I do know that memories are at their weakest when they are being recalled."

"Tell me more," I urged.

"That's why, in therapy sessions, when someone is trying to rid themselves of a traumatic experience from the past, the therapist would ask them to recall the memory. And as that memory is being recalled, you intervene with drugs, or you unpack it and try to build new memory structures around it to replace the old ones."

"Interesting," I paused. "So...you're saying I should not avoid it?"

"No, you shouldn't. Avoiding it will only make the feeling stronger. Also because it takes a lot of energy to suppress an emotion," he continued.

"But it feels counterintuitive..."

"I know."

"But I guess it makes sense..."

In those agonizing post-breakup moments, when my own mind seemed like an indecipherable puzzle, a logical insight—precisely like the one given by the Neuroscientist—was what I needed.

I pondered his words long and hard, attempting to apply that theory to my current question: *To go to Bali or not?*

The decision to go to Bali or not was still hanging in limbo, much like the unresolved emotions swirling within me. I still had my ticket. But the mere thought of my ex-fiancé had the power to cripple me, and I couldn't fathom what Bali, the place where we were supposed to get married, would do to my fragile emotional state. Bali held the remnants of countless memories, a terrain we had once joyously explored while planning our now-canceled wedding.

On one hand, I yearned to reunite with friends flying in from Europe, who already booked non-refundable tickets for the wedding. On the other, fear clutched at me—what if every corner of Bali echoed with memories of my ex-fiancé, sparking an emotional avalanche? The prospect of reliving those moments gnawed at my core, and I found myself desperately seeking a way to erase or at least mute those haunting memories.

But the Neuroscientist told me to not avoid those bad memories. *Could he be right?* Could going to Bali, recalling the memory of the relationship and triggering it to be at its weakest state—be a strategy? Could I create new memory structures around such triggers, effectively replacing the old memories with new ones? It made sense. But it felt risky.

Okay, Mira. Let's think this through carefully.

All my closest friends were going to be there. Technically, what was supposed to be the wedding trip could be reimagined as a Bali reunion trip—a restoration in my memory. What would have been the wedding villa could be rewritten as the summer reunion holiday villa. But the wedding day itself loomed as a daunting challenge. I thought long and hard about what it could be rewritten as because I refused to let that day linger as the tragically canceled wedding day.

You know what? I could throw a party!

Yes. I'm going to throw a frickin' wedding cancellation party!

Yeah, screw it. I'm going.

And with that decision, I messaged all my friends. "Guys, The Trip is on. I'll see you all in Bali!"

***

The last thing I wanted to do after canceling a wedding was deal with the financial aftermath of it. Talking about money, even under the most ordinary circumstances, can be rather icky. So when two brokenhearted souls, still navigating their own post-breakup depression, had to sit down and discuss who owes how much, it was a recipe for disaster.

After we had both taken a much-needed three-week breather to let the breakup settle in, the ex-fiancé and I had to crunch some wedding spending numbers. It was the only way we'd be able to move forward.

In Indonesia, it's a customary practice for the bride's family to foot the bill for the wedding—a final gift as if to say, "Here's one last present from us; now she's your responsibility."

My mom took charge of the major wedding expenses. We agreed that she would handle the essential components: the venue, catering and decor. Anything considered an extra luxury—such as the alcohol, the after-party and even flying our favorite DJ duo all the way from Scotland—was left for us to cover. Fair.

In the months leading up to our wedding, my ex found himself unemployed, and this prompted me to shoulder his costs initially. At the time, I didn't doubt that I'd eventually get the money back. After all, we were getting married. However, when the decision to call off the wedding was made, not only did our relationship unravel, but so did the balance sheet. He ended up owing me a considerable sum of the non-refundable wedding expenses.

At that point, post-breakup communication between the ex-fiancé and I had dwindled to nothing. Drafting an email filled with financial calculations felt like it might explode into a new wave of heartache. I painstakingly itemized every single wedding expense we agreed to cover together, meticulously calculating the total amount he owed. I made sure to include the 10 million rupiah that he took to pay for his flight out of the country, ensuring it was boldly highlighted at the end of the payment request email.

Considering our history as formerly betrothed, I aimed to avoid adopting the role of a stern debt collector. Instead, I opted for a more compassionate approach. I granted him a reasonable six-month window for repayment and offered flexibility in currency options, accepting either IDR or euro (EUR). To facilitate the process, I even provided both of my bank account details, allowing him the freedom to choose the method that suited him best. I basically offered him the best (interest-free) loan repayment plan one could ever ask for.

Anticipating a response to my email within a couple of weeks, I was taken aback when he replied within the hour. Initially optimistic that the financial matter would be resolved sooner than expected, my optimism took a nosedive the moment I opened his email.

Written in what seemed like a hurry, his response was riddled with typos and inconsistent capitalization. To my disbelief, he asserted that it was, in fact, me who owed him money. Attached to his email was his own financial calculation sheet, complete with the non-refundable Bali flight cost for his entire family (something we explicitly agreed that he would cover) and various household items purchased together in the past (which had nothing to do with the wedding!).

Seriously?

He is now demanding money for the juicer we bought last year? He could take that juicer to Amsterdam for all I cared!

Out of principle, my sole focus was on reclaiming the wedding money he owed me. Moreover, I expected him to exhibit the decency of trying to act like a responsible adult and repay what he owed. So, when he dragged the juicer and started sending me invoices for things that were *never* my responsibilities, I went mental.

"NO," I wrote assertively. "NO FREAKING WAY," I added, my frustration seeping into each word. "Your count is absolute rubbish. I demand all the wedding money that you owe me."

At that point, it was clear: If he wanted to play hardball, then the gloves were off.

Even with a full dose of anti-anxiety meds coursing through my system that day, no chill pill could have possibly tamed the storm. As anger bubbled up, I couldn't help but channel my inner Liam Neeson from the first *Taken* movie.

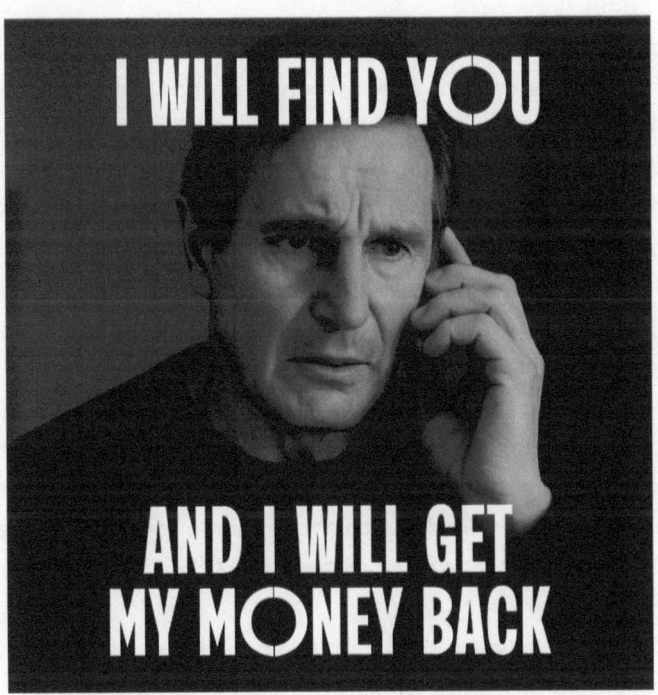

IMAGE 11: *A Liam Neeson meme*

***

"I'll be in Jakarta this weekend. Are you around for coffee or something?" The Neuroscientist casually dropped the message on one lazy Tuesday afternoon.

"Wait, what?! You're coming this weekend?"

"Yeah, and I'll probably go to Bali after Jakarta," he added.

Hold on. *We'd be in Bali at the same time?!* I questioned whether it was fate at play, a random twist of events or if he intentionally orchestrated his plans upon learning of my travel schedule. I decided to let the mystery linger and enjoy the unfolding events without reading too much into them.

"Well, I'm off to Bali on Monday for that wedding cancel—I mean, reunion trip I told you about! But yes, I'm free this Saturday. How about brunch?"

Little did the Neuroscientist know that Saturday held more significance than just a casual brunch proposal. It was the day originally earmarked for my Jakarta akad nikah ceremony with my ex—the official exchange of vows for Muslims. This ceremony carried immense weight in the eyes of my family, serving as a pivotal step exactly one week before the Bali wedding reception. It was to be held in front of an imam and our closest family, the akad ceremony would have formally recognized me as a married woman in the eyes of God and my country.

But, instead of partaking in the solemn rituals that would have sealed my marital status, I found myself preparing to meet a Tinder date on the very same day. It left me pondering whether the universe was attempting to convey some sort of message.

"Brunch on Saturday sounds good," he said. "Shall I let you pick the place?"

"Perfect. Yes, leave that to me. Where are you staying, by the way?" I would pick somewhere convenient for both of us.

"I got an Airbnb in the Kuningan area. Is that close to you?"

"I live in Kuningan!" Another unexpected alignment by the universe, perhaps? "Let me book a brunch place nearby then."

"That would be nice. Thank you."

"No worries. Safe flight and see you Saturday!" The anticipation built for our Saturday brunch rendezvous.

The possibility that maybe the Neuroscientist was coming to Indonesia to see me was exciting. Regardless of the direction our meeting might take—be it a passionate romance, a platonic connection, a blossoming friendship or even evolving into an online shrink-patient dynamic—our interactions provided a much-needed confidence boost. It reminded me that, despite the recent tumultuous events, I could still be liked by someone else.

***

"Don't bother coming back to Jakarta. By the time you get here, all your stuff will be gone." The mounting tension had led to a series of email exchanges with my ex filled with more curse words than I care to admit.

It had become painfully clear that he had zero intention of settling the wedding debt. The realization hit hard, adding a layer of betrayal to the already tangled mess of emotions.

I've always seen myself as a nice, smiley and generally good-tempered person. That is until someone decides to mess with me. When that happens, they're pretty much dead to me. So, when it came to the financial battle following the canceled wedding, I had zero intentions of being the one left at a disadvantage. I needed to reclaim the upper hand.

In a bid to assert control, I gathered the items that he had left at my apartment—clothes, shoes, DJ mixers and his precious vinyl collection. I wasn't about to break a sweat or lift a finger in the process, though. Instead, I gave explicit instructions to my cleaning lady to box up all his stuff and transfer it to storage, a place my ex couldn't easily access. I notified him that he can have all of his belongings back once the debt is settled.

While I didn't get the chance to theatrically toss his belongings off the balcony like any enraged ex-fiancée might dream of, I did inject a bit of drama into the process. Picture this: Beyoncé's "Irreplaceable" playing on repeat as my cleaning lady did all the heavy lifting, physically removing his remnants from my apartment—and my life. I played the director's role, pointing at things to pack and ensuring that nothing was left behind. All the while, my manicure remained unscathed. Beyoncé would be proud.

The purge took a solid three hours to complete. And once it was all said and done, I plopped down on the sofa and surveyed the apartment with a deep sense of relief. It felt as though a colossal weight had been lifted off my chest. No more facing those countless little reminders of him—from his denim shirt that always looked effortlessly good on him to that limited edition Henrik Schwarz vinyl or even his chocolate-flavored protein shake for the gym. All gone.

I could finally reclaim my apartment, the space that used to be ours, and transform it into mine again. The echoes of him were replaced with a newfound tranquility. Out of sight, and I was determined to make him out of mind as well.

To the left, to the left.

***

"You look exactly like your photos!" I exclaimed as the Neuroscientist and I met up for brunch at Loewy, the open-air café around Mega Kuningan. *Okay, maybe just a bit shorter and skinnier in person.*

"Thank you. I'll take that as a compliment," he replied with a grin. "You also look like your photos."

Meeting someone in real life for the first time after weeks of digital interactions can play tricks on your mind. Your brain has this funny way of making you think you can assume exactly how they will be like. But you can't.

So, even though physically the Neuroscientist closely resembled most of his photos, there was still that 5 percent difference—a bit of reality distortion—that I only noticed when we finally met. He was not as tall as his photos made me believe. And yes, he was skinnier in real life, a revelation that could have been due to the angles in his photos or the fact that they were taken more than a year ago.

"So, are you ready to tell me what happened?" the Neuroscientist dove right in once our food orders had been placed: fried chicken and waffles for me and scrambled eggs on toast for him.

"Well, truth be told, we hadn't been great for months. Jakarta didn't exactly work out for him. He left his solid job in Amsterdam to come here and be with me, but he ended up unemployed for a while. Eventually, he landed a startup gig, but things went south when he didn't get along with his manager and he lost his job just six months before the wedding. Things pretty much spiraled downhill from there."

"That sounds like a lot for both of you to deal with," he said compassionately.

"Yeah, it was a lot. I mean, planning a wedding is stressful on its own. Then you throw in the stress from a new life in Jakarta to adjust to, my work being super busy and having an unhappy, unemployed fiancé at home. But not a lot of people knew we were struggling. I didn't tell anyone. People just assumed I was stressed because of the wedding planning, you know? But no, I wasn't. We had an amazing wedding organizer, so everything was quite smooth on that front."

He nodded, and I continued, surprising myself with how honest I could be in front of him. "I was stressed because our relationship was in a really bad state, but we had a wedding date looming. Honestly, at first, I didn't even feel the stress. But my hair was falling out, my period schedule was a mess and I was dealing with acid reflux. Those physical symptoms were the wake-up call, making me realize I was actually under a lot of stress."

"It seems to me you had an emotional burnout," he concluded, steering the conversation to a more reflective tone after our food arrived.

Emotional burnout.

The sizzling symphony of fried chicken and the sweet harmony of waffles became a backdrop to my contemplation. Emotional burnout wasn't just a buzzword; it encapsulated the exhaustion, the weariness and the mental fatigue that had subtly crept into every facet of my life. It was like the puzzle piece I didn't know I was missing, fitting seamlessly into the complex picture of my emotional state. As I savored each bite of chicken, I appreciated the clarity that a simple phrase had brought me.

I'd encountered a *physical* burnout once in my life, back when I first joined Google. It was a combination of adjusting to a new high-paced job, readjusting to life in Indonesia after my stint abroad and trying to navigate a Jakarta-Amsterdam long-distance relationship all at once. A perfect recipe for exhaustion. My workdays were grueling and each commute was a marathon (like, three hours a day, no joke). To keep the flame alive in our long-distance relationship, I'd often stay up late, sacrificing precious sleep hours just to have a couple of hours of talk time with my ex-fiancé after he finished his work. The weekend rolled around and I'd drink and dance to let off a little steam. Not exactly the picture of self-care. So, when the Tinder Neuroscientist dropped the term—a burnout—but for my emotions, it just clicked. It made sense.

Yes, I had an emotional burnout. My ex and I both had a massive emotional burnout. We'd been trying to run on fumes, expecting everything to magically fall into place.

I grabbed another piece of chicken, savoring not just the crispy goodness but also the acknowledgement that what we went through had a name. It wasn't just chaos; it was burnout.

"Tonight was supposed to be my akad reception," I said.

"What's an akad reception?" he asked, showing genuine curiosity.

"It's essentially the official Muslim exchange of vows, done in front of an imam. You can think of them as Muslim priests, I guess. After that, you get officially registered by the country. We had planned to do it in Jakarta with an intimate gathering in front of close family members before flying to Bali for the main reception. But, obviously, we had to cancel the venue for the akad too," I explained, a tinge of wistfulness in my voice as I revisited the plans that now lingered only in the realm of what could have been.

"Was it hard to manage all the cancellations?" he asked.

"Well, the restaurant for akad was surprisingly very understanding. And they refunded the deposit money as restaurant credit," I casually mentioned, forking a piece of waffle into my mouth. I then laid out my revised plan with growing enthusiasm "So my akad reception tonight is morphing into a group dinner with my friends at Plataran Dharmawangsa, one of my favorite Indonesian restaurants. You should definitely give it a try while you're here. The place is beautiful, and the food is fantastic. The deposit amount was quite substantial, so I guess I just have to order a lot tonight to finish all that refunded credit!" I proudly shared my plan to repurpose every single element of the canceled wedding into something else—anything else—other than a wedding.

"And you're still going to Bali, yeah?" he asked.

"Absolutely! None of my friends canceled their tickets, so we decided to turn it into a reunion trip. I haven't seen my Amsterdam friends for almost a year," I said, taking a sip of my iced tea, the silver lining of the reunion adding a touch of excitement to the altered plans.

"Is your mom coming?"

"No, she's not. She insisted that I should just go and have fun with my friends. She doesn't want to bother us."

"How did she take it? I mean, the whole wedding cancellation thing," he asked while casually cutting a piece of toast.

"To be honest, she took the whole thing surprisingly well. When I first approached my mom about canceling the wedding, I was genuinely scared that she would've told me to just go through with it," I paused, taking a moment. "You know, I've heard so many crazy stories from friends of friends where the bride had a change of heart, but the mom got angry and forced her to go through with the wedding simply to avoid embarrassing the whole family since invitations had already been sent."

"That's crazy," the Neuroscientist remarked, his disbelief at the cultural pressure was evident.

"I know, right? But it happens. So I'm just grateful that my mom isn't like that."

"What did she say when you told her?" he continued.

"She told me, 'Mira, you should decide for yourself. If you want to continue with this wedding and later realize it's not working out and you get a divorce, I know you're a strong lady, so you'll eventually be fine. But if you want to cancel, then just cancel. Don't worry about me. I don't care what people might say. If you're unsure and thinking of going through with it and taking your chance, please remember that marriage is not something you should gamble on.'" I felt a lump in my throat as I repeated my mom's words.

"You're lucky. You have a really nice mother."

"I know!" I exclaimed, feeling genuinely grateful.

"And so what are you going to do with the wedding day in Bali?" He eventually asked the most important question of all.

"Well, in the spirit of not letting any non-refundable items of the wedding go to waste, I'll be throwing a party. A wedding cancellation party!" I answered enthusiastically.

"That sounds lovely! What will be the party lineup?" He joined my enthusiasm.

"Hmm...I haven't thought of it in detail yet. But I have several DJ friends coming. There's my friend Paulo from Brazil and Bergas from Jakarta and several Indo DJ friends who are living in Bali. I'm sure I can ask them to play. And maybe I'll play a bit too. Not sure yet. I need to see first what state I might be in on that day. Hope I won't be a mess," I said.

"You DJ? That's awesome. I'm sure you'll be fine. The party sounds like fun," he said.

"Do you want to come? You'll be in Bali too, right?"

"When is it again?"

"It's next Friday, the sixth."

"Ah. Unfortunately, I can't. I will only arrive in the evening of the seventh."

"Ah, too bad," I felt a little disappointed.

"Will you still be there on the eighth? Maybe I can come by and check in on how you're doing after the party?" he suggested.

"Yeah, I will be. We'll all be checking out at different times that day, but I think I'll be there till the evening. I like that idea of meeting up. Let's do that! Hope I'm still alive," I answered.

"You will be. You know, you're doing a great job upcycling your wedding," he looked at me as he put his cutlery down.

Upcycling the wedding. *Oh, I like that term. Another good one from him.*

"Thanks for saying that. I'm really just trying to make the best out of this whole shit show. After my plans blew up, my brain basically needed a hard reset. And this is what it came up with."

"Not bad for a romantic."

"A romantic? Me?" I laughed a little. "Most people think I'm cold, remember? My ex definitely would've said I have no heart."

"Hmm, I think you're more of a pragmatic romantic," he offered with a smile.

"Oh wow...Yeah, that term fits way better than I'd like to admit."

The whole brunch with the Neuroscientist felt like a surprise therapy session. He just listened, asked the right questions and somehow the weight on my shoulders started to feel lighter. The fact that he actually thought my whole wedding-upcycle plan was cool made me feel like my therapist just gave me a gold star for handling this breakup mess. Progress, right?

At that point, I didn't even care anymore if he was in Jakarta for me or it was just truly a coincidence. I didn't care if our connection was simply going to be a platonic one. To be honest, I had zero capacity for romance anyway. All I wanted—and needed badly—was someone to talk to. Someone who would listen. Someone who could help me make sense of all the fucked-up things that were happening in my head. And as fate would have it, I met a kind Neuroscientist on Tinder.

After our three-hour long brunch, we shared a ride back on a Blue Bird taxi. And as I dropped him off at his Airbnb, he gave me a hug and wished me "Good luck next week."

"Thank you, I will be needing that!"

***

When I called off the wedding just five weeks before the actual day, any hopes of recovering my expenses seemed like a distant dream. The venue had been fully paid for, and canceling flights came with hefty penalties. The 50 percent down payment for the catering? Non-refundable. No matter how heart-wrenching my breakup and the subsequent cancellation story were, a wedding, it turns out, is a business and vendors need their due payments. In the grand scheme of things, I wasn't the only person on earth who had called off a wedding, and vendors weren't about to offer compromised cancellation terms just because my world felt like it was crumbling.

But, oh, the silver lining! Enter Cyra, my rock star wedding planner—truly amazing at what she does. In the midst of the financial wreckage, there was a glimmer of hope, a possibility for some magic.

The moment the news reached her ears, our wedding planner wielded her expertise like a wand, weaving through the complexities of cancellations and negotiations. While the venue and flights were etched in stone, she managed to salvage some aspects, finding creative solutions where others saw dead ends. In a world where "non-refundable" echoed like an unyielding decree, she found loopholes, renegotiated terms and even persuaded vendors to bend a bit. It felt like a Herculean feat, but with her, the impossible became a challenge to overcome.

With a flicker of brilliance, she decided to reallocate my booking fee for hair, makeup and decor to another one of her new clients who happened to be eyeing the same vendors. This ingenious move not only ensured a seamless transition for the new client but also translated into a full refund for me on those specific items. In the grand scheme of things, the monetary value might not have been astronomical, but the mere fact that she went above and beyond—working her magic to make things a tad easier for us—meant the world.

With most of the wedding cancellation admin squared away, all that lay ahead for me was embarking on The Trip—the destination wedding travel to Bali, sans the actual wedding. My friends probably thought I had lost my mind. Why proceed with the wedding trip that had already been canceled? Why willingly return to places saturated with painful memories? Why subject myself to such emotional turmoil? Yet, during those turbulent times, no one dared to voice objections to the heartbroken (ex) bride navigating through the depths of pain.

I wasn't entirely delusional though; I knew The Trip would be a challenge. It was like willingly pouring acid on an open wound or stepping into a Facebook photos throwback twilight zone where, despite the breakup, every corner teased memories of my ex. *Seriously, Facebook, with all the information you have on me, can't you do better? We've broken up, alright?*

Amidst the doubts about my decision to still venture to Bali, I held onto the wisdom imparted by my Neuroscientist Tinder friend: *Memories are at their weakest when being recalled.* It became my mantra, my anchor in the storm of emotions. Yes, it was going to be tough, but maybe, just maybe, revisiting those places would dilute the intensity of those memories. After all, resilience sometimes means confronting the pain head-on and emerging stronger on the other side.

The Trip was my very own experimental emotional exposure therapy. I compelled myself to relive every nuance of our relationship, subjecting myself to the sights and sounds that once encapsulated our shared journey. From the dark sand beaches where we savored cold fresh coconuts to the narrow side streets of Canggu, where I clung tightly to my ex on the back of a motorbike, to our cherished Bebek Tepi Sawah joint in Ubud—each locale whispered fragments of our story. Even the radiant Bali sunsets, once the backdrop to our wedding plans, became part of the emotional landscape I needed to navigate.

Armed with the comforting presence of my nearest and dearest friends, I ventured into the challenge. *Bismillahir rahmanir raheem*—in the name of God, the Most Gracious, the Most Merciful—I whispered as both a plea for strength and a commitment to the journey ahead. With this mantra, I embraced the uncertainty, ready to rewrite the narrative of Bali and, in doing so, reclaim a piece of myself from the wreckage of a broken relationship.

***

Before landing in Bali, I buried myself deep in work as a coping mechanism. From chasing the ever elusive inbox zero (an impossible feat!), crafting the marketing plan for the next year (I love to do) and reluctantly following up on vendor payments (a task I'd rather avoid) work became my daily refuge. For a solid nine to 10 hours each day, my mind found solace in tasks that had nothing to do with the breakup. Despite the usual work-related stresses and pressures, they provided a much-needed escape from the melancholy engulfing my thoughts.

But during that week on The Trip, it was an entirely different narrative. I found myself on holiday, liberated from the shackles of my day-to-day obligations. No more 7:30 am alarms piercing through my dreams, no more 8 am video calls with the regional team, mercifully free from the tyranny of my 200 plus unread emails. I should have been in a state of blissful relaxation, right? But well...*Fuck me*. That's exactly when everything started to creep back in. Because for the first time ever since the breakup, I had the luxury of time to just...feel.

No more distractions to keep the emotions at bay. It was like the floodgates of suppressed emotions had burst wide open. The picturesque Bali landscape became the backdrop to my emotional unraveling. The freedom from obligations also meant the freedom to confront the pain.

One morning, the cruel grip of insomnia dragged me out of slumber at 5 am. Despite the company of my friends in the villa, an overwhelming sense of loneliness settled over me like a heavy fog. A haunting thought that the breakup was entirely my fault loomed large. I convinced myself that I was the one who had driven my ex crazy, sentencing myself to a lifetime of singlehood. The words echoed in my head like a relentless refrain: *I drove him crazy, and now I will be alone forever.*

On another day, I opened Spotify first thing in the morning, sought out the Spice Girls and played their song "Mama" on repeat. The acoustic guitar's gentle opening, followed by Baby Spice's soft singing, wrapped me in a cocoon of warmth that felt as if it emanated from my own mother. Though physically absent, I could feel her love and unwavering support, a reassuring embrace that transcended the digital waves.

Then came a morning enveloped in a suffocating sadness, a weighty feeling I couldn't pinpoint. I found myself unable to muster the strength to leave the bed, lying there in the shadows, curtains drawn, lights off and concealed under the security of my blanket. It was as if I had plunged into a pit of despair, my body heavy with an indescribable sorrow. Hours slipped away as I lay in the dim room, tears streaming down my face, until the persistent knocks of my friends shattered the suffocating silence and forced me to emerge from the darkness.

Depression, as I discovered, is undeniably real. It doesn't discriminate, and unfortunately, it doesn't take a break—not even when you're on vacation. It clings to you, casting shadows even in the most picturesque settings, reminding you of its relentless presence.

I eventually acclimated to my holiday-induced depression and decided to adopt a strategy of having zero expectations and planning absolutely *nothing*. It was a sort of preemptive strike against the looming cloud of uncertainty, ensuring that my holiday plans couldn't be completely derailed—because, well, I had no plans to begin with! Hah!

***

Allow me to introduce my friends in the villa: Mouna and Michael, the first duo in our eclectic mix from Amsterdam. Mouna, a Swedish-born beauty of Eritrean descent, quickly became my best friend through work. We shared a unique bond, both navigating the delicate balance between our open-minded, liberal outlook and our efforts to reconcile it with our Islamic religion and, at times, culturally conservative backgrounds (pork? A big NO! Ramadan? We gladly observe. Sex before marriage? Absolutely, as long as your parents are blissfully unaware!). Oh, and did I mention she was my fantastic maid of honor?

Now, onto Michael, Mouna's boyfriend and also my ex's Best Man for the wedding. A German-Singaporean engineer turned consultant, Michael harbored a not-so-secret dream of becoming a DJ. His life unfolded with the precision and accuracy you'd expect from someone raised in the fusion of two of the world's most efficient and unbending cultures. It was a consensus among our friends that if Mouna and Michael were to have a baby, that little one would be bestowed with the most enviable combination of genes.

Next, Linda and Robert. Linda, a striking German-Jamaican mix, proudly stood as another beauty in our wonderfully diverse Ethnic Squad™ gang. Much like Mouna, my introduction to Linda happened through my work at Adidas. Our shared love for techno beats and the cult movie *The Room* wove the threads that bound Mouna, Linda and me together as the best of friends. "You're tearing me apart, Linda!"

Now, let's talk about Robert, her boyfriend. A genuinely nice and steadfast German guy, his heart matched the kindness of his soul. And his biceps? Solid. As Linda gracefully danced from one dancefloor to another, Robert served as her unwavering anchor, the steady rock she always came home to.

The next dynamic duo? Boy and Willem. Boy and I go way back to our innocent days as two young Asian students navigating university life together. He's like my Filipino brother from a distant Pinoy aunty. We've lived together, we've traveled together and we probably had an encyclopedic knowledge of each other's exes. Boy, with his "forever 25" appearance, embodied the epitome of what it meant to have excellent Asian genes—whatever you think his age is, add 15 years to it. Annoyingly youthful looking, I know.

And then there's Willem, the Dutch half of the equation. A solid guy with green fever (he loves gardening), undeniably Dutch, with a last name that might tickle your throat as you attempt to pronounce the G as *gggggeeee*, complete with the quintessential Dutch directness we've all come to appreciate.

This eclectic crew, this mishmash of friends, became my anchor and emotional safety net amidst the unexpected twist of a canceled wedding-turned holiday trip. Over dinner one night, I laid my cards on the table, telling them, "Please don't expect anything from me. I'll try to be there as much as I can, but if I suddenly disappear without saying anything, even in the middle of a conversation, please forgive me. It's not you guys. It's definitely me. My brain might be crashing, and I just need to be alone."

My friends, the seasoned companions who'd known my quirks from our years in Amsterdam, took my disclaimer in stride. They didn't bat an eye at my sudden withdrawals during dinner, my incoherent ramblings or my insistence on doing nothing more than lounging by the pool. Instead, they patiently knocked on my door every morning, ensuring I didn't spend too long stuck in bed and miss out on the scrambled eggs whipped up by Mouna and Linda.

Their understanding and unwavering support made those initial days in Seminyak, waiting for the rest of our gang to join later in the week, a comforting prelude to the main event of The Trip: the wedding cancellation party and a four-day stay at the Morabito Art Villa in Canggu (a.k.a. the actual wedding venue). The presence of the three couples provided the companionship I needed, and with their reassuring nods and watchful eyes, it felt like they were prepared even if I were to suddenly have a mental breakdown.

As we transitioned from Seminyak to the Morabito Art Villa, the backdrop for the canceled wedding, the emotional journey deepened, marking a turning point in The Trip. It was a blend of solace, understanding and the unwavering camaraderie of dear friends, turning a potentially devastating experience into something bearable and, dare I say, memorable in its own unique way.

**

As we concluded the initial leg of The Trip and ventured northward, we bid adieu to the hustle and bustle of Seminyak, exchanging it for the laid-back, hipster-filled and gentrified surf town vibes of Canggu. Leaving Sunset Road in our rearview mirror, our car cruised through the streets of Petitenget and Batu Belig, infamous stretches dotted with international eateries, Ibiza-style beach clubs and luxurious hotels that had mushroomed side by side over the past decade. Nestled among these upscale establishments were a handful of local, low-key spas and warungs, valiantly striving to maintain their relevance amid the ever-changing landscape of their high-profile neighbors.

As the wheels turned and memories flickered, we passed by landmarks that triggered a cascade of recollections and anxiety. Each place bore witness to bittersweet memories of Bali, shared with my ex.

Potato Head. *Our first Bali trip together.*

Bebek Tepi Sawah. *Our favorite fried duck joint.*

Merah Putih restaurant. *The caterer for our ill-fated wedding.*

The car navigated through the narrower streets of Canggu, where açai bowl joints and yoga barns coexisted peacefully. The route to the Morabito Art Villa unfolded through a familiar shortcut, a road my ex and I had frequented countless times in the months leading up to the wedding. We had traversed this path, visiting and revisiting the villa with our wedding planner, meticulously planning every detail of what should have been our wedding day.

Along this narrow, poorly paved road in Canggu, rice paddy blocks were nestled between the newly developed modern Canggu homes, poised to bulldoze through the remaining minted lands still occupied by the lush, green and soon-to-be-gone rice fields. The prospect of change loomed on the horizon, and in about a year or two, the view would be transformed entirely.

The Circle K in Batu Bolong. *We almost ran out of gas there one time.*

The skate bar at the end of the street. *A place we had yet to visit.*

That small street in Berawa. *Our favorite Bali Airbnb.*

Each location whispered stories of our shared history, etched in the fabric of our relationship.

Honestly, there were moments during The Trip when I questioned my own sanity. Most depressed and brokenhearted ex-brides would run as far as they could from places that echoed their shattered relationships. Yet, I found myself doing the exact opposite—revisiting every single painful memory. It felt like being an emotional masochist, purposefully subjecting myself to the agony of reliving the past. Or, perhaps, I was just plain crazy.

"This feels so weird," I confided in Mouna as the car meandered through the familiar streets.

"Oh, it must be, darling," she responded, casting a sympathetic glance my way.

"The last time I passed this street, we were—" I faltered, unable to complete my sentence.

"Hey, don't worry. We're all here," Mouna reassured me, reaching over to grab my hand for support.

As we approached the last left-turn leading to the small, gated street where the wedding villa awaited, I announced to the group, "We're here."

The road narrowed, and the anticipation built. We entered the property through its roundabout entry. Stepping out of the car, we were immediately greeted by the villa's striking entrance hallway adorned with dozens of intricate white, dove-like wooden statues stretching from the milky high ceiling.

Making our way inside the villa, we passed through a doorway crafted from black stone and gold-painted carved wood, shaped like a replica of a Balinese temple gate. Flanking the entrance gate were two white and yellow fringed traditional ceremonial umbrellas, standing tall on each side, extending a warm welcome to the tropical haven that was Morabito Art Villa.

Morabito Art Villa was part art gallery, part luxurious resort, part best place to throw a wedding (cancellation) party. Owned and curated by the artistic French soul Pascal Morabito, this villa was more than just a temporary abode; it was one of his family's Bali homes that graciously opened its doors for private wedding ceremonies, among other moments of celebration.

Stepping into the main building, we were immediately greeted by a grand, wide, open living room area that offered a panoramic view of the lush and exotic beachfront garden, stretching toward the Indian Ocean. Nestled in the heart of this immense garden was a large, white swimming pool, bordered by an array of charming exotic plants that probably only my botanist friend Rama could identify.

With nine eclectic rooms, each boasting its own unique design and a collection of antiques that could make even the most devoted collector green with envy, the property felt like a hidden sanctuary. Scattered across several charmingly mismatched buildings, every space carried its own personality, as if infused with stories from another era. It wasn't just a place to stay—it was a haven, a retreat that promised not just comfort, but a touch of magic in every corner. It all felt like a curated exhibit from a tropical modern art museum, seamlessly woven into the fabric of the villa.

Returning to the villa, this time without a fiancé by my side, I still felt its charm, its warmth wrapping around me like a familiar embrace. The sense of belonging lingered in the air, undisturbed by time or circumstance, reminding me once again why this place had carved out a special corner in my heart.

"The party should be here," I jumped straight into party planning mode, gesturing towards the area beneath the wooden steps of the patio. "And the DJ booth should be up there."

"When will the speakers arrive?" Michael inquired, eager to assist.

"Sometime tomorrow morning. I'm not exactly sure what time. Could you lend a hand with setting up and sound checking?" I delegated the task to him.

"Sure thing!" he replied with enthusiasm.

"And over there," I indicated the far end of the garden, where palm trees loosely dotted the landscape, "that's where we would have exchanged vows. At sunset, between those two trees in the middle."

We stood in silence, collectively envisioning the majestic scene that could have been.

"Mira, this is getting really sad," Mouna interjected, breaking the sombre silence.

"Oops, my bad. Let's focus on the positive. Follow me, I'll show you the rest of the space," I suggested, leading the group to explore the rest of the estate.

"What's that?" Linda pointed towards a white structure resembling a tall terrace adorned with antique outdoor chairs and tables.

"I'm not entirely sure," I confessed, casting a glance towards the mysterious white structure. "But I think it's some sort of terrace for sunset viewing. You get a panoramic view of the beach from up there."

As we walked beneath the structure, I continued, "That building next to it is where the Morabito family stays when they're in Bali. And behind it, there's this massive warehouse where they store all their crazy art and antiques! It can feel a bit creepy in there, so don't wander in if you're high! Who knows what might come out!" I playfully warned them.

"This place is truly stunning," Mouna remarked, her eyes sweeping across the estate once more before heading to her designated room.

She was right. Despite the painful end to my relationship, one thing remained undeniable: We had chosen an incredible venue for our wedding. And I couldn't help but feel excited for the journey that awaited us in this magical place.

***

Over the next 48 hours following the arrival of the Ethnic Squad™ at Morabito Art Villa, more of my friends from Europe and Jakarta touched down in Bali, adding to the lively atmosphere of our tropical retreat.

First, there was our beloved Brazilian duo: Paulo, another DJ and colleague from Adidas, and his ever-so-sweet girlfriend with the biggest heart, Tati.

Then, there was Lieke, the second Dutch member of our group: a fellow single, 30-something lady who had recently experienced her own breakup. Our friendship had blossomed over the years as we shared our love life's struggles and triumphs.

Next up was Daniela, affectionately known as Ela, my former flatmate from our basement Amsterdam flat, "The Dungeon," and a kindred spirit from Austria. We bonded over our love for wearing black, mastering the perfect cat-eye eyeliner and indulging in copious amounts of sweets.

Another familiar face from The Dungeon era was Marieke, our upstairs neighbor. Born in Sri Lanka but raised by Dutch parents, her passion for food was infectious. Marieke was destined to become the next Johannes van Dam.

In addition to the Amsterdam crew, more and more friends from Jakarta began to arrive in Bali. The final additions to our Morabito gathering were my Indonesian dance floor partner-in-crime—and Disco Queen—Natasha, along with her husband, Jakarta's infamous disco DJ Bergas.

Staying together at a villa near Morabito were my *halu*[2] high school best friends Andara, Tia and Nurul, along with their plus ones. These ladies had known me longer than anyone else attending the wedding cancellation party. We go way back to a time when our facial skin didn't need the daily touch of Biologique Recherche's P50 to stay supple and youthful.

Also staying nearby were my Indonesian bros, Mario and Teguh, and their then-girlfriends. Mario and Teguh were my Indo BFFs. Together, we were the Bekasi Boys and Girls comrades. They would have been my bridesmaids had they been born female.

And last but not least there was probably the most unique friend I've ever had, Rama. A high school desk mate turned BFF, Rama was a botanist and a Javanese dancer with a tan to die for. Rama followed his own path: breeding orchids using artificial lights

---

[2] Halu, short for hallucination, is the Indonesian way of saying delulu (delusional). They are always optimistic about something but unrealistic (like wanting to be frugal for a year when they ended up booking two European trips in the same year).

under his desk and exclusively listening to traditional angklung and gamelan recordings.

These were my people. My quirky crew. My support system during the best and worst of times. They were the reason I dared to come back to Bali and confront all those memories head-on. With them by my side, I knew I'd always have someone to lean on, no matter what happened during The Trip.

As the party day drew nearer, each and every one of them lent a helping hand to make things happen. It didn't feel like my party anymore; it was our party. It was a collective effort put together by the village of "Mira's Really Really Nice Friends," with a population of less than 20.

"Two compact disc jockeys (CDJs) and one turntable are coming in an hour," I told Paulo and Michael, who would also be DJing at the party.

"Awesome. Who's playing vinyl tomorrow?" asked Michael.

"Bergas will. He brought some solid disco tunes," I answered.

"Sweet! So how do you want to arrange the timetable?" Paulo followed up.

"Hmm...To be honest, I haven't thought about that yet. I was hoping it would just be an open deck where everyone just plays whenever they feel like?" I ventured.

"I think you should set some rough timings," Michael, channeling his structured German side, suggested.

"Hmm, okay. What about you guys open at noon with a chill deep house set? And then maybe Amir can play in the afternoon and Bergas and Archie after sunset?" I suggested.

"Okay. And are you going to play?" Michael asked.

"Hmm...I'm not sure about that. Depends on my state of being tomorrow." I answered.

"You just let us know, yeah?" said Paulo.

"Okay. Thanks guys," I responded.

"Mira, what should we do for food?" Mouna came over with Linda as I wrapped up my music setup discussion.

"I think we should just get pizza from the villa." Linda chimed in. "It's easy for people to eat while partying. No need to prepare plates and cutleries," added Linda.

"Yeah that's a good idea. But no pork salami please!" Mouna reminded us of her Muslim dietary restriction.

"Yes. Good call. And let's make sure we order enough vegetarian ones for Linda," I added.

"What about snacks?" Linda asked.

"There's a bigger supermarket 10 minutes away from here. We can take the car and buy some stuff there. A bunch of chips and cookies would be enough I guess?" I answered as I scribbled all the food notes on a piece of paper.

"Don't worry. We'll go there and shop for the snacks. You just stay here. What else do you want?" Mouna suggested.

"Okay. Thank you ladies. I think everything that's written here would be enough." I gave her my note.

As Mouna and Linda headed out with the driver, I walked over to Marieke and Ela who were lounging by the pool, enjoying the warm Bali sun.

"Can you guys help me write this Facebook message invite? I want to send it to all the wedding attendees this afternoon." I joined them as I sat next to Marieke.

"Yes of course!" said Ela, coming out of the pool to join us.

"Make sure you tell people to bring their own booze," Marieke reminded me.

"Ah yes, good point." I typed that point into my phone.

"And have them bring their swimsuit and towel so they know it's a pool party!" added Ela.

"Yes! I don't think we have enough towels for people here. They definitely should bring their own," I said.

As I drafted the final party invitation, a WhatsApp message came in from Andara. "Mir, we have five bottles of gin, three bottles of vodka and two bottles of whisky with us. Shall we drop them off at your villa already?"

To optimize on alcohol cost, I had asked guests who were coming to the wedding to each get a bottle at the airport Duty Free. And I was glad to know that most of them did just that, despite the cancellation of the wedding.

"Yes please!" I answered. "Come anytime. I'm here the whole day."

"Do you need us to get mixers too?" she followed up.

"Uhm, no, no. I'll sort the mixers out. Don't worry. Can you just tell the rest of the people who came with bottles to come early to the party tomorrow?"

"Sure. Leave that with me." Andara reassured me.

That afternoon, Cyra the wedding—turned party—planner came by to check on everything and delivered the sound system.

"If you need anything else just let me or the villa staff know. They are very helpful!" said Cyra as we ran through the plan for the party.

"Yes they are! They are literally the nicest people ever."

"Well, I think you're all set now. Have a blast tomorrow!"

"Thank you Cyra. Thank you for everything," I hugged her tightly in the lobby as I walked her out of Morabito.

I walked back inside the villa to the hustle and bustle of party planning. With everything falling into place, anticipation bubbled inside me. My heartbeat faster. But this time it felt different. Unlike the anxious knots of earlier days, this excitement was palpable. It was happening—the party I'd envisioned was taking shape before my eyes.

***

03/05/2016, 11:04

> Dear friends who are currently in Bali / are still coming to Bali this weekend,
>
> To turn the cancelled wedding around, I would like to invite you all to an impromptu pool party on Friday, May 6th at Morabito Art Villa in Canggu (yes, it's the initial wedding venue on the original wedding date!). Venue deposit can't be returned, so there's no reason to not use it to have a little party while everyone is in Bali! 😊
>
> We'll start at 2pm till midnight. Friends will be DJing, I'll have some booze and snacks but feel free to BYOB and don't forget to bring your swim suit, sunglasses and towel! 😊
>
> See you!

> PS: If I might have missed anyone that are still in Bali, please pass the message along! Hope to see you all this Friday! x

IMAGE 12: *The wedding cancellation party invite*

As the day of the wedding cancellation party dawned, sleep eluded me. Knowing that breakfast wouldn't be served until 8 am, I realized at about 5 am I couldn't stay in bed any longer. My body seemed to crave movement, urging me to heed its call. So, without further ado, I slipped into my trusty running gear, a complete ensemble from head to toe, proudly branded with Adidas, my former employer. With each stride, I felt the anticipation building, propelling me forward as I embarked on a sunrise run along the tranquil expanse of the Berawa beach.

Venturing onto the beach, I encountered only a young couple strolling hand in hand along the shoreline, their presence adding a touch of sweetness to the quiet scene. With each step I took on the soft sand, I realized that I had never truly experienced a beach run before, especially not at such an early hour when the remnants of the tide still lingered, forming pockets of water along the shore.

As I continued my jog, heading left along the coastline, I encountered other early risers engaged in their morning routines, each one enjoying the invigorating salty breeze. However, my Baywatch-worthy morning run didn't last long. With the rising sun came a rise in temperature, causing me to quickly break into a sweat and struggle to catch my breath in the humid heat.

Deciding it was time to turn back, I acknowledged that even a 35-minute workout was a significant achievement, especially in the sweltering conditions. As I made my way back to the villa, I spotted Paulo and Michael up and about, their surfboards laid out on the grass as they stretched.

"Morning, guys," I greeted them with a smile as I passed by. I couldn't help but feel a sense of pride in my morning accomplishment. After all, no matter what the rest of the day held, I had started it off on the right foot.

***

"Good luck today :)" a message from the Neuroscientist, offering a wave of support, illuminated my phone screen as I emerged from the refreshing shower.

Wrapping my hair in a towel, I settled onto one of the deck's ornate metal chairs, the cool breeze of the morning brushing against my skin. With a sigh, I called him expressing my nerves and the restless night that had preceded the day.

"That's normal. It's a big day for you," came the reassuring reply from the Neuroscientist, his words offering a semblance of comfort.

"Yeah. I still can't believe that I made it here. This was supposed to be my wedding day! Everything feels a bit surreal still."

"Maybe in another alternate universe you are already married," he mused.

"Yeah, maybe," I replied, contemplating the idea of parallel realities. "Or divorced already," I chuckled.

"So what time does the party start?" he shifted the conversation.

"Noon. Well, I asked people to come around two."

"Do you think your ex will come?"

"I hope not!!! I mean, I know he is also in Bali. And I'm sure he knows about the party. And a bunch of his friends will come too. But yeah, he better NOT come," I added firmly.

"Oh, so you invited his friends too?"

"Yeah. I mean, they are already here, and they were supposed to come anyway to the wedding, so I figured why not invite them too," I explained, trying to stay nonchalant.

"Ouch. He might not be too happy about that."

"Yeah, well...I don't really care haha. I guess it's up to his friends if they want to show up or not."

"That's true. You're just being a generous inviting party host."

"Exactly!"

"Well, I'm sure you have a lot to prepare so I will leave you to it." He sensed my need to focus.

"Thanks :) And you're still flying into Bali tomorrow night?"

"Yes. I'll see you there in two days," he confirmed.

"Great! Looking forward to it!" I felt a surge of excitement as I rose from the pool deck's chair and descended the stairs to officially kick off the wedding cancellation party day.

***

Downstairs, the aroma of freshly made toast and scrambled eggs greeted me as I joined Boy and Marieke at the breakfast table. They were already indulging in the morning feast, savoring each bite amidst the tranquil ambiance of the villa.

"Morning!" I greeted them cheerfully, taking a seat and helping myself to some cut fruits and watermelon juice.

"Oh hey," Marieke responded, her mouth full of toast, her surprise evident at my early appearance, especially after my morning jog.

"What time did you get up?" Boy inquired.

"Quite early. I couldn't sleep anymore so I went for a run."

"I literally just woke up!" Boy chuckled.

"Did you guys sleep alright? Where's Lieke, by the way? She arrived last night, right?" I asked, curious about the whereabouts of our friend.

"Yeah, she's probably still sleeping from the jet lag," Boy replied.

"Well..." Marieke's voice trailed off mischievously as she exchanged a playful glance with Boy and me. "I had company last night, so I didn't sleep much I guess," she teased, her wink suggesting an eventful evening.

I gasped in mock shock. "Shut up! Don't tell me that Colin stayed over?"

"Yeah, he did," Marieke smirked.

Boy exclaimed. "I knew it!"

I looked around the breakfast area. "Where is he now?"

"Still sleeping in my room," Marieke replied, nonchalantly.

"I love it!" The whole thing felt so carefree.

"By the way, are you ready for today, Mir?" Boy asked.

"Yeah, I think so. Why wouldn't I be?" I responded with a shrug, trying to mask my lingering doubts.

From a distance, I spotted Willem strolling toward the breakfast table, his cheerful greeting punctuating the morning tranquility. "Goede Morgeeen!" he called out, his enthusiasm infectious.

"Morgeeen!" We responded in unison, welcoming him with warm smiles.

"Here, babe, come sit here," Boy beckoned to Willem, gesturing to the seat beside him.

Willem hesitated for a moment, then teased, "Naaahhh...I'm going to sit next to Mira this morning," as he playfully claimed the chair next to me.

"Hey!! Niet leuk!" Boy protested to the affectionate teasing.

"Grappig schaatje," Willem reassured him, taking Boy's hand from across the table. "I'll move over in a bit," he promised.

"Okay, fine," Boy relented.

"Gooooooood morning, lovely people," Mouna chimed in, entering the scene with Linda in tow. "Has anyone seen Michael?"

"Yeah, I saw him and Paulo this morning about to surf," I said.

"Ah, I thought he was back already," Mouna replied, settling into her seat alongside Linda.

"Colin stayed over!" I couldn't resist sharing with the group.

"Aww...Ck ck ck...Marieke...Well done," Linda commended her with a playful wink, prompting laughter from the group.

"How many people are we expecting today?" Boy inquired, shifting the conversation to logistical matters. "And who else do you think will hook up today at the party?"

"I'm not sure how many will show up later. I sent the party invite to most of the 150 original wedding invitees. Minus his family, of course. And oh, I'm definitely NOT hooking up with anyone!" I replied, preempting any speculation.

"Oh god no, Mira. No, no, we need to protect you today. Don't hook up with anyone, please," Mouna added.

"Yeah, don't worry. I won't," I assured her.

"And Mira..." Mouna's tone softened as she reached out to grasp my hand, her eyes locking with mine. "If at any point of the day you don't feel good about the party, or you change your mind about having that many people over, you just let us know, ya?"

Her concern made me emotional. I felt protected.

"Yeah, I'll kick everyone out," Linda jumped in. We all laughed.

"And then we all can just chill by the pool all day again," Mouna said.

Feeling the warmth of my friends' support, I squeezed Mouna's hand, my heart brimming with gratitude as I glanced around the breakfast table. "Thank you guys," I said sincerely, overwhelmed by their unwavering solidarity.

"So, is the party still on?" Boy's hopeful gaze met mine.

"Oh, hell yeah!"

***

Since my university days, throwing themed house parties has been a cherished hobby of mine. There's something about hosting gatherings, especially ones where people can let loose and have fun, that truly energizes me. Costumes have always been my go-to icebreaker for getting people to relax in new surroundings, hence my love for themed parties blossomed. Throughout my twenties, I took pride in orchestrating some epic events.

One standout was The Dungeon Halloween bash at my old Amsterdam flat with Ela. Queef and Dave, my then silly riot girrrl band (I played bass), rocked out in the living room while over 100 guests showed up in spooky attire (our neighbors weren't too pleased, but we made it up to them with cake!).

My knack for party planning didn't go unnoticed at work. My manager dubbed me the Party Marketing Manager (PMM), a role I embraced wholeheartedly alongside my official position as a Product Marketing Manager. Outside of office hours, I was responsible for ensuring that any work-related social events or visiting guests from other regions had an unforgettable time in Jakarta. My boss trusted me to show them the best of Jakarta's nightlife, with the expectation that I'd keep the party going until the wee hours. Talk about the best of both worlds!

But throwing my own wedding cancellation party was a whole new ballgame. Gone were the elaborate themes and costume dress codes, replaced by uncertainty and nerves. Should it be a jubilant celebration? A sombre acknowledgement? Or perhaps a fiery display of indignation directed at my ex? I had no playbook for a wedding cancellation party. All I had was a wedding villa, an open deck and an invitation to whoever still wanted to join. Oh, and there was me, an ex-bride who might have a nervous breakdown in the middle of it all. *This is going to be fun!*

※※※

That day, Bali graced us with perfect weather. The sky stretched out in a flawless shade of blue with wisps of white clouds that drifted lazily by, offering intermittent relief from the tropical sun. I slipped into my new black two-piece swimsuit and threw on a loose, unbuttoned white shirt for some added coverage, slathering on a generous layer of SPF 30 to ward off sunburn while still allowing for a golden tan.

Although guests weren't expected until 2 pm, Paulo and Michael decided to kick off the festivities early, spinning their warm-up deep house beats from noon onwards. Their music filled the air, setting the stage for what promised to be a groovy day. I found myself slowly getting into the party mood, lounging by the pool with my feet dipped in the water, soaking in the vibes.

As I glanced around, I spotted Ela emerging from her room in her signature black and white tube top adorned with an oversized bow—200 percent cute, as always. Meanwhile, Marieke reclined on a pool bed, cigarette in hand, exuding an air of effortless coolness. Boy stood under the sun's rays, chatting with Lieke, who was determined to catch up on her tan after arriving fashionably late. Each person seemed to be in their element, fully embracing the relaxed atmosphere of the day.

"Guys, pizza's here. I think we should eat now before everyone else arrives," Linda announced as the Morabito staff brought out boxes of warm, fresh pizzas.

"Mir, let's dance!" Natasha pulled me away from the poolside when she heard Michael playing a familiar tune. I grabbed a slice of pizza and took it with me onto the grass—the makeshift dance floor. Joining Natasha, I began to move to the music, trying to balance eating my pizza while grooving to the beat.

"Michael is good!" Natasha exclaimed as she danced around me.

"Yeah, he is," I agreed, taking another bite of my pizza.

"What do you want to drink?" Natasha asked.

"Just ginger ale for now," I replied, mindful of pacing myself for the long day ahead.

"Be right back!" Natasha headed over to the makeshift bar area manned by the Morabito staff to grab some drinks.

By 2 pm sharp, the first guests started to trickle in. It was Amir and his friends. *Germans*, I thought. Always on time. I quickly finished my pizza and made my way to the entrance, arms open wide. "Amiiiir! It's so good to see you again!" I exclaimed, embracing him tightly.

"How have you been?" Amir asked, giving me one of those amazing hugs.

"Well...I'm alive!"

"You look well,"

"Aww...Thank you! I'm definitely better than those days on your sofa in SF!"

"That's good to hear. You remember my girlfriend Nivan," he said, introducing her.

"Yes, of course!" I hugged Nivan warmly.

"And these are my friends from Berlin and Amsterdam. Ben, Eliese and Stefan."

"Well, nice to meet you all! Welcome!" I greeted them with a handshake and a smile.

"Amir told me that today was supposed to be your wedding," Ben said.

"Yeah...that's not happening anymore. I guess you can call today a wedding cancellation party!"

"That's even better!"

Over the next few hours, many more friends and colleagues—old and new ones—trickled into Morabito. With each arrival, my worries about whether people would show up to a rather sorrowful wedding cancellation event slowly dissipated.

Everyone I'd hoped for showed up: new friends from Jakarta like Erlend and Pooja (with her baby bump!), my Google crew, including my boss Veronica with her husband and my teammate Farrah, who brought the youngest guest of the day, little Liam, and even old friends like Markus, who flew in from New York with his girlfriend.

In addition to them, more Amsterdam friends made it too. Thomas came with his new girlfriend, along with Khan, Suzanne, Colin and many others. To my surprise, some of my ex's friends also decided to join the festivities (I couldn't help but wonder how he felt about that). And last but not least, DJ friends from Bali who had promised to grace the deck also made an appearance. Apparently, people *do* show up to a wedding cancellation party!

Before I knew it, the pool area was buzzing with conversation and laughter as my nearest and dearest mingled. For the first time, my Amsterdam and Jakarta worlds collided around the Morabito pool. This support system provided me with the energy and strength I needed to navigate through the day.

By 4 pm, my Jakarta high school BFFs crew—Andara, Tia, Nurul—showed up, along with Mario and Teguh and their then-girlfriends. Mario and Teguh were my Indo BFFs. Together, we were the Bekasi Boys and Girls (BBG) comrades. Had they been born female, they would have been my bridesmaids. Everyone fulfilled their promise of bringing all the alcohol bottles.

"Where's Rama?" Tia asked.

"Not sure. He said he'd come in the afternoon," I replied, scanning the area for any familiar faces.

"Seems like a good turnout! How many people are here?" Nurul asked.

"Not sure. Maybe 60 so far? But I think more people are coming later, so I guess I'll end up with 80 people?" I said, giving it my best guess.

"Congratulations, Mir," Andara chimed in.

"Eh? What for?" I asked, puzzled.

"For dodging the bullet on this one!"

"Yeah, you're right. I think I really should celebrate the fact that I was almost married!"

"I bet he's crying by himself in Bali at the moment, seeing that his friends are all here," Tia speculated.

"I hope so, too!" I chuckled. I liked the idea of him getting a taste of his own medicine. "Anyhow, you guys make yourselves at home! The bar is over there, and the toilets are behind that area. Food...oh, seems like they're finished. Shoot. I should order some more food." My mom's voice echoed in my head, reminding me of the importance of proper hospitality: "You need to give your guests good food if you invite them," she always said.

"Mira, relax. Let us handle this," Andara said.

"Oh, okay. Thank you," I sighed, relieved to feel so supported.

***

The sun began its descent, casting a warm, golden glow over everyone gathered at Morabito Art Villa. What started as a wedding cancellation event blossomed into a vibrant celebration reminiscent of a summer festival. The bar buzzed with activity as drinks flowed freely. By the poolside, friends laughed and shared stories. Couples found moments of intimacy on the grass, lost in each other's embrace. It was a scene of pure joy and camaraderie, where love radiated in every corner, despite the absence of a wedding ceremony.

As I moved from one group to another, ensuring I connected with each guest, I sensed palpable ease and contentment. Morabito had worked its magic. I swapped stories, spontaneously danced with friends and lounged by the pool in equal measure. Far from being a sombre affair, the atmosphere was infused with the carefree spirit of summer love.

When I finally checked my phone, I couldn't believe it was already nearly 6 pm. *It was time*. With a sigh of anticipation, I set my gin and tonic aside and made my way towards the row of palm trees at the edge of the garden. As I reached the two towering palms in the center, I came to a halt. Standing there, I let the gentle breeze caress my skin, mingling with the salty tang of the ocean air. I closed my eyes and took a deep breath.

In another universe, I would have been a bride. I would have stood atop the raised ground between the palm trees, my chiffon gown billowing in the breeze, its delicate fabric forming a dreamy silhouette around me. I would have clasped my soon-to-be husband's hands, gazing into his eyes as I spoke my vows—promising to cherish, to remain faithful, to love until the end of time—surrounded by those dearest to us. And then, we would have shared our first kiss as husband and wife.

For a fleeting moment, I allowed myself to step into that wistful vision, to exist in an alternate reality. I felt bittersweet longing. But I opened my eyes and anchored myself in the present. I stood among the same palm trees, surrounded not by wedding traditions, but by the people who truly mattered. There was no grand ceremony, no exchanged vows, but the love that enveloped us was undeniable, authentic, unburdened and strengthened by the raw beauty of honesty.

Andara came by and grasped my hand firmly. "Only you could pull this off, Mir," she said, gesturing towards the exuberant crowd. "Who else could rally every single guest to still show up for a canceled wedding? Everyone is here because of you."

Her words made me feel a deep, affirming rush of gratitude and pride. I looked around, taking in the scene. In the absence of a wedding, we created something even more meaningful. It was proof that love endures, that bonds can strengthen even in the wake of disappointment and heartache.

Forget the wedding. Love was undeniably in the air, woven into every laugh, every embrace, every shared moment. And in that sun-drenched haven, I knew that Bali was not going down as a sad reminder of my loss. Bali was being rewired in my memory as a symbol of resilience and renewal—a testament to the transformative power of love in all its forms.

***

My therapist emphasized time and again in our sessions the importance of steering clear of mixing my anti-anxiety drugs and alcohol. But, being the quintessential rebellious middle child, I chose to ignore her advice.

As the sun dipped below the horizon and darkness descended upon us, the atmosphere called for a shift to a more intense beat. Don't get me wrong—I thoroughly enjoyed Michael and Paulo's daytime deep house set. However, it was time for me to step into the DJ booth and transition the vibe from Café Del Mar to Panorama Bar.

"I've been drinking all day. Should I still take my chill pill?" I asked Natasha.

"Uhm, not sure. Heard you can't mix those things." she replied.

I hesitated, contemplating the familiar admonishments from my therapist. But then, a defiant thought asserted itself: Why the hell not? It was my wedding cancellation day, and I was entitled to do whatever I pleased. So, with a shrug, I took a bite of the pill and washed it down with my gin and tonic. "Can you hold onto the rest for later?" I handed her my drink.

"Of course, just let me know when you want it."

"Thanks, Nat."

I had never spun tracks while under the influence before. Sure, I had played gigs with a slight buzz from alcohol (those were the days!), but never with added anti-anxiety drugs in the mix. What if I got too messed up? What if my mixing became a total train wreck?

Screw it. If I botched my own set, there were plenty of DJ friends on standby at Morabito who could seamlessly take over at a moment's notice. And so, with a sense of reckless abandon, I hit play.

※※※

I couldn't recall how long my set lasted. Once that pill hit, time became a distant concept, irrelevant in the midst of the music. It could have been three hours or three minutes for all I cared. It was as though I had received an instant upgrade in my DJ skills, with my mixing flowing seamlessly and my track selection hitting all the right notes. It felt like I was being guided by some elusive music deity, effortlessly led from one perfect track to the next. Honestly, I couldn't say if I was actually that good or if it was just the substance doing its magic. Ha! But damn, I have to admit, that was probably the best set I've ever played—EVER!

Plus, it was my own damn party. So, I had the freedom to play what I wanted. No obligations to please a bar owner who paid me to perform. No discerning crowd to cater to. None of that. The circumstances were just perfect for a stress-free set with no expectations.

Natasha returned to the DJ booth and grabbed the mic, her voice cutting through the music to call out to more people. "Guys, you all better be dancing here now!" Her energy was infectious, drawing more friends to the grass where Teguh and Natasha had been dancing nonstop since the first track of my set.

As 8 pm approached, darkness descended, casting a tranquil atmosphere over the gathering. I glanced around and noticed that half of the guests had gravitated towards the pool, their laughter mingling with the gentle lapping of the water. The warm glow of the garden lights, mirrored by the pool's calm blue surface, beckoned me. It was time for me to wrap up my set. I queued up Moralez and Kings of the Universe's "Acid is The Answer" for the final track and passed the DJ booth reins to Amir before shedding my white shirt and heading straight for the pool.

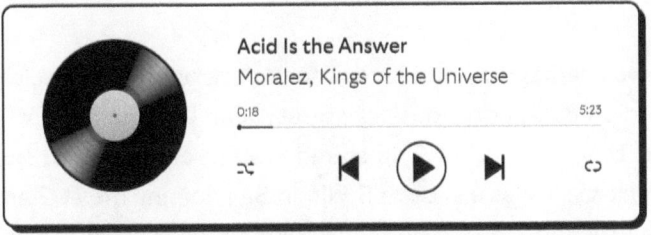

Entering the water, I was enveloped by its warmth, like a liquid blanket. I leaned back, allowing the water to support me as I closed my eyes and surrendered to the sensation of weightlessness. The sounds of the party faded into a comforting hum, muted by the water filling my ears. I let go, allowing the sorrow and tension to dissolve with each gentle wave.

I looked up at the night sky and was captivated by the brilliance of the stars, their twinkling like a celestial lullaby. I was happy to be alive. Happier still to be with my friends.

A familiar voice called out from behind me, and I turned to see Rama, finally joining the festivities. With his eclectic style, he wasted no time in making his presence known, launching into his signature Javanese rave dance move. It was a sight to behold, and I couldn't help but laugh with joy.

"Rama!" I rushed out of the pool to greet him with a wet hug.

"Hello my dear. Congratulations once again for dodging the bullet!"

"Hehe, thanks Ram. So glad you could make it." I replied.

"Where are we headed after this?" he asked eagerly.

I shrugged. "I haven't even considered it."

"How long can we keep the party going here?" Rama inquired.

"I think the main speakers need to be off by midnight, for the neighbors' sake," I recalled, repeating what Cyra had told me.

"Perfect. Let's head to KOH afterward. There's a great DJ playing tonight," Rama suggested.

"Sounds good to me. I'll just follow your lead. I'm up for anything!"

**

KOH was dark, grimy and loud. The underground techno club was nestled on Bali's notorious gay street, Jalan Dhyana Pura. With its unisex toilet, Funktion-One sound system and a crowd buzzing with energy, it was a slice of Berlin in Bali. Joining me at 2 am was a small techno crew, including Rama, Natasha, Amir, Lieke, Boy and a few of Amir's friends, all of us unwilling to let the night end prematurely.

The love and positive energy I had soaked up from my friends throughout the day kept me buzzing. Sleep was the last thing on my mind; I was wide awake and ready to channel my energy into more dancing. I needed to release all the pent-up emotions swirling inside me, and there was no better way than losing myself on a techno dance floor.

As we entered KOH, I made a beeline for the front of the dance floor, positioning myself in front of the DJ and the towering industrial fans behind him. Without a word, the Morabito crew formed a protective circle around me, shielding me from any unwanted interruptions. It was exactly what I needed—a safe space to lose myself in the music.

Long before I discovered somatic therapy, I found solace in the dance floor, using it as a tool to process and release emotions trapped within me.

That night at KOH, with the Morabito crew providing a barrier from the outside world, I danced and danced. I surrendered to the pulsating techno beat, letting it purge my grief, anger and frustration. With each sway and step, I felt my emotions lightening, replaced by a sense of liberation.

As the night wore on and my companions gradually called it a night, I danced on, eventually accompanied only by Rama. My body ached from the relentless movement, but my heart overflowed with contentment. We danced until the last track faded away and the lights came on, signaling the end of an unforgettable night.

***

The morning sunlight filtered through the master bedroom curtains, gently nudging me awake. Relief came over me as I realized I was back in my own room, in solitude.

Stepping onto the balcony, I gazed out over the expansive Morabito garden, feeling a curious sensation stir within me. With a deep breath, I felt a subtle expansion in my chest and a gentle fluttering in my stomach—an unfamiliar yet oddly comforting feeling. And as Mouna and Boy waved up at me from the pool below, a smile tugged at the corners of my lips. It dawned on me—I felt...happy.

It wasn't a jubilant, exuberant kind of happiness; rather, it was a quiet, contented one. It was like the warmth that spreads through you when a stranger's smile brightens your day or when you stumble upon a forgotten treasure at the bottom of your purse. It wasn't life-altering, but it was undeniably pleasant.

I was grateful that I had mustered the strength to host the wedding cancellation party. Dancing through the day and night had been exactly what I needed to shake off the heavy cloak of depression. Now, as I basked in the gentle glow of contentment, I felt a glimmer of hope. Though I knew there was still a long road ahead in my healing journey, it felt like the worst was behind me.

"How was it?" The Neuroscientist texted.

"You were right," I typed. "I'm so glad I went through with the wedding cancellation party. It was exactly what I needed to create new memories and move past the canceled wedding."

"Seems like you had a lot of fun?" He responded with a smiley.

"Yes! Surrounded by all my friends, it was such a loving atmosphere. It was sooo nice!"

"That's amazing. How are you feeling now?"

"Well, I'm nursing a bit of a hangover," I confessed. "But it was worth it. It truly felt like one of the best days of my life!"

"I'm so glad to hear."

"Thank you for nudging me in the right direction. Without your encouragement, I might still be wallowing in despair back in Jakarta."

"No need to thank me. You're the one who took the leap and made it all happen."

Chapter 3

THE REBOUND

🎵🎵🎵
I'm just looking for a good time
And I think it's in your sheets
She likes to cuddle
I just want some heat

She wants Mr. Right
I want Mr. Right Now
Now that we're standing on even ground
Do you wanna be my rebound?

REBOUND
by **JOHSA MANZANILLA & LINDSAY DUNCAN**

I had my first rebound when I was 21. I was young, naive and freshly brokenhearted after the end of a three-year interfaith relationship. He was a devoted Christian Indonesian young man, and I was a Muslim. And despite him having had a profession that made the list of "Jobs Approved by Asian Moms"[3] (tax lawyer), my mom never blessed our differences in religion. So we had to end things.

Prior to age 21, I hadn't been single for longer than a month since I got my first boyfriend at age 12. Since then, it was one steady relationship after another, mostly with much older guys who refused to grow up and/or were in a band (adult realization: I had daddy issues). I'm not saying it was healthy, but it was clear. I always knew my relationship status.

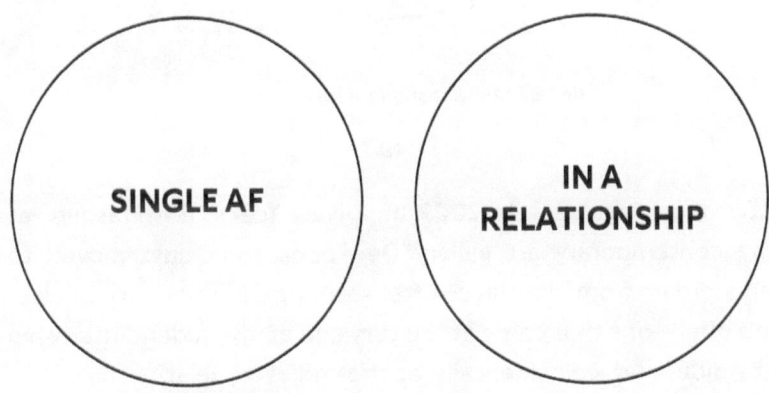

IMAGE 13: *Relationship status before (pre-2012)*

In my late twenties, I began to notice that things were becoming more complicated. Friends of mine were sort of dating someone but still seeing other people, or they had "friends" who didn't seem like just friends. The lines were blurry, and grey zones were everywhere.

My own dive into this intricate grey area began on a cold, post-breakup December night in Amsterdam—an unforgettable night that led me to KDY (a.k.a. Mr. Best Rebound Ever) and my very

---

[3] 'Jobs Approved by Asian Moms' are engineers, doctors and lawyers. But these days entrepreneurs and startup founders would be acceptable too

first lesson in navigating and understanding the complexities of that in-between space—and the unexpected beauty that could come from it.

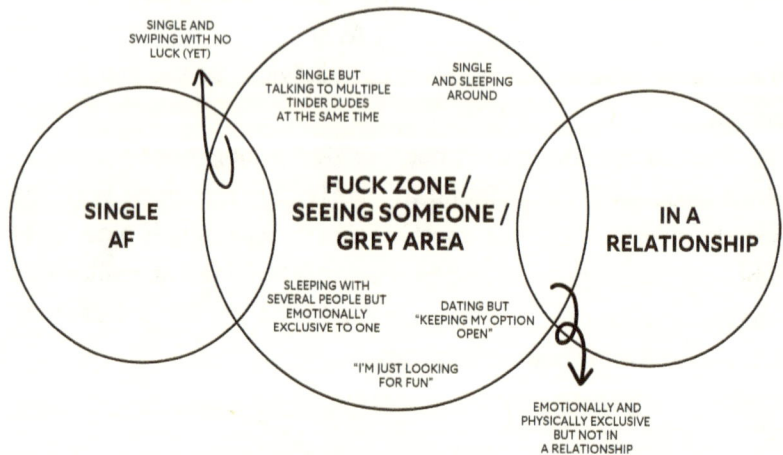

IMAGE 14: *Relationship statuses nowadays*

***

KDY and I met back in 2009 at a New Year's "Bal Masqué" at the contemporary art gallery De Appel. I had just moved to Amsterdam from The Hague after securing a permanent-contract job offer—one that came at the very end of my student internship at Adidas and, coincidentally, at the end of my relationship.

I was eager to start my new life and new year in Amsterdam. So I decided to come to De Appel's artsy, masked-themed New Year's party with my Queef and Dave bandmate, Vina (she was the singer, I played bass). I wore an avant-garde leather outfit, a cat woman mask and a fuck-it-I'm-gonna-party-and-flirt attitude.

KDY immediately caught my attention when he walked into the room. Unlike every other party attendee, he came in dressed casually with no mask. His nonchalant can't-be-bothered-to-dress-up attitude and lack of theatrics ironically made him stand out in a sea of extravagantly dressed art students. *Hmm, that guy is cute.*

His jet-black eyes locked onto mine as I moved through the crowded dance floor, subtly inviting him to follow. Two Michael Jackson ("Thriller" and "Beat It") and one Amy Winehouse ("Valerie") songs later, we were dancing together, weaving between sets of large fluorescent braided ropes hanging from the ceiling, making out to the remixed sound of the King of Pop.

***

KDY turned out to be a Korean-born, Dutch-adopted, art school graduate and karate master who worked as a baggage handler at Schiphol airport. A pretty random mix of professions, I know. But this experience gave him strong lean arms and a mind filled with eclectic wisdom. With his Adidas ZX sneakers and North Face jacket, he dressed like a hipster graffiti artist, yet he carried himself with a quiet presence. He spoke with the precision of someone who had spent years in disciplined practice (must be his karate!), as if every sentence had been thoughtfully weighed before leaving his lips. His monk-like demeanor made him seem both detached from and attuned to the world around him, a paradox I found intriguing.

He also let me in on some travel industry secrets: Before Rimowa was all the rage, those classic zipperless Samsonite hard cases were *the* toughest and most durable suitcases you could ever get.

After our hell of a fun, intoxicating New Year's rendezvous, we decided to go on a second date where we ended up at his place by the Waterlooplein flea market. Tipsy after dinner, I decided to do a little walkthrough around to give his place a proper scan.

KDY didn't have much furniture at his place. These days he would probably be called a minimalist. But back then it felt like he was just squatting in the apartment temporarily. My eyes landed on the only photo frame on his desk. Inside the wooden frame was a photo of a curly, brown-haired little girl in a green dress. She looked like she was about two years old. *Cute. Must be his niece.*

"Who's that?" I pointed at the photo.

"That's my daughter."

"Oh…" came out of my mouth. But, *WHAT THE FUUUCK???!! HE IS A DAD? HOW DID I NOT SEE IT COMING? WHAT THE FUCK AM I DOING WITH MY LIFE SLEEPING WITH A DAD? I'M 21! I'M NOT READY FOR A DADDY! OR TO BE A STEPMOM! CODE RED!! LEAVE!! IMMEDIATELY!!!! AAAAA…BUT IT'S SO COLD OUTSIDE!* was what went on in my head.

"Are you okay?"

I immediately sat down. "Can I get a drink?"

He poured me a glass of red wine and joined me on the sofa to calmly tell me everything. Long story short: He and his ex-girlfriend, who lived in Milan, had already broken up when they found out that she was pregnant. Despite the split, they decided to keep the baby and give an Amsterdam-Milan long-distance co-parenting relationship a try. *Seriously, how the fuck do you even do that?!*

Obviously they knew that kind of arrangement was never going to be sustainable in the long run. But Amsterdam was not an option for her and Milan was not an option for him. Fast-forward to that day, when he told me that he was in the final process of getting his green card and moving to New York City, the chosen location where they both could co-exist in the same place as co-parents for their little girl.

Damn. That's a lot to handle for a 21-year-old.

What the hell am I doing here?

There's ZERO future with this guy, so why am I even still here on his sofa?

Even if I'm able to deal with the whole baby mama situation, he is also leaving the country!

So there is absolutely no point in continuing our night, right?

Or is there?

Obviously, neither of us were in a long-term relationship mindset at that point. I just came out of a breakup and him, well, he had *that* whole situation going on. But we knew we genuinely enjoyed each other's company. And there were still so many Amsterdam art parties and Michael Jackson dance floors that we wanted to crash. Also, this was pre-Tinder. I couldn't just swipe my way to the next match.

Maybe...we could just keep enjoying each other until the natural deadline of separation arrived? His green card was set to arrive in a couple of months, and once it did, he'd be gone anyway. It was the perfect built-in exit—an organic, civilized way to end something that was never meant to be forever.

So, we contemplated long and hard that night. We listed out all the pros and cons, debated them with the kind of seriousness usually reserved for life-altering decisions. And then, after all that deliberation, we looked at each other and thought—*why the fuck not? Let's do this.*

And so over the following 4.5 months, we had a lovely, undefined relationship filled with yummy Surinamese food, visits to various Amsterdam art galleries, competitive board games and many fun disco nights. And when the positive news of his green card eventually came, we knew exactly when he was going to leave Amsterdam for good. This allowed us to pin exactly the last weekend we were going to have together.

We decided to go for one last dance at Club Up (RIP). Our final night together carried a bittersweet weight, the kind that lingers in the air when you know an ending is inevitable.

After more than four months of spending time together—dancing, laughing and navigating the grey area—we had kept things casual, light, uncomplicated. At least, that's what my rational mind told itself. But no matter how much I tried to maintain that detachment, some tender feelings had crept in.

And as we swayed together on the dance floor, serendipitously, the DJ played "Valerie" from Amy Winehouse, a monumental song from our first night together. It felt like it was written in the stars that *that* night was really meant to be our last night together—like a movie ending. So we put our arms around each other's shoulders, shared our last dance and made a promise: "This has been really lovely. But we can't do a sequel."

"I know. Because the sequel always sucks!" he smiled.

"Yeah, you're right. Definitely no sequel." I nodded and smiled back at him.

He grabbed me tighter, held me closer and whispered in my ear, "And I just want to let you know that if circumstances were different, you are totally girlfriend material."

My heart instantly felt warm. Those words were all I needed to hear.

I smiled, kissed him one last time and let go.

Not everything good is meant to last forever. Sometimes, the beauty of something lies in its impermanence—in knowing it was special *because* it had to end. And as for KDY, wherever he is now, he will forever go down in my book as the best rebound ever.

***

So, after the positive emotional breakthrough I had from the successful wedding cancellation party, I figured maybe it was *finally* time for a rebound. And before I embarked on my search for a rebound, I wanted to be absolutely sure on what I had to look for. Thinking back to KDY and why he was the perfect rebound, it all came down to a few critical things:

Criteria	Rebound Material	Long Term Material
He is nice and understanding of your post-breakup situation	✓	✓
He is cute	✓	✓
He is a lot of fun	✓	✓
He has major deal breaker (i.e. He has a baby mama, or different religion)	✓	☐
There is natural deadline (i.e Leaving the country)	✓	☐
He wants something serious	☐	✓

IMAGE 15: *The rebound criteria table*

As you can see, certain things—like deal-breakers and deadlines—that might doom a normal relationship actually provide the perfect foundation for a temporary (but loving) rebound. Those very deal-breakers act as safeguards, keeping me from falling too deeply at a time when I knew I was still in the process of healing my broken heart. Instead of being obstacles, they became gentle reminders that this connection, however enjoyable, was never meant to last—allowing me to embrace it fully without fear of getting lost in it.

And after the Neuroscientist returned to Melbourne, our connection shifted into something different, one that revolved mostly around him scientifically dissecting what was happening in my depressed mind. With that, he officially became my mental rebound—good for my state of mind, yet conveniently confined to the safe, controlled distance of digital communication.

Now I needed someone in person. Someone around to hold hands with. Someone I could go to the cinemas with. Someone I could have a hangover cuddle session with.

And so, in search of a rebound, I went back on Tinder.

***

After swiping for a few days, I identified the most common types of Tinder guys you will encounter when swiping in my beloved city, Jakarta.

#1 THE ALAY

The Alay guys are corny and cringeworthy. "Alay" basically means "cheesy." Their overly filtered and badly taken profile photo will be paired with very limited (or no) bio information. As you swipe to see their other photos, you'll notice selfie-stick selfies at questionable places (like on riverside or next to a chicken cage—completely random!) are very common among them. If you wonder what these guys do, all you have to do is pay close attention to the background of their photos because they're always taking selfies at work—a stack of laundry in the corner? He's a laundry guy.

#2 THE BULE JALAN JAKSA

"Bule" is a term we use for white people. It's the Indonesian version of "gringos" or "ang mohs." Most of the time it's a rather neutral term, but when paired with Jalan Jaksa, which is a street in Jakarta where the backpackers go, it takes on a different meaning. So Bule Jalan Jaksa is a general term people use to call cheap-ass white people (usually older and bald or with receding hairlines) who come to Indonesia with questionable intentions (the dream of finding a submissive young Asian bride to bring home).

#3 THE CHINDO WHO STUDIED ABROAD

Chindos (Chinese Indonesians) are well-off kids who went abroad for their higher education (usually in English speaking countries such as Australia, the US and Canada). Their profiles will be in English, and you will find Western culture-influenced hobbies or interests (like drinking or American football or hip-hop) prominently shown and written in perfect English, to show just how well-integrated they are in Western culture. They know you're a fellow Indonesian, but they will still chat with you in English. *What's up, dude?*

#4 THE TECH BROS

The startup world exploded in Jakarta during the tech boom, as it did in many other cities around the world. And with that comes also the influx of founders, co-founders, CFO, CMO, COO of whatever obscure start up you've probably never heard of. A lot of them are foreigners who think they can conquer the next frontier of emerging markets: Indonesia. I mean, don't take the grandeur of their title at face value because you can literally call anything a start-up these days. Like how I am the CEO of my own YouTube Channel.

#5 THE SERIOUSLY-LOOKING-FOR-PARTNER

These guys are mad serious about finding a *wife* on Tinder. You know this because, well, they write it on their profile. (i.e. "Looking for a soulmate to spend the rest of my life with," "Looking for a Muslim wife."). In Indonesia, civil weddings don't exist, which means you can't legally marry inter-religiously. So these guys put their religion prominently on their profile to attract matches of the same faith. The more desperate ones don't even want to wait for swiping to find the one. They just put their contact info directly in their bio in the hopes of their future wife sliding into their WhatsApp inbox.

#6 THE "VISITING BUSINESSMAN"

These guys are not from Jakarta, and they make it very clear that they are in town on a temporary stay. They will write down on their profile precisely how long they will be in town by listing out their exact travel dates. Also, to make them look more legit as businessmen, 92 percent[4] of the time their first photo will be a photo of them in a suit. These guys are looking for "a classy lady" who is up for a "nice dinner" and some "fun time." They mainly ended up being the target of *ayam*, which literally means "chicken" in Indonesia, but is also slang for young ladies looking for rich sugar daddies.

#7 THE SEEMINGLY NICE AND NORMAL-LOOKING GUY, BUT WITH AN EXPIRED MARRYING AGE

At first glance, there's actually nothing wrong with this last group of guys. They went to good schools, they have a solid job and their photos are relatively normal. But what makes you suspicious of them is their age (between 26-35). As a background, the average marriage age in Indonesia is 24 for girls and 25 for guys. So because most Indonesian eligible bachelors would be taken by 25, whenever a single guy has passed that age, you can't help but wonder. *What's wrong with you? Did someone hurt you badly?*

Obviously, none of these guys fit what I was looking for: a cute and fun guy with a kind heart and a deal breaker serious enough to make me *not* want to be with him for the long run (but acceptable enough for a short period of time). Ideally, they'd also work in the creative field (so we could talk shop), well-dressed and smart. *Well, okay, maybe I am asking for too much?*

***

---

[4] Data came from the robust study of 'Men with suits on Tinder.' Sample size 7.

I've always had a thing for film directors. My encounter with them started off early in my career. I started my marketing career at Adidas in Amsterdam when I was 21, and by 23, I was on set in Los Angeles shooting one of their global digital campaigns. I loved everything about being on set—the energy, the creativity, the meticulous planning yet unexpected turns of the day. Especially interesting are the people on set: from the fashion stylist to the art director and the set producer. But to me, the most interesting of all is the director, who has that alluring mix of technical skill and original vision that aligns with my creative impulse and my analytical brain. On set they act as a leader (as they direct the whole crew) and a team player at the same time (because they can't do it alone without their DoP, the sound guy, the art department and more).

A director creates films that can make you laugh or cry and transport you to places. Or he makes a piece of well-made advertising that can sell lots and lots of products. There's creativity in every film medium but also a persuasive logic to how it all comes together.

So, when I stumbled upon a Tinder profile of this cute Italian guy who seemed to always wear black (plus point!) *and* was a director (demonstrated by one of his pictures while holding a camera on set), of course I had to swipe right.

And it was a match.

***

"Love your *Planet Terror* photo!" read the first message I got from the Director.

OMG. Yes! Not only did he comment on my favorite Halloween photo, but he also knew exactly the movie my character was from. Double points! My Tinder profile strategy of putting a semi-obscure movie reference in my photos to filter out the Tinder swindlers and filter in matches who have the same cultural references worked!

"Thanks :) I love Tarantino movies!" I immediately responded.

"But Rodriguez directed that one, not Tarantino."

He was right. "I know! Tarantino produced it though." Extra points for having that knowledge alone. "So what are you doing in Jakarta?"

"I'm shooting a car commercial! A Honda ad."

"Oh cool. Which agency do you work with?"

"Hakuhodo. Do you know them?"

"I've heard of them, but I never work with them. Are they good? I'm always on the lookout for new creative agencies."

"Yeah, they are alright. It's a car ad, they're all the same," he sarcastically replied.

"Haha. Okay,"

"And you? What do you do?" he asked.

"I do marketing for Google. That's why I work with a lot of agencies too."

"Oh that's cool. Maybe you can hire me!"

"I don't make car commercials! Hehe. Also, I need to review your reel first!"

"Oh, sure. Here's my website." I liked his confidence.

"So are you based here?"

"To be honest," he said. "I don't really have a base! 😊 I live out of my suitcase, and I will just travel based on where the job takes me."

"Oh wow. I really don't know how you do that."

"I don't own much. So it's pretty easy to pack my life and move somewhere for a couple of months," he said.

"And how long are you in Jakarta for?"

"For this project two months. And then I'll head back to Italy for a couple of weeks before coming back to Jakarta for another project: a Nissan ad. And maybe Dubai after that, if I get the job with Toyota," he said.

"Oh wow. You're really a car specialist yeah." I opened his website at the same time to check out his past work. *This guy is pretty good.* Audi, Maserati, Jeep, Pirelli, Ferrari. *He has done them all.*

"Yes, sort of. I would like to do more non-car lifestyle projects though. But I keep on getting booked for car commercials because of my reel."

"Yeah I can see that. Your work is really good though!"

"Thank you 🙂. So, tell me. What are you doing on Tinder?" He immediately followed up.

"Well, I just got out of a relationship," I said. "I canceled my wedding about a month ago." I wanted to be honest. I had nothing to lose anyway.

"Oh wow." He paused. "What happened? If I may ask."

"He left just a few weeks before the wedding."

"What an asshole! I'm sure you're better off without him."

"Well, obviously the story was a bit more complicated than that. But I'm okay. I had a wedding cancellation party! Haha. That was super fun." I replied.

"You probably made the right decision."

"Yeah, I think so too. If not, we would probably have gotten divorced within a year."

"We should meet. You're interesting!" he said.

If being almost married made me an interesting person, *I guess I'll take it as a compliment.* "Sure. Let's meet. You don't seem to be a weirdo 😆."

"Don't worry. I am not a serial killer. So, coffee sometime soon?"

"Sounds good. Maybe next weekend? "But before we meet, can I have your full name, please? I need it so I can Google you and verify your existence 😆."

"Of course! Do you want a copy of my passport too? 😄."

"Haha it's okay. Just the name will do."

***

The Director was a solid eight in my Googleable scale. His website featured his bio with additional interesting details (BMX rider turned film director), a lot of past work portfolio (cars, cars and more cars) and of course, a photo of himself. With landscape shots of the desert of Dubai to the skyscrapers of

SWIPE THERAPY 125

Hong Kong and a few artistic shots of him on set, his Instagram account gave me the impression that the Director was a pro and that he was constantly being flown in to do all kinds of international jobs. He must have been really good at what he did.

Besides their Googleable score, another bare minimum threshold when deciding to meet someone is by asking myself "Can this person at least be a good LinkedIn contact?". So even if there is no romantic, sexual or friendship interest with the person, at the very least I added someone new to my network. Therefore: No CV, no coffee.

***

How to pick a location for a first Tinder date

When choosing a time and place to meet a Tinder match in person, several important factors and criteria should be considered for the first meetup.

1. It's a public space (safety first!).

2. The place is somewhat casual (so you don't have to put too crazy of an effort in dressing up).

3. It's daytime and the place has to be well lit (so there is no escaping the no-filter IRL).

4. The timing needs to be a drink/meal time that does not have to involve alcohol (brunch is a pretty good choice).

5. BUT, the place needs to have a bar (in case your initially 'sober' date does go well and it feels right to continue with alcoholic drinks). Then you can turn that Brunch into a boozy one.

Point #4 is especially important to start with because we all know that
a) everyone can be our best friend with alcohol, and
b) your vision gets 3% more blurry with every glass.
So, by the time you hit your 7th glass, you could be on a date with a monkey, and it wouldn't matter.

So, in order to avoid regretting any decisions you make while intoxicated, I highly suggest meeting a stranger from the internet sober (at first!). This way your gut feeling (very important!) is not clouded. I prefer that I have my full sober ability to analyse and scrutinise a human being *before* deciding to get drunk with them. Well, of course unless I have quickly made up my mind that all I want from them is some sexy time in bed and nothing more.

IMAGE 16: *A Tinder tip*

He was late. *Ugh.* Frickin' Italians. It seemed like they adopted a similar sense of elastic time[5] like my fellow Indonesians. If this was his way to make an impression on a first date, *well,* he wasn't off to a good start. *Where's that German punctuality when you need it?*

Twenty minutes and many mindless Instagram scrolls later; the Director finally emerged at the entrance of Potato Head at Pacific Place. He showed up dressed all in black. *Okay, right choice of color.* Plus point. A well-fitted black v neck t-shirt paired with a meticulously double-folded black denim. *I have to admit this guy understands a good fit.* I gave him another point for that. On his feet were a pair of beaten-up grey Vans. *Hmmmm.* I'm more of an Adidas kind-of-girl, but his Vans were vibing well with the whole monochromatic mature skater-boy look he got going on.

His messy dark hair, scruffy beard and introverted grey eyes were the same as how I saw them in his profile. If it weren't for the extra white hairs that I was only able to notice in person, I would have thought that all of his Tinder pictures were taken as recently as last month.

I gave him my right hand to initiate a handshake, but he went in for the hug. And it wasn't just a hug. He went for a proper five-long-seconds one—tight squeeze and all.

"Okay, that's enough," I awkwardly pulled myself away. "I'm just not really a touchy person, especially with strangers."

"Oh, I'm sorry," he immediately pulled away. "But don't worry, after being with me you will love hugging!"

Nice confidence.

"Let's see about that," I said. "But no more touching!"

It's not that I don't like physical touch. But having been brought up in a predominantly Muslim country where you're taught from a young age that men and women are not supposed to come into physical contact unless they are *muhrim*[6], the act of

---

[5] "Elastic time" also known as *jam karet* in Bahasa Indonesia, refers to the habit of always arriving 1.5 hours late, which is generally accepted as normal because you can always blame it on the traffic

[6] *Muhrim* refers to a state of familial or marital relationship between a man and a woman in which physical contact and close interaction are permitted under Islam.

showing affection by touch to the opposite gender simply never came naturally for me. I need more warm-up time to be able to be comfortable with physical contact and intimacy with someone.

We absolutely love each other to death in my family, but we simply don't hug. We're more about making sure everyone is well-fed—caring and loving at a little bit of a physical distance.

"What do you feel like drinking?" the Director asked as he sat down right next to me. Our thighs touched. My heart rate rose a bit as he entered my sacred personal space. *Why is he sitting next to me when there is an empty chair there?*

I put in my request for "something non-alcoholic, please," as I tried to inconspicuously shuffle an inch to the right to create space between us.

"So tell me about your wedding cancellation party! How was that?" I was glad that my "almost-married" status didn't stop us from meeting.

I took my phone out. "Shall I just show you the video?"

"You have a video of it?!" he sounded enthusiastic, shuffling once again closer.

Oh no.

"Well, when you cancel a wedding one month away, there's really not much refund you can get back. Everything and everyone was paid for. So I got the film crew to shoot a wedding cancellation party instead!"

The Director took his white Apple earphones from his backpack, plugged them into my phone and pressed play. I waited silently as I tried to read his facial expressions from his smirks and the movement of his brows.

"Seems like a great party!" He returned my phone. "But tell your editor I have comments on the editing. Please cut a couple of frames from the rooftop dancing scene. And then on that pool scene, he could edit it closer to the beat. That will make the video tighter." He was funny. I liked him.

Maybe he could be my rebound?

***

"Almond eye! I'm near your office. Are you still working?" read a text from the Director one early Wednesday evening. He called me "almond eye" because of the shape of my Asian eyes. I wasn't sure whether that was kind of cute or borderline racist (probably racist by today's standards). But back then, I just let him.

After that initial meeting at Potato Head, we'd been on four dates over the course of three weeks. I wasn't sure yet if we were able to say that we were "seeing each other." We hadn't even kissed yet (he said we should take things slow, given the fact that I just had a canceled wedding), but we knew we loved spending time with one another.

"Yeah. I'm still in the office," I responded. There was nowhere else I was going to be on a midweek evening. The breakup seemed to turn me into a workaholic, antisocial, single Jakarta girl. So if I wasn't doing my night run or hot yoga, of course, I would have been at the office, slaving away until bedtime because, well, no one was at home waiting for me.

"Can I come visit you?" He was at Plaza Senayan, the mall next door.

"Errr...I guess so." His request surprised me. "There are still some people at work, but yeah, sure come by. I can show you my office."

It didn't take long for him to show up—head to toe in black of course.

"The receptionists left at 5 pm," I explained the empty reception while I keyed in his name on the guest registration machine. "Here," I passed him the personalized visitor badge along with a red tag to hang it. "You need to wear this tag visibly at all times."

"Okay boss!" He winked and hooked the tag onto his shirt.

The Google Indonesia office was already quiet by 7 pm. The few remaining people were either working overtime or simply waiting for Jakarta's traffic to die down before heading home.

"This is the Marketing corner, and that's where I sit!" I pointed to the desk at the end of the last row. I had a wide, white desk with adjustable standing legs that faced the open-plan space. Through the three-meter-high floor-to-ceiling windows behind my desk you could see Jakarta's classic night scene: Dazzling lights from skyscraper buildings fused together with the illumination of hundreds of cars fighting through the traffic.

"You have a great view," he said.

"Yeah, we do. I can just sit and watch the traffic from up here. It's quite handy to be honest to figure out when it's a good time to go home. But wait till I take you to our big training room. The view there is pretty sick. You can see our national stadium."

I had to give it to Google. The company sure knows how to find good locations for offices. I have never been to a Google office with a less-than-desirable location. New York? Chelsea Market. Singapore? CBD. Tokyo? Shibuya & Roppongi Hills. San Francisco? By the pier. With the exception of the mothership Mountain View campus (that's just frickin' far!), I would be happy to work from any of the other offices around the world.

"And this is where they feed us." I opened the door to the most important part of every single Google office: the (free) canteen.

Google Jakarta's canteen was a two-storied, high ceiling, mezzanine-shaped cafeteria decked with colorful floral ceramics. On the mezzanine floor above, which was accessible through the circular metal stairs, was the wellness and game area. That compact but delightfully decorated area was filled with Android bean bags, various gaming consoles, an elliptical machine, TRX ropes and a ping pong table. You could say that all those facilities were set up there to ensure employees' well-being, but you could also say that it was simply another way to keep you focused on *just* work. Because whenever you need a quick stress release cardio between meetings, you don't even have to leave the office!

"Who drew all the illustrations?" The Director walked around to observe the painted brick wall of the mezzanine. It was an illustration of Indonesia's very first President Soekarno, along with a "merdeka atau mati" speech bubble.

"Er...To be perfectly honest, I don't know. Some local artist, I'm sure."

"I like the style. And what does this mean?" He pointed at the speech bubble.

"Independence or die," I said.

"Cool. I like this guy," he remarked. "Nice office."

"Thanks! Oh, there's one more you haven't seen. The nap pod!"

"You can sleep in the office?"

We left the canteen and headed to the mezzanine above the reception. We passed through the booths until we reached the far end of the area, which was walled off with a room divider and a plexiglass Google logo. I pushed the door with a red vacant sign on as we entered the most comfortable corner of the office, filled with mattresses and Google colored pillows and comforters: The nap pod.

"How many co-workers have you made out with here?" teased the Director.

"Hey! Of course, none." Semi-offended, I squinted my eyes at him. "I don't date co-workers. I like to keep a clean distinction between my personal and professional life! It's not good to mix it up."

"Why not? I met my ex at work, on a set in LA," he responded.

"Well, that's you! I would never date a cowor...oh wait." I put my finger on my lips. "Nah, I lied. One of my exes in Amsterdam also worked at Adidas. Okay, never mind." I blushed. "But no, I've never made out with anyone here!" *But maybe we will?*

"I'm sure many people have used this place for making out." He looked straight into my eyes as he took a step forward.

Okay, he is getting...close.

My heart started to race. It felt like tiny bubbles were bursting inside my belly. He was getting really close! *Uhm, what do I do? What do I do?* I sat down abruptly and tried to keep my cool.

"I mean, yeah, this is actually the only corner in this office where there is no CCTV camera. This room was not initially built as a nap room. It used to be just a chill corner but then they built that wall to create a partition and converted this whole area." I kept on blabbering to hide my nervousness. "I think they did a good job with the construction. You can't even tell what it was bef..."

He silenced me with a kiss.

As if I had a "FRAGILE Handle with care" sign on my forehead, he went in cautiously. His soft, thin lips gently caressed mine.

Fuck, I miss this so much.

He knew not to intrude on my space hastily. He took his time as he gently touched my hand and tiptoed his lips around mine. With his breath brushing my face, I could feel the wall that I put up to shield myself from another heartbreak slowly crumbling down.

This feels so good. I took a deep inhale as I started to bite his lips.

I can go on forever. I held his hands tight.

Oh shit. I didn't turn the door sign to Occupied.

What if someone walks in on us? My mind started to panic. The fear of getting caught mixed with the excitement of doing something forbidden in the office caused a major stir in me. *Mira...shut up and just enjoy this.*

I put my hands around his neck. As I moved my hands up along his jawline, I grazed the stubble of his beard. Our tongues met, then he teasingly pulled his tongue away. *Hey, come back!* I slowly bit his lip.

Then we were both lying down, with him on top of me, on one of the colorful mattresses. We continued to make out passionately until suddenly an intense feeling of guilt took over. It felt like someone splashed cold water on my face to snap me out of the steamy situation.

"I...Uhmm." I let my hand go and pulled back.

"Are you okay?" Puzzled, he pulled his hands away.

"Yes, I'm fine." I sat down slowly. "I just need a breather. I think this is a bit much."

"Did I do something wrong?" He looked worried.

"No, no. You didn't do anything wrong. It was really nice. This whole thing is really nice actually. But I just feel like, uhm...can we just take things slow? I don't think I want to have sex yet." *And especially not here in the office!*

"Oh, I see." He took a deep breath of relief.

"It hasn't even been two months since my canceled wedding. Maybe it's all a bit too fast, too soon for me. I told myself to give it at least three months before sex," I explained.

"Mira..." I liked it when he called me by my name. "Don't worry about it. Trust me, I understand. I'm not in this for sex. I love our chitchat. I love the time we're spending together. For me, you're a long-term investment you know, so I can wait." he wrapped his arms around me and pulled me in for a hug.

"Thank you. That means a lot." I looked at him before I rested my head on his shoulder. "And you're right," I continued.

"About what?" he asked.

"I'm really starting to like your hugs."

"I knew it!" He held me even tighter in his arms.

"This is really nice, but can we continue to make out more though?" I looked up to him with a cheeky smile. "But just making out! Nothing more."

"Of course, as you wish!"

And we leaned back in.

***

Jakarta felt like a brand-new city after the Director and I got together. All the painful memories of the city that reminded me of my previous relationship evaporated as I re-explored my own hometown with someone new.

The Director loved taking photos, so we explored architecturally interesting places and drove through captivating small streets that I had never seen before in my own hometown.

He was also a vegetarian (he couldn't bear to think about animal slaughtering) and I wasn't, so we ended up trying out all the vegetarian-friendly restaurants that I had never been to before.

In a lot of Indonesian people's minds, even the concept of vegetarianism doesn't completely make sense to them. When you say you want vegetarian food, they will give you a "vegetable" dish, but they may still use shrimp paste in the sauce and they will still insist that it's a vegetarian dish. But there are a lot of true vegetarian-friendly dishes in Indonesian cuisine. My favorite: the yummy *gado-gado*. It consists of blanched vegetables, bean sprouts, beans, kol, tempeh, egg and is topped with spicy peanut sauce. It's absolutely delicious! But yeah, there's only so much gado-gado you can eat every day before you start getting sick of it. So the Director often resorted to ordering some Burgreens with Gojek when he ran out of vegetarian ideas.

Because the Director and I worked in the same field of marketing and advertising, we related to each other's work lives. Whenever one of my creative agencies showed me reels of directors, from which I had to choose for a campaign, I came to the Director for his professional advice.

"What do you think of this guy?" I showed him the reel of Zahir, a young Malaysian director. "It's good," he said. "But I can probably do a better job," he teased.

"What about this one?" I showed him some films from Desmond, another Malaysian director. "He did a lot of artsy cigarette ads. I like his style. Feels quite fresh and contemporary," I added.

"Yeah, I agree. Go with him. But why are there so many Malaysian directors here in Jakarta?"

"To be honest I don't know. A lot of the good ones just seem to be Malaysians," I said.

"Make sure you also check his editor and the post house he will be using," added the Director.

"Who do you usually use?" I asked.

"I usually do the first edit myself. It's faster."

"Oh wow. That's cool."

"Babe, do you want to see the storyboard that I just got? You won't believe it."

"Sure, show me."

He got his laptop and opened up the file.

I studied the board carefully and arched my brow as I saw tacky drawings of a car jumping from a bridge onto a gigantic record player and started spinning. "A client actually approved this?" I looked at him with disbelief.

"Yep." He shrugged. "Shooting next week."

"I really don't know how this is going to sell more cars. If I were the client, I would not have gone with that idea."

"Well, not all clients are as smart as you." He closed down this laptop.

"Aww, thanks, babe." I gave him a hug.

"Maybe we should work together sometime."

"You know what, I think that could be really fun!" My eyes lit. "But I am not sure if I will ever be your client because I don't think I will ever work for a car company! I can't even drive!" I admitted one of my major flaws as an adult.

"You don't have a driving license?" He didn't believe me.

"Nope," I answered proudly. "But I also can't drive! I've decided that I will just wait until self-driving cars become commercial!"

"Not a bad idea." He smiled.

Even though I didn't care about Porsche, BMW or Honda, I could appreciate how he artistically captured whatever he shot. With his keen eye for details, through his films, he was able to create a strong, intimate desire towards an inanimate object like a car. He had this amazing ability to bring out all the highly technical parts of the car while making them feel organic at the same time. The way he worked the camera to highlight a car's curve was like the work of an erotic filmmaker. He made those damn cars look bloody sexy! And that was sexy to me.

His great visual aesthetics also came in handy for my own Instagram feed. It didn't take long for him to become my unofficial #instagramboyfriend.

"Look, I got a great shot of you. But that electricity pole behind is distracting my eyes." He showed me the photo he just took. "I would probably Photoshop it out later."

"No! That's cheating! Too much manipulation. I will never do that for my feed!" I protested. "In my feed everything needs to be real. There's already way too much overly filtered, highly edited stuff on social media!" I argued, trying to defend my Instagram feed principle.

"But, babe. Who cares about reality these days? Reality sucks!" He shrugged. "My feed isn't a reality. It's my vision," he added. "Plus, I get jobs from it. So the photos better be perfect."

Besides all our fun little adventures—the work chats, the photo taking and the Jakarta vegetarian restaurant exploration, I was most grateful for how he was there when I needed emotional support.

His kind nature allowed me to open up and be honest with him as I went through months of therapy, yet his sarcastic Italian humor allowed me to laugh about my own post-breakup misery in his company. Whenever my ex sent an email (the never-ending argument about how much money is owed) that shot up my anxiety and drove me to the brink of tears, I ran to the Director's place, and he would welcome me with open arms.

"What an asshole! Babe, you're lucky you didn't end up marrying him."

He was damn right.

***

We'd been seeing each other for about three months when the Director decided to head back to Italy to see his parents for a three-week stint. Like a child being left by her parents, I started to spiral into anxiety.

What if my ex suddenly pops up? Who can I run to?

Who is going to hug me whenever I feel sad and lonely?

Who am I going to go to the cinema with? I want to watch Finding Dory.

What if I have panic-attack-inducing nightmares again?

My mind was racing out of control, and I needed a quick way to calm it down. I knew I should have meditated or gone for something mindful like a yoga class or something. But of course I chose the foolish way to get out of a spiraling mind by numbing it with the easiest mindless distraction within arm's reach…swiping on Tinder.

Yes, the Director and I were *kind of* seeing each other (or whatever definition you could give to the situationship we had), but I figured since we were not *officially* a couple, there was nothing wrong with me continuing to swipe on Tinder purely for the entertainment (and distraction) value of it. And to throw in a little Descartes to make it sound pseudo-philosophical: *I'm bored, therefore I swipe.*

For a short while, the swipe-to-kill-anxiety method worked. My fear of being left alone again calmed down with every new match I received. Despite having had no intention of starting a conversation with any of those guys, to know that there were people who found me attractive and interesting enough to match was more than enough. It felt like I had plan B, C, D and E lined up in case the Director never came back.

But after a while, like a junkie taking cheap drugs, I needed more to get the same high. One day, I realized I had spent two hours on the app for nothing more than getting a low-grade hit of self-validation. *What the fuck am I doing with my life?!*

Well, the truth is, I was doing a lot less. I was avoiding people and a lot of social obligations so that I could avoid being forced to tell the "what the fuck happened?!" story over and over again. I didn't want to relive the pain, the departure, the what could have been.

I reserved my time and space for only a select few—close friends who truly knew me, the ones who would understand if I suddenly decided to leave in the middle of a meal when anxiety struck. My social circle temporarily shrank. All other acquaintances faded away, and I officially disappeared from the larger social scene. After work, all I wanted was to curl up on my sofa with Netflix or a book until I passed out, only to wake up in the morning regretting that I hadn't dragged myself to bed. *Sigh.*

Post-breakup, my time spent with the calm and quiet Director seemed to rewire me. His introverted nature rubbed off on me. And when he wasn't around, I found myself, unexpectedly, enjoying my weekends alone. Recovering from heartbreak while managing a full-time job and trying to stay relatively sane had drained me, leaving little energy for people or socializing. By the end of each day, all I craved was solitude and peace.

It felt like I had finally met my introverted side—and honestly, I was loving it.

With the Director away and my social life on pause, the only constant thing that was anchoring my life was…work.

To be honest, being in the office was actually good for me. Like dragging yourself to the gym when you have a massive hangover, the hardest thing was only the getting-there part. But once I was in the office, I would actually feel okay-ish. Back-to-back team meetings with regional and global counterparts that used to suck up all my energy had somehow turned into a blessing. The nonstop demand of being "on" at work became the best distraction from my own emotional misery. Whenever the slightest bit of sorrow rose, there was always an email or work chat to respond to, giving me a constant flow of emotional numbing drip throughout the day.

Work left me no time or space to grieve. I had to shut off my feelings, swallow them whole and push through. Every day felt like an emotional bulldozing just to keep things on track—physically and mentally exhausting. By 5 pm, I was drained, brain-dead, running on empty.

I could have just called it a day and gone home to rest, but that was the last thing I wanted. I wasn't ready to unplug from my numbing routine. Being alone at home for an extended period meant giving my mind the freedom to wander—to replay every painful memory of the relationship that had crumbled.

So yeah, *nope*. I'd rather be at work.

Drinking Red Bull every day at 5 pm might have been one way to extend my battery life into the evening, but I knew that wasn't sustainable. Instead, I tapped into one of the few high school physics lessons I actually paid attention to: Newton's third law of motion and the concept of energy conversation.

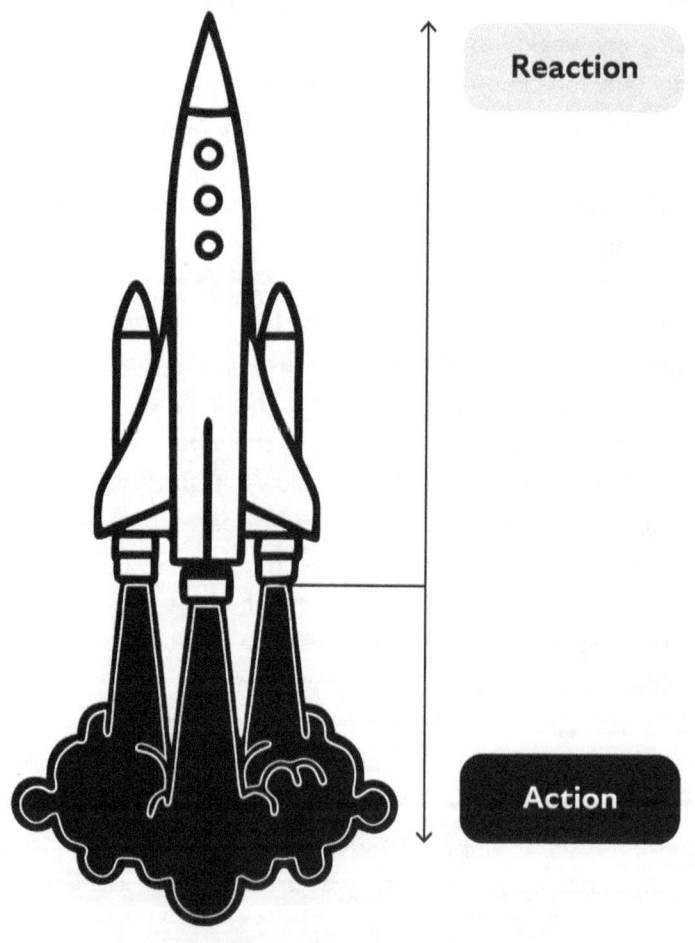

IMAGE 17: *Action and reaction illustration*

Energy is all about action and reaction: the idea that depleted energy can be replenished by generating new energy. *Aha!* So, every time I hit an afternoon energy slump, I dragged myself to the nearest yoga studio for a 90-minute intense hot yoga session or powered through a 5K run around the national stadium. And just like that, I'd return to work recharged, pushing through a few more hours until bedtime. Maybe I wasn't leaving much room for fun, but for now, my own company was exactly what I needed.

***

I cut down a bit on my mindless Tinder swiping, but it was still my go-to while stuck in gridlock traffic. One Friday afternoon, on my way back home from work, in the middle of Semanggi's rush hour traffic, the one thing that any brokenhearted millennial would dread happened: "bumping" into my ex on Tinder.

The sight of him was enough to trigger some sort of repulsed feeling in my stomach. My thumb froze and my heartbeat crazily like I was running a marathon. If I were at home, my first natural reaction would be to run to the toilet and start throwing up. But alas, I was stuck in traffic with no escape.

Why is he showing up here?

Fuck. Is he in town?!!

WHY THE HELL IS HE IN JAKARTA??

Ever since the breakup, I've unfollowed and unfriended him from all social platforms we were connected on, erasing his presence from my digital life. So I had zero idea about his whereabouts. But at that very moment, I needed to know where he was. I needed to confirm if he was really in town or if he was swiping in Jakarta from another location (I prayed to God it was the latter!). I typed in his Instagram account to confirm. *Ha! He hasn't blocked me.* Cautiously I scanned through his latest posts while I reminded myself: *Do not accidentally double tap!*

There it was: The latest picture posted is a photo of a ramen bowl from our favorite Jakarta joint dated...*today*.

Shit. He is in town.

What is he doing here?
He left this so-called "shithole of a place," so why is he here again?!
I wasn't entirely sure what troubled me more. Was I freaked out by the fact that he was in town which meant that we may bump into each other? Or was it the fact that seeing my ex on Tinder confirmed that he had moved on, because he was actively looking for...something, someone. Though...I was *also* on Tinder myself. So technically it shouldn't matter, *right?* But my heart rate said otherwise.

"MY EX IS IN TOWN. HELP!" read my desperate text message blast to a few of my closest friends. Within 90 minutes (which was pretty remarkable given Jakarta's Friday traffic) four friends were at my apartment accompanying me as I drank my third glass of vodka and Coke.

"I really don't know what he is doing here! He fucking left this city! What if he is going to suddenly show up at my door? Thank god I've changed the lock." I took a big gulp of my drink. "Can we please go out to a party? I really need to dance." I begged my friends.

"Are you sure you want to go out?" Natasha didn't sound convinced.

"Yes, I do. Please. I would rather not be here in case he suddenly rings my door. I don't know what to say to him!" I paced back and forth in my living room.

"We can also just hang here, you know. We're happy to wait with you until you fall asleep," said Jaka as he poured himself another drink.

"No, no. I can't. I think I'm too anxious. I really need to dance. Please."

"Hmm, okay. If that's what you want. Where do you want to go?" said Mayo.

"Who's playing tonight?" I asked.

Asa quickly checked his phone. "I think Ojon is playing Enter The Void at Colo. Do you want to go there?"

"Yes. That's perfect. I can just dance my anxiety away in Colo's darkness."

Natasha grabbed her purse. "Alright. Let's go then."

***

The next morning I woke up with one of the worst hangovers I could remember. It felt like someone took my brain and put it through a blender while piercing its bits and pieces with ultra-sharp, thin needles. The thumping sound of the bass from Colo also seemed to have gotten stuck inside my head, reverberating a never-ending pressure onto my skull. And to top it off, my memories of the night were, at best, patchy. Ouch. I really should have known better than to mix alcohol (especially vodka!) with anti-anxiety meds. Yes, I know. Once again, I should have listened to my therapist.

My hangover self-pity also quickly turned into intense worry when my hands also started to tremor uncontrollably. Shit. What have I done? I didn't know what happened, but I knew it must have been a dangerous side effect of my own stupidity. So I told myself: "No more, you dumbass."

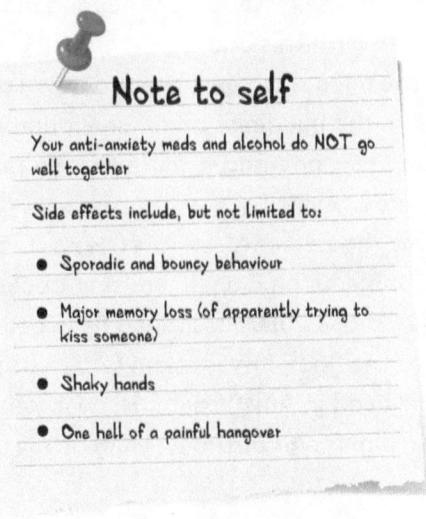

IMAGE 18: *A note to self*

After a brutal yet much needed morning kickboxing session, I decided to spend the rest of the weekend hiding at home. At that point I couldn't care less anymore if my ex were still in Jakarta. I've changed the door lock, and I have intended to not open my door to anyone, except for any Go-Food delivery guy who came to bring me my trusted emo pacifier: A box of Ovomaltine-flavored martabak manis tipis kering[7]. Yum.

As I spent hours moping at home by myself, while bingeing on the romantic yet edgy series *Love* on Netflix, the smallest traces of the canceled wedding (and my failed love life) started to make me feel claustrophobic. I still had bridal magazines on the coffee table and some copies of the wedding invite. It was all too much. I grabbed a trash bag and did a much needed and overdue wedding cancellation purge.

Bridal magazines? Trash.

Wedding Invites? Trash. Well, okay, maybe I'll keep one just to commemorate the beautiful design.

Wedding website? Subscription canceled.

Invoices? Trash.

Wedding dress? Hmm...Do I donate it? Refund it? Give it away? Keep until my next wedding? I needed more time to think about what to do with this one.

I grabbed the filled trash bag, headed down to the basement and dumped it in the building's communal dumpster. In the end, a wedding that took one-and-a-half years to plan took merely two hours to throw away.

Back in my apartment, still restless, I absentmindedly rearranged the objects on a shelf, shifting books from one side to the other. As I did, a Polaroid slipped from between the pages and fluttered to the floor. It was taken two years ago, back when my ex and I still lived in Amsterdam. He was wearing the denim shirt I had given him for his birthday; I had on my usual black shirt

---

[7] This crispy, thin, and utterly addictive sweet pancake is the love child of a crêpe and a waffle, often filled with chocolate, cheese, or nuts, and guaranteed to send your taste buds on a wild, sugary ride.

with red lips. We were in one of Amsterdam's many brown cafés, leaning into each other, caught in a moment of laughter. Not yet engaged, not yet living in Jakarta—just happy, in love.

As if I haven't had enough of an emotional roller coaster of a weekend, I went from freaking out about my ex being in town to experiencing the worst hangover ever to this: tears streaming down my face onto this little Polaroid. Once upon a time we were happy, and it felt like a lifetime ago.

With my puffed-up eyes, two empty boxes of martabak and no more episodes of *Love*, I hit a turning point. As much as I dreaded having to become one of those brokenhearted cliché, I knew I had no other option but to finally give in to watching *Eat, Pray, Love*.

Sigh. I really wished the Director was there to give me one big cozy hug.

IMAGE 19: *An Eat, Pray, Love meme*

✳✳✳

Ask any young Indonesians what they dread more than being single, and they'll tell you that it's being single *and* being forced to attend a family gathering, especially the likes of Lebaran.

Lebaran a.k.a. Hari Raya can be seen as Christmas for the Muslims. After a whole month of Ramadan, sans food, sans water, sans many sinful things from sunrise to sundown, it is the time to get together with your big, multi-generational family and stuff yourself with a whole range of Lebaran delicacies that include *opor ayam* (a kind of chicken curry), *ketupat* (rice cake inside woven palm leave), *gulai sayur* (vegetable stew) and a whole range of existential-crisis-inducing-inquiries from your family.

That year's Lebaran, which came about four months after the breakup, was special for me. To say that I was scared shitless was an understatement. Up until that point, I hadn't really communicated any details of my breakup to my extended family except for the fact that the wedding was canceled. Period. They didn't know why. They didn't know what happened. They didn't know if we were still together. And they for sure didn't know where my ex-fiancé was at the time. And I wasn't sure I needed to tell them the whole truth anyway.

"What should I tell the whole family?" I asked for guidance from my younger sister as we got ready in the morning.

With everything that had been going on, and all the money that had been lost to the canceled wedding, I didn't even have the time to think about buying a new Lebaran outfit (a tradition you would usually do). What I had left with were six tailored, green floral batik skirts that were supposed to be worn by my bridesmaids. Luckily, one of them was my size and one fit my sister. So I said *yay* for being able to upcycle something from the wedding into my makeshift new Lebaran outfit.

"I don't know. Just tell them the truth, maybe?" my sister ventured.

"I don't think they need to know that we both had a major emotional burnout."

"Okay. Yeah, that's probably too much information."

"Why do people always need to meddle in everyone's personal business?" I continued to grumble as we made our way to our aunt's house, where that year's Lebaran gathering was happening.

"You know, they probably don't mean it that way. They just want to find topics of conversation. Asking about relationship status is pretty much like asking about the weather for them."

My sister was right. Most Indonesian people are straightforward conversationalists. Saying, "Oh, you've gotten fat!" or "When are you getting married?" seemed to be the easiest way to strike up a conversation if you haven't seen each other for a while.

I mean, try to introduce a new boyfriend at any family gathering. I bet you that by the end of lunch he would have been grilled about how much he is making (because they need to know if he can provide for a family), where his father went to school (because of course he had better have gone to an equivalently prestigious uni to the one that your father went to) and what he thinks about the food (and he better say it was delicious).

Indonesians live in a communal society. So when you marry, you simply don't just marry your partner. You marry the *entire* family. Usually, I would have been able to take on my family's intense inquiry into my personal life any other day. But not this time. Not this Lebaran. My wounds were still way too fresh.

Every "What happened?" and "When are you going to find someone new?" cut deeper than the last. It didn't seem to matter how much I had achieved—my career, my friendships, my personal growth—all of it felt overshadowed by the one thing I had lost. No matter what I did, I was still just the girl who had somehow failed at life.

***

Over the course of the next few months, the situationship I had with the Director (yes, he did return to Jakarta) steadily grew into what felt like a full-on relationship, minus the official status (we never had the official conversation!). He became my trusted confidant of all my emotional troubles, my rock as I powered through the nonstop grind of corporate life and my trusted cuddle partner. I even started to wonder if maybe there was a possible future for us. But as with any relationship, especially a rebound one, the honeymoon phase eventually ends. And once those rosy-tinted glasses were lifted, I slowly started to notice a shift in how I felt and how I saw him.

From his Instagram, you will see a super accomplished, young, international director who jet-setted all over the world (from LA to Milan to Bali to Dubai) for the most coveted car advertisement jobs. It looked like he lived a life full of glam. But through the times we spent together I got to see what really went on behind all that facade. What I started to see was a hyper-focused, overworked and borderline manic person who could power through two weeks (or more!) of production time with little to no sleep. And this cycle would repeat over and over again in every single location he was in. Every single job consumed every waking hour of his life.

"You know you should take some breaks in between projects, right? Your working hours are crazy!" I started to worry.

"I don't take holidays, babe," he answered adamantly. "I don't want to be shooting cars all my life. I want to retire when I'm 40. I don't want to be like those 50-year-old directors still pitching projects to clients like you," he continued.

"What do you mean, clients like me?!"

"Well, I don't mind if my clients *are* like you. You're smart. But my usual clients are not. They can just be so dumb sometimes. Just look at this script I just got. It's so stupid. You have this car going through a ring of fire and ending up on a giant turntable. I'm not even going to put this in my reel. I'm just doing it for the money," he ranted as he aggressively typed on his laptop.

I also started to catch sight of all his insecurities. Behind all his conveyed confidence came to light one of his biggest fears in life, that because he is just so good at creating one type of commercial (in his case, cars and motorbikes commercials), he will forever only get booked for car commercials and forever be known as *just* a car director. His specialty in the business seemed to be a double-edged sword.

"I want to make movies with stories," he shared one of his dreams. "And get paid for it!" he added.

His beautifully curated Instagram feed also went from artistic and cool to somewhat fake and vain as I saw the amount of hours he took editing every single photo into perfection.

"My feed is my business card," he often justified. "I need to compete with all those 20-year-old so-called directors who don't know how to handle a camera but have millions of followers!" His frustration about the industry was apparent.

I understood what he meant, and I empathized with the pace he felt like he had to keep up and the constant manicuring of his online presence to get picked for jobs. It was exhausting. To be honest, it was too exhausting for me. And if you're used to "faking" it on your feed, *what else is not real?*

I use social media for connection. For authentic sharing of my life with my close circle of friends. For keeping in touch with my nearest and dearest. And yeah, sure, for some occasional humble brag of a good hair day selfie. The moments when I've lost sight of that use of social media have been some of my darkest days.

Right before canceling the wedding, I was guilty of over-curating my life on the platform to only show the best and most rosy side of things: The holidays, the quirky Google offices around the world, the summer festivals in Europe, the engagement ring, the seemingly perfect fiancé. And all that facade continued despite the already deteriorating state of my then relationship. Until one day, I received a message from a friend who was supposed to attend the wedding: "Can't wait to see you guys in Bali. From what I see on Instagram, it seems like you guys are having the best time of your life!"

When she said that, all I wanted to do was to scream and say: "Actually no. We are going through some really tough times now." But I simply couldn't. Those images that I have put out on Instagram about my seemingly perfect life had prohibited me from being able to be honest. And it made me feel trapped and suffocated by my own stream of #couplegoals photos. I didn't want to live like that anymore.

If I have to think too much before I post something, then it's not worth it. Sharing is for connection. And since over-curated sharing seems to deprive us of the ability to really connect at times when we actually need it the most, then I would rather not. I didn't want to live in that kind of feed prison. And I didn't know if I could be with someone who did.

The Director's Instagram feed was undeniably beautiful—at first, it felt genuinely impressive. But over time, the carefully curated perfection started to feel a bit overwhelming. What once seemed like a charming appreciation for aesthetics gradually came across as more of an obsession with appearances.

I started to wonder if my initial attraction to the Director was clouded by the fact that I was simply...sad and lonely. No doubt his presence made me feel good. It made me feel better than the miserable state my ex-fiancé left me in. But after my craving for some feel-good intimacy was somehow fulfilled by the Director's presence, I slowly got my sensible mind back and started to see things differently. There were definitely flaws and red flags.

He never wanted to get married or have kids, which was the complete opposite of what I wanted for my future. He said things like, "Why would you want kids? They're so loud and smelly." When it came to marriage, he dismissed it as an outdated tradition, mostly useful for tax benefits. "I'd rather be alone than stuck with someone forever," he once told me. It made me wonder: What drove him to work so relentlessly, especially since he didn't dream of having a family?

"I want to make a lot of money and be rich," he said, like a mantra.

"But why?" I asked him once. "You don't even spend it."

"So I can stop working at 40, get a big villa in LA and have all the young girls come and party all the time," he joked.

I laughed. "Yeah, right." But I could sense there was some truth there. Beneath it all, it felt like there was a quiet fear, an insecurity about not having enough. It reminded me of what he once shared about his father, an architect who went bankrupt mid-career. That experience shook his whole family, and I could see how deeply it shaped him. I understood where he was coming from. Still, I found myself yearning for something more—a deeper purpose beyond just the chase for wealth.

I started to realize that our core values didn't quite align, and that gap would likely cause tension down the line. I could already imagine the arguments, over finances, over how to spend our money, over what really mattered in life.

The more I got to know him, the clearer it became: We were probably not meant to go the distance. Maybe it was time to step back before things got too serious.

***

"Babe, you know that sooner than later you will realize that you will not find anyone better than me," said the Director as he went down on me.

"Shut up. Just keep on going," I pushed his head down again.

I sighed. He was not wrong. Sure, he was pretty excellent down there, but more than that, he was so great precisely because of the very flexible relationship arrangement he let me have.

"We don't need to define this," the Director said. "You don't need to introduce me to your friends if you're not ready or you don't want to. If during your next Amsterdam trip, you feel like sleeping with other people from a party, do it. Just don't forget to wear a condom and please don't tell me about it."

$$\text{A LOVER} = \frac{\text{An awesome fuck buddy} + \text{romance}}{\text{the relationship}}$$

IMAGE 20: *The lover equation*

After the end of my intense last relationship, I really wasn't ready to be tied down in a traditional relationship. But I also didn't want to be completely alone. So when the Director came along, it was like a blessing. He was the perfect arrangement for me at the time. I was getting romance and intimacy without the pressure of a relationship. He was a lover! And a really damn good one. *So maybe I should just enjoy it while it lasts a little longer?*

***

"Maybe I should move to Jakarta," the Director said out of nowhere one morning.

"Uhm, why?" I didn't see that one coming.

"A lot of my shoot jobs these days are from this region. And you know, you're here. And you're just as messed up as I am, so maybe we should just move in together!"

I wasn't sure if he was serious or if he was being sarcastic, but either way, all I knew was that the idea he proposed suddenly shot my anxiety up. It reminded me of my ex-fiancé's decision to move to Jakarta with me from Amsterdam and how it all became the beginning of the end. It reminded me of the suffocating feeling of being in a broken relationship that was falling apart. It reminded me of the many terrorizing sleepless nights post-breakup.

I felt my body tensing up even just at the thought of being in an official relationship again that soon, even if it was with someone that I had grown to care about in the last couple of months. Looking back, I should have told him then how I was feeling. But all I could do was brush off my feelings and respond to him with another joke.

"Seriously babe, is that your romantic idea of how to ask someone to move in together?" I tried to play it cool and push my anxiety aside, but deep down, I knew that I needed to have a serious conversation with him.

***

"How's your shoot going?" the Director checked in on me in the middle of the week.

"It's really good! But I'm super exhausted!" I sent him a couple of photos from the set. "We're on set number three today. We started at four this morning to catch the sunrise and now we're in this Dutch cemetery to capture a spooky scene for the campaign."

"Looks really good! I'm proud of you, almond eyes!" He never failed to be my number one cheerleader.

I was in Surabaya with my creative agency Bujukrayu and our production team LYNX shooting our first nationwide campaign for Google search in Indonesia. It was actually my first time in Surabaya, even though it's Indonesia's second largest city after Jakarta.

"I can't wait to see you at the Airbnb this Saturday!"

Yes, we were going on our first official holiday together. We had been seeing each other for four months, and had our undefined relationship been a normal functioning one, we would not have hesitated to plan a holiday together. But it wasn't a normal relationship, so we did hesitate a bit. We talked about it for a long time. *Should we? Should we not?* We weren't officially together, so what did it mean if we went on holiday together?

The first official holiday together is a significant moment for any couple, official or not. Because when you're just dating, you have in-between time to escape from each other, but not on a holiday, because you will be together 24/7. You'll sleep together, eat every meal together, travel together and you can't really leave. Habits that were unseen before may suddenly pop up, and you don't know whether you're going to like them or not. And if you don't, well, you're screwed.

The slightest thought of an official relationship was enough to trigger my anxiety and fear of commitment. What about a week-long holiday where I couldn't escape from someone? But I also needed a break, and I didn't want to go on a holiday by myself. I'd been working a lot—especially leading up to this shoot—so, in the end, I said, "Why the heck not."

We decided on Bali as our destination. It made sense. We wanted somewhere close yet relatively familiar, and it was only a 50-minute flight away from Surabaya, so I could fly straight to Bali after my shoot was done. The last time I was in Bali was for my wedding cancellation trip, so I thought maybe this trip would be good for me. I could create more new memories that weren't related to the canceled wedding.

What was the worst thing that could happen, *right?*

***

The shoot in Surabaya had just wrapped up the night before, and in the morning I packed and went on to catch my flight to go to Bali to meet the Director. I should have been excited about our Bali break, but all I could feel was a sudden rush of panic and anxiety.

Should I cancel?
This is too much. I am not ready.
Fuck, I feel like canceling.
Is it too late to cancel now?
Maybe it's better to tell the truth now than lying during the holiday?

I couldn't sleep the night before. I didn't know what I was so scared of. I had known him for more than four months and he'd been nothing but nice and understanding with me, so I tried to convince myself that even if I did have another mental breakdown in Bali, he would be able to give me my much-needed space. Plus, canceling last minute would be such a cold-hearted bitch move, even for me. So I told myself to shut up, pack my bags and just go.

So I went.

***

We were laying by the pool of the villa when I said, "I think we should end this after the holiday."

"What do you mean?" He looked at me as he stood up from his lounge chair.

The night before, I hadn't slept again. I thought it might just be the fatigue from the shoot, and that I would feel better in the morning. But I didn't. The anxiety only grew bigger and bigger.

"I think this is too much," I continued.

"What's too much?"

"All this. Us! I didn't realize it until I got here. But being here together on a trip with you, it feels like we are in a relationship, an item and I don't think I can do that at the moment. I just can't. I'm sorry." I looked at him, hoping he would once again understand my situation. I was hoping he would tell his sarcastic jokes and make fun of my stupid mind to help calm my anxiety down.

He looked at me for a moment, and then he walked away.

"Wait, where are you going?" I got up.

"Why did you have to say that now?" He didn't take it well and raised his voice, throwing his hands up in frustration. "Couldn't you wait until the end of this holiday? I'll head back to Milan next week with no foreseeable future project in Jakarta. Why did you have to ruin this?"

"But we can still have fun together for the next couple of days, no?" I tried to salvage the situation.

He looked at me dead serious. "That's very selfish of you!" He slammed the door to his room.

I stood there in shock.

He wasn't wrong. I had been selfish. There I was with one of the sweetest guys ever. He had literally supported me through all of my worst: my anxiety attacks, my rage and my sadness after each therapy session. And not only did he stay, but he also tried to understand me, comforted me through it all and gave me all the space I needed to heal. And what did I do? I ran away as fast as I could. What a bitch.

I thought our Bali holiday would be a chance to say goodbye to each other. That it could top my list as the new most beautiful rebound story of my life. That the Director and I would cherish every single last moment that we had together because we knew we were about to say goodbye to each other, forever. I imagined us staying up all night until sunrise, giving each other one last kiss to remember and cement all the beautiful times we had. But that idea was completely one-sided. Maybe he had a different idea about our relationship, and I completely blew it.

He turned cold, and I knew it was over. We agreed to be as civil as possible during the rest of the holiday, but it was hard. The days dragged on, and the hours were filled with tension. We went through the motions, going out to eat and visiting beaches, but as soon as we got back to the villa, he would bury his head in his phone and avoid me. It felt like we were a separated couple still living together waiting for a divorce to be finalized.

I started to wonder if I had made a mistake. Maybe I should have tried to fix things with the Director. Maybe I would regret this decision for the rest of my life. Maybe my relationship trauma was clouding my judgment and I would never be able to be in a healthy relationship again.

What if I can't find anyone better than the Director?
Am I broken for life?
Should I take my words back?

But then I remembered all the reasons why we weren't right for each other. All the deal-breakers that I knew would never make us work in the long run. So I stuck to my gut and swallowed the bitter pill. It was hard, but it was the right thing to do.

As this trip came to an end and we arrived back in Jakarta in silence, we said our goodbyes. All I could muster was a simple "I'm sorry."

Chapter 4

THE MISTAKE

"So, how do you cope when insomnia strikes and it's 4 am?" my psychiatrist probed during one Friday evening session.

"I just lie in bed," I said, wracking my brain to recount my most recent dawn routine. That recurring insomnia had steered me toward biweekly therapy appointments and an ever-fluctuating regimen of anti-anxiety medication.

"I also curate this playlist on Spotify. I call it my 'Life Soundtrack.'" I offered her a peek at my phone. "It's a collection of songs that represent my emotions during the more melancholic moments of my life. So, I just hit play and cry for an hour or two, maybe."

"And afterwards, how do you manage to drag yourself to work?" she asked.

"To be perfectly honest, I am also not sure. After a few hours of crying, I just feel...empty. It's like having my battery completely drained, leaving me in a state of numbness, you know? But I just remind myself that there's only one thing I have to do: take a shower." I pressed on, noticing her diligently scribbling down notes. "Perhaps it's the act of getting out of bed. Or maybe the cold water, but once I've showered, it's as if my drained battery gets a small jolt of life, maybe like a 5 percent recharge. And that tiny 5 percent charge is just enough to propel me into the day, to get dressed and drag myself to work."

"Fascinating. Could you elaborate?"

"It's tough, you know? Mustering the strength to take that shower is *really hard*. Sometimes, I just let myself linger in bed for a few hours. I just let myself feel all the sorrow." I lifted my gaze from the carpet, allowing our eyes to meet. "I become immobilized. I can't do simple tasks. But, after hours of tears, I do eventually feel calmer. Maybe I've simply cried it all out."

She paused her notetaking, setting her pen and notepad aside to meet my gaze with an empathetic one. "Alright, you don't require an antidepressant," she declared. "You've displayed the ability to persevere through these murky mornings. And that's quite an accomplishment! I think we'll reduce your dosage. Just half a tablet per intake for the upcoming fortnight, and we'll evaluate your progress from there."

No need for an antidepressant.

I can lower my anti-anxiety pill dosage.

And my shrink is seeing progress!

If my ex could see me now, I'd have proudly tossed my hair and smirked: "Ha! Take a look! I'm nearly back on my feet!" (Well, at least that's what I thought).

In the wake of the breakup, I was dead set on not letting that sorry excuse of a man destroy my life. I'd come across enough tales of breakups and canceled weddings that turned lives upside down. Like that girl my sister knew, who ditched her job, blew up her savings and took off on a globe-trotting escapade with a fling when her fiancé canceled things off (bad idea; she came back broke). Or my pal Mabuk, who bolted to NYC when his engagement went bust. And of course, there was the iconic breakup saga of *Eat Pray Love*, which I embarrassingly watched, sobbing alone at home on that post-breakup night.

They say a breakup can either make you or break you, and while I was still figuring out which category I fell into, I was doubly sure that it wouldn't ruin my career. So, my psychiatrist's positive feedback was a much-needed booster shot right before a critical work offsite in Tokyo. My assignment was to prepare and present Indonesia's Google Search Marketing annual plan to our global VP. This was a pivotal moment that would decide our marketing budget for the upcoming year. I was in dire need of that reassurance that no matter what, things would eventually fall into place.

***

"Hey, I'm heading to Tokyo next week. Are you in town?" I sent Satoshi a text. He was a Japanese ex-Googler I'd run into in Singapore a couple of years ago. We clicked from the get-go. We had heaps in common, and hanging out with him was always a blast. From our common interests to our undeniable chemistry, my bond with Satoshi had always been effortless and filled with shared laughter.

I still had a clear recollection of his Google goodbye bash last year in Thailand. We'd lost ourselves in the rhythm of Justin Bieber's "Sorry" amid a sea of teenagers in a teeming Bangkok nightclub. Allegedly, we'd even hitched a ride on a tuk-tuk back to our hotels at the crack of dawn, though that part was a bit foggy in my memory. Waking up with a befuddled "Did something happen last night?" look on our faces when we saw the cryptic text history on our phones, hinting at the exchange of hotel room numbers. But as it turned out, it was all just harmless, inebriated banter. We both woke up solo in our respective rooms, concluding it was just a classic case of drunk texting. *We've all been there, right?*

"Yes, I'll be around! How about we catch up over the weekend?" Satoshi shot back.

"That would be awesome! It's been too long since the last party ;)"

"I know! How have you been?"

"Life's been a whirlwind. Remember that wedding talk I shared? Yeah, that's not happening anymore now."

"I heard. Really sorry about that."

"It's okay. I think it was for the best…"

"Still…I really hope you're in a better place now? And how's the world of Google search?" he deftly shifted the conversation.

"It's good! Actually, I'm in Tokyo for a search offsite! I'll be presenting our country plan to the global team. I'm pretty sure I'll be needing A LOT of drinks once the week is over!"

"Don't worry, I'll take you out ;)"

"Yay!"

The previous time I visited Tokyo, I was still sporting my engagement ring. My ex-fiancé and I were there for an Amsterdam reunion and to celebrate our friend Kamil's milestone thirtieth birthday. It was a week-long extravaganza of merrymaking and revelry. I was aware that Tokyo's nightlife had a lot to offer. Given the rocky few months I'd endured, I was convinced I could do with a generous dose of fun in Tokyo once all the work commitments were fulfilled. So, the news of Satoshi being in town and willing to play tour guide for the weekend got me all excited! Instead of rolling the dice with a stranger from Tinder in Tokyo, I decided to play it safe, steering clear of potential drama and sticking to the familiarity of known faces from the past.

***

Every Google office around the world felt like home. I had to hand it to them! Even with a staggering workforce exceeding 100,000, they had brilliantly managed to retain a consistent cultural vibe across all offices. The quirky nap rooms, vibrant and lively cafeterias, fully stocked Micro Kitchens on every corner and plenty of hot desks available anytime made visiting a different Google office a welcoming, safe and satisfying experience.

In stark contrast to many conventional firms where paying a visit to another office necessitated a string of pre-arrangements, at Google, our badge was our passport. It was a running joke among Googlers that if we ever found ourselves lost in a sprawling city, we would only need to have three things at hand:

1. Our passport (to leave the country when needed),
2. Our phone (to use Google Maps and find the nearest Google office),
3. Our Google badge (to access the office and all the amenities like food, showers and rest areas).

Perched on the top of Roppongi Hills, the Tokyo office offered an unobstructed 360-degree view of the city and the majestic Mount Fuji. It was adorned with Kimono-dressed Android figurines, featured an izakaya-style cafeteria with sushi and ramen stations and boasted a capsule hotel-style nap room with a shower room equipped with luxurious Japanese amenities. Honestly, if it weren't for the Ritz Carlton hotel where they accommodated us during this trip and its incredible view, I wouldn't mind sleeping and showering at the office!

My boss, Veronica and I touched down in Tokyo early in the morning, our bodies weary after a grueling 7.5-hour red-eye flight straight from Jakarta. We made a quick detour to our hotel just to stow our luggage before bee-lining to the office. They flew us business class, which meant that there were no viable excuses for not having slept soundly the night before. Plus, time was of the essence because the presentation was scheduled for the next day. While we were dozing off in our flatbed seats up in the air, our Director Sapna had left a few last-minute crucial comments on our presentation deck that demanded prompt attention. There was no time for rest.

Working for an emerging market at Google often gave me the vibe of being part of a cash-strapped startup in bootstrap mode, perennially vying for marketing funds every quarter. The only difference was that our source of funds wasn't external venture capital; it came from internal management, mostly from the mothership (a.k.a. Mountain View HQ).

When I enlightened people about my job at Google, which was essentially marketing Google search, they often seemed puzzled. "But everyone already uses Google. Why does Google need marketing?" they asked. This was a perfectly reasonable question, particularly if you hailed from a developed country or were a part of the elite upper crust of urban societies in developing nations. Likely, you've been acquainted with a computer since your tender childhood years and fostered a long-term relationship with Google, harking back to the desktop era.

However, for users from emerging markets, such as Indonesia or India, who were introduced to the internet for the first time via smartphones, they might have been aware of Google's existence but not necessarily adept at using it as fluently as the rest of us. The conventional marketing strategies we employed for the first billion internet users would not suffice for the next billion. That's why the infusion of investment was so pivotal—to expand our growth to cities beyond the urban areas. That was precisely what was on the line for Indonesia at that Tokyo offsite.

***

"I think I'm still drunk," I confessed to my boss, being completely honest about my condition while also trying to conceal the pounding pain at the back of my head.

We met for breakfast at the office's 27th-floor café for a final huddle before *the* presentation, the upcoming 45 minutes of intense discussion and relentless Q&A that would ultimately shape our work for the next 12 months. And there I was, resembling a zombie with a throbbing headache and a massive hangover. *Shit.*

"What time did you get back last night?" she asked, sounding worried, referring to the big team dinner we all went to last night. Veronica had left by midnight, and as usual, I had continued with the rest of the group, who decided to hit up a bar. And another bar. And another.

"I think...I was in bed at around 3 am." It had actually been 5 am. But obviously, I didn't want her to know that I was about to do the most important country presentation of the year with only two-and-a-half hours of sleep.

"I seriously don't know how you do it," she shook her head in wonder.

"I don't know either," I replied, chugging down a whole bottle of cold water as quickly as I could to relieve my dehydration. Not sure if it was the hangover or because it was Japanese, but the water tasted *so good*. I knew my body was probably begging me to go to bed, but I was fueled by the adrenaline of the presentation. And there was no way a hangover was going to come between me and the budget for my country.

"If you nail this presentation, I'll personally campaign for you at this year's Golden Panda Award," she reminded me of what was at stake.

Ah yes, the Golden Panda Awards. It was our annual culture award for Google's Asia-Pacific Training Program (APAC) Marketing team. The categories ranged from serious ones like "Most innovative" to funny ones like "Most likely to be mistaken as a YouTuber" all the way to absurd ones like "Most likely to go on stage with a hangover and rock the show." And that one, my friend, was the category I wanted to win the most.

Last year, the second and third places had gone to two notorious party animals who (fortunately) had left the company since. Their departure had created an opening—an opportunity for me to make it to the top three! All I needed was a stage to showcase that particular skill of mine in front of a lot of Google marketers who could later support and vote for me. And what better opportunity did I have than proving myself as the master of presenting with a hangover than on the most significant stage of the year: presenting in front of Marvin.

Ugh, I feel like I'm gonna puke.

***

I took a deep breath, steadying my nerves as I entered Andromeda, the conference room that had been booked for the presentation. The room was sleek and modern, adorned with vibrant Google-themed decorations that added a touch of playfulness to the otherwise formal setting. The aroma of freshly brewed coffee wafted through the air, providing a hint of comfort amidst the mounting tension. Inside, I noticed Rachita and the whole India team packing their laptops and bags, a clear sign that they had wrapped up their presentation. I tried to read their expressions to gauge how it went, but their poker faces revealed nothing but a sense of relief that it was all over. Did they get their budget? Did they tank it? No one knew.

As the attendees settled into their seats, my confidence began to waver. I could feel the butterflies fluttering in my stomach, and my hands grew slightly clammy. Veronica, seated to my right, gave me a reassuring thumbs-up and whispered, "Good luck."

In the center of the room, surrounded by his trusted team, sat Marvin, a smile playing on his lips as he said, "Alright, Indonesia. Whenever you're ready."

Marvin made me nervous. Well, actually, he made *everyone* nervous. He was our big boss. Our Global Marketing VP. The holder of our budget. The man we named the week after (which was called Marvin's Off-site, duh). He rocked a pair of transparent thick-framed hipster glasses, along with his Comme des Garçons polka dot shirt, neatly folded raw selvedge denim and some limited edition bright purple Nike collab. If you didn't know any better, you'd probably mistake him for the CEO of Hypebeast. With the lethal combo of Jack Ma's brain and Kevin Ma's style, Marvin was super cool and friendly yet intensely intimidating.

Before I started, I chugged a big glass of cold water. The pounding headache reminded me of my terrible choices last night, but I had to push through. At that point, I was fueled by the need to prove to myself (and my ex, to some extent) that I was just fine. That my career would never take a hit from the breakup, no matter how many nights I drowned my sorrows in alcohol.

My presentation began on a strong note. I was shocked at how well I managed to hide my dreaded hangover state. My voice sounded steady, and my hands stayed calm as I clicked through the slides that I had practiced tirelessly. The confidence I had in my material pushed me forward. The room seemed to respond positively, and I convinced myself that I had everything under control.

You got this, Mira.

However, as time passed, Marvin's infamous questioning session kicked off. Sure, I could have mentioned that I preferred to save questions for the end, but Marvin didn't seem to care about that. He would interrupt and grill me whenever he pleased. Each of his inquiries felt like a spotlight shining on my pounding headache and uneasy stomach.

He would ask questions that made me go, "Why the heck didn't I think of that before?!" The unspoken rule with him was to expect questions about anything at any time during the presentation.

"And what's the breakdown for Gen Z in that data? Where exactly is Surabaya? What kind of retention are we seeing from that feature?" His questions kept pouring in.

I fought to keep my composure, determined not to let my discomfort show. But the more questions he asked, the more my nerves churned and the harder it became to keep up the act. I glanced at my team, desperately seeking support. Veronica and Rita noticed and jumped in to help when they saw me struggling to recall a specific data point.

Honestly, I wasn't the best at memorizing numbers sometimes. But thank goodness for Rita. She was our data powerhouse, straight from Russia. She was the yang to my yin. While I handled the creative aspects, she tackled the data side of things. She could answer any data-related question with confidence, and she never took "I don't know" for an answer. I seriously believed she had the potential to be the Russian Prime Minister one day. She was probably the only person on our team who could intimidate Marvin *just a little*. So, every time I hesitated for even a second while trying to answer one of Marvin's questions, Rita would swoop in to save the day.

Finally, the presentation came to an end, and I let out a shaky breath. The room fell into an uneasy silence, as if holding its breath along with me. I awaited Marvin's judgment, a knot of anxiety tightening in my stomach. He leaned back in his chair, his expression unreadable.

They say Google's interview hiring process, which came with a minimum of five rounds, was tough. Honestly, the interview process was probably made that way as a teaser. Because the moment you got accepted, that kind of grueling questioning simply became part of your everyday breakfast. And that day with Marvin, combined with my hangover, was like the Google interview process put on steroids. I was mentally and physically drained. I just wanted that session to end so I could crash in bed and continue being...hungover.

Marvin stood up and started walking back and forth at the end of the room. With his hands in his pockets, you could see him thinking about everything he had just heard from us. For a moment, I feared the worst. But then, a slight smile spread across his face.

"I like the plan. It's a good strategy," Marvin said, his tone surprisingly gentle. "How much were you guys asking again? Three million dollars for a whole year?"

"Yes," I answered.

"I want to go big in Indonesia and see what we can achieve. So what can you guys deliver if I give you 10 million for this second half of the year?"

"Wait, what?" His response stunned all of us.

Damn. Ten million dollars. None of us saw it coming. It was going to be Google's first major investment in Indonesia Marketing. I guess my hangover presentation skills were on point. Golden Panda Award, here I come!

Marvin's announcement made me feel like I'd just been injected with a double shot of adrenaline. All the headaches and body pains from the alcohol faded away in an instant. My heart was racing. If they had turned off the lights and played some techno music, I might have started dancing right then and there. I saw big smiles on everyone's faces, especially Sapna's and Veronica's. We did it! All those late nights crunching numbers and fixing slide alignments paid off!

And at that very moment, I couldn't help but think how kind God was to me. My personal life fell apart that year, but somehow, in a crazy turn of events, my professional life took a turn in an exciting direction. I moved into a newly expanded role right after the breakup, and I was about to handle the most significant budget I'd ever gotten to manage in my entire career!

Thank goodness I don't have a boyfriend, was the first thing that came to my mind after we finished the whole presentation. I could already sense that I wouldn't have had any time for a romantic relationship with the massive workload that was about to come from that budget injection. So maybe, just maybe, the breakup actually happened at the perfect time. Otherwise, I would have had to deal with one very unhappy and unemployed husband at home while I worked like crazy.

After leaving that meeting, I called all my creative and media agencies for an urgent meeting to share the news before everyone headed off for the long weekend.

"How did it go?" asked Peyi, one of my creative partners from the agency, eagerly awaiting an update.

"First of all, I want to make sure each and every one of you has a good break planned. Because I have to apologize in advance, but as soon as you guys return, we're going to be on one crazy ride until the end of the year. We just secured $10 million in funding!"

During the video call, I could see a mix of joy and fear in my agencies' eyes. They knew it was going to be an exhilarating time, but it also meant a lot of hard work at breakneck speed for them. And they were absolutely right.

Once that call was over, our main mission at Marvin's Offsite was officially accomplished! It was now up to us to deliver on the plan with the most impactful, creative, innovative and best-in-class campaign the country had ever seen. Bring it on!

Alright, now it's time to take care of my hangover.

***

Imagine a traveling businessman right now. What comes to mind? Perhaps a white middle-aged man in a sharp black suit rolling a silver carry-on Rimowa through the airport, discussing crypto and company acquisitions on his phone. Or maybe a senior Indian executive squeezing in a final supposedly important call loudly at the airport lounge while waiting to board his flight.

After hours of business flight, in service to their corporate lords, these men would likely end up in a city far away from home, only to find themselves alone in their five-star hotel rooms at night, munching on room service hamburgers and toiling away on their laptops until the late hours. Some of them might be single, with never enough time to properly date and find a life partner, while others would be married and desperately missing their wives and kids back home. The rest would be more than happy on the road nonstop because business travel provided them with an escape from family life, a legal excuse to temporarily leave their wives and kids behind.

And then you also hear stories of husbands cheating on their wives during business trips. Perhaps these men are simply lonely, you might say. Being far away from their families due to never-ending work obligations, they yearn for companionship and a bit of intimacy to keep their sanity intact. Or perhaps the life (and the people) that awaits them at home are precisely the reason why they needed the escape in the first place.

Is that why sites like Miss Travel, a platform supposedly designed for "sugar babies" to meet traveling businessmen, exist? There must be a substantial market for it, considering the multitude of lonely businessmen out there seeking company as they jet set their way in and out of luxurious five-star hotels, accumulating Marriott Bonvoy and KrisFlyer points they can later use for their own vacations.

And there I was, perched on the bay window of my 56th-floor room at the Ritz-Carlton. The sun had already set, revealing the mesmerizing night scene of Tokyo. I couldn't help but soak in the captivating view, basking in the glow that cascaded from the towering buildings, as the city's evening soul sprang to life.

The sight was simply enchanting. I could feel the electric energy in the air, as the neon lights flickered and painted the cityscape in vibrant hues. The streets below teemed with activity, and the distant sounds of laughter and conversation floated up to my lofty perch.

After the presentation that morning, I ended up dozing off for a solid three hours. I woke up and sat at the bay window of the room, and I found myself lost in my *Lost in Translation*-esque view when a familiar twinge of melancholy began to seep in. It was as if I could somehow relate to the lives of those traveling businessmen—at least the single ones.

It wasn't the physical distance from home that weighed on me; it was the emptiness of not having someone to call or return home to that tugged at my heartstrings. Even in the midst of that ache, I found myself wrestling with a whirlwind of conflicting emotions.

It was a strange mix of privilege and loneliness that swirled within me. On one hand, I was fortunate enough to find myself in the luxurious Ritz-Carlton hotel, surrounded by all the comforts and opulence one could imagine. The breathtaking view from my room alone was worth celebrating. Yet, despite the lavishness, I felt a void.

Also, I don't look like your typical "businessman." And because of that glaring difference in appearance, I often grappled with a sense of unworthiness. I mean, who was I to indulge in the same sense of loneliness as those suited-up professionals? I was just a single girl who had recently gone through a breakup. According to society's expectations, I should have been jumping for joy that work was sending me off to exciting places.

I had just accomplished a major milestone at work, and it couldn't have gone any better. The sense of achievement should have overwhelmed me with joy, but instead, a tinge of sadness seeped into my heart. There was no one to share the news with, nobody on the other side of the world who would be as thrilled about my big work win as I was.

As I skimmed through the contacts on my phone, desperately seeking someone to spill the news to, I paused on the Director's number. The thought crossed my mind—should I call him? Maybe I shouldn't have ended things with him. Could I still reach out, just to share what's happening in my life? But then, doubt crept in. Would reaching out be selfish of me? And where was the equivalent of Mr. Travel for supposed traveling businesswomen like myself? After all, I, too, experienced bouts of loneliness. I craved companionship, someone with whom I could share snippets of my life.

Meanwhile, Veronica was probably managing to squeeze in a quick 15-minute FaceTime session with her two little boys, catching up on their day before we all reconvened for dinner that evening. To be honest, that's all I yearned for—a person who would check in on me before dinner.

***

I wasn't entirely certain about Satoshi's relationship status. There was a vague memory of stumbling upon his profile on Tinder a while back when we happened to be in the same city. And then there was that harmless flirt we exchanged at his Google farewell party, over a year ago now. Curiosity piqued, I found myself scrolling through his sparsely updated Instagram account, where, aside from some captivating travel snapshots, there was no trace of a significant other in his life. The dots started to connect.

Since he didn't seem to have a girlfriend, perhaps we could indulge in some harmless flirtation once again? It seemed like exactly what I needed—an intimate and fun moment with someone I sort of knew. Plus, having worked at the same company, I trusted him.

To be absolutely sure, I could have directly asked if he was single, but that would have felt awkward. We were two former colleagues, reconnecting for a fun weekend in Tokyo. Did his relationship status even matter? We had agreed to meet up and have a good time, whatever that might entail.

I wondered what the weekend held in store for us. Would it be a friendly gathering between (ex) Googlers? A networking opportunity for two tech-savvy individuals? Could it potentially develop into a long-term friendship? Or, deep down, was I secretly hoping for a Tinder-like encounter, with the possibility of a casual hookup?

Honestly, I found myself yearning for the latter. I wanted a chance to let loose, to enjoy a carefree rendezvous with someone I could trust. My mind buzzed with anticipation, contemplating how to approach this weekend and what outfit would be appropriate. I really had to strategize.

Determining the potential Date Lifetime Value (DLV) of someone is indeed a crucial step before embarking on a "date." You might be wondering why this matters, but trust me, it plays a significant role in shaping the entire dynamic of the encounter. From the choice of venue, time of day and even your outfit, the DLV of your date sets the tone. Not to mention, it also dictates the level of alcohol consumption, which can greatly influence the level of flirtation involved.

DLV	Location	Time	Outfit	Alcohol Consumption	Flirt Level
Maybe a good hangout friend	Semi outdoor cafe with lots of natural light	Brunch	Athleisure	(Healthy smoothie)	(Bro vibe with a high five ending)
A great guy to have in my professional network	Coffee shop	Afternoon	Casual formal attire	(Coffee or tea)	(Keep things work related)
Fun night with a sexy time potential	A dimly lit romantic restaurant with a fun dancing bar nearby to continue the night	Early evening that goes on till late at night	Subtle sexy attire (Low cut / sheer top, tasteful high slit skirt, etc.)	🍷🍷🍷	🔥🔥🔥
Straight up booty call	My place or yours (Preferably mine)	10PM or later	Whatever that is easy to take off	🍷🍷🍷 🍷🍷	🔥🔥🔥 🔥🔥
I like him but I'm not sure if he has a GF or not	A brightly lit, fun and casual restaurant with a darkly lit bar nearby to continue the night (if confirmed no GF)	Early evening that has a potential for extension	Casual on the outside, sexy on the inside i.e jeans and tank top with lace bra inside (Need to figure out the GF situation first)	🍷🍷	🔥🔥

IMAGE 21: *The Date Lifetime Value (DLV) Chart*

If you anticipate that your date's DLV falls within the realm of a potential hangout friend, you'll want to keep things PG-13. This means scheduling the meet-up during the daytime, preferably for brunch, with no alcohol in the equation. You can rock your casual athleisure attire, knowing that you have plans to hit the gym right after the friendly rendezvous. You can also adopt a relaxed and chill demeanor, exuding a friendly "bro" vibe to ensure they understand that the whole thing is purely platonic.

On the other hand, if it becomes evident that your date's DLV screams "booty call," you'll need to design the date in an entirely different manner. Late-night encounters work best in this case, ideally past 10 pm. The location should be either your place or theirs (although I personally prefer mine, so I can kick them out later on).

As I planned my weekend hangout with Satoshi, I found myself contemplating where he would fit on my DLV chart. Also, the fact that I wasn't sure if he had a girlfriend or not made it tricky. Was he a potential hangout friend, or did he fall into the realm of a fun night with a potential sexy time?

***

I had no idea what to expect when Satoshi mentioned that we were heading to Black Rose. He described it as a "special bar," his words delivered in a hushed tone reminiscent of a secretive dealer unveiling his hidden stash. "Trust me, you'll like it," he assured me with a mischievous grin.

After finishing our delicious sushi dinner that Saturday night, we stepped out onto the bustling street near Roppongi's infamous intersection. We raised our hands and patiently waited for one of those iconic shiny black Tokyo cabs to pull over and whisk us away.

Finally, a cab came to a halt. We eagerly hopped in, ready for our adventure. "Is it far?" I inquired, curiosity getting the best of me.

"No, not really. The place is somewhere between here and Shibuya," Satoshi replied, his voice filled with a hint of excitement.

I was still nursing a hangover from our previous night, a wild techno party at Circus Club, where a young French boy (I use the term "boy" because he appeared barely 21) persistently tried to flirt with me. Throughout the night, he was cautiously asking, "Is he your boyfriend?"—referring to Satoshi.

My response remained the same, "No, we're just friends." It was true; nothing happened between Satoshi and me that night, even with the copious amounts of alcohol we consumed.

As Saturday rolled around, exhaustion began to set in. The intense work week, combined with consecutive nights of revelry and lack of sleep, had left me drained. I had no mental capacity left to consider alternative plans for the evening. I placed my trust in my local friend, Satoshi, and without even bothering to Google the place, I allowed him to lead me to this enigmatic establishment called Black Rose.

The cab driver pulled over at the corner of a side street, veering off the main road that stretched from Roppongi to Shibuya. A nondescript grey, seven-story building stood before us. My Japanese language skills were practically nonexistent, and the cab driver's command of English was limited. In response, he resorted to using universal body language, politely gesturing towards the upper levels of the building, indicating that we had arrived at our destination.

Strange. The building appeared like any other typical mid-sized Tokyo office, likely filled with salarymen during the day, but was now closed for the night. I strained my ears, hoping to catch a faint bass sound that would indicate the presence of a bar or club, but there was nothing.

"Are we in the right place?" I asked Satoshi as we approached the building.

"Yup, it's on the fifth floor," he replied confidently.

We entered the building and stepped into a narrow, dimly lit hallway on the ground floor. I followed Satoshi as we made our way towards the back, where a small elevator awaited us. On our way I noticed a row of plaques displaying the names of the building tenants and there it was, carved in black Gothic font on a silver plate: Black Rose, 5th floor. "I guess this is it."

The elevator was tiny and rather claustrophobic. I estimated it could barely accommodate four average-sized people, or perhaps five smaller Japanese individuals if they squeezed together.

As we pressed the button for our floor, the doors closed, enclosing us in silence. No cheesy elevator music to break the stillness. At this point, I half expected to hear some distant music emanating from the bar's sound system, but there was only silence.

I glanced at Satoshi, giving him a look that clearly asked, "Where on earth are you taking me?"

He responded with a mischievous smirk. *Ding*. Finally, a sound to signal our arrival.

The elevator doors slid open, revealing another Black Rose metal plate, larger in size, softly illuminated against a backdrop of red velvet drapes. A Japanese man, dressed in a studded black leather vest, approached us and greeted us at the door. Satoshi made a gesture to indicate that it was just the two of us, and the man motioned for us to come inside leading us to our designated seat.

We turned right after exiting the elevator and followed the leather-clad man down a short, dimly lit corridor that led to the main room. As we stepped inside, my eyes widened in disbelief. It was a long and narrow bar bathed in red light, with a peculiar sight in the center, a human cage adorned with metal chains. Behind the bar stood seven Japanese women, fierce and commanding, all dressed in dominatrix leather outfits.

At that moment, it finally dawned on me: *Oh my god. This... is a bondage bar.* Satoshi had brought me to a real-life Japanese bondage bar!

We made our way to our seats, the last two at the end of the bar. Along the way, we passed intoxicated Japanese men eagerly downing their drinks and engaged in lively conversations with the women behind the bar. I handed my coat to the patron and settled onto a floor-mounted metal stool with a comfortable red leather cushion, conveniently positioned next to the enigmatic 'cage'.

Though the cage was empty at the moment, my mind couldn't help but conjure up all sorts of wild scenarios that might have taken place there.

"Just wait and see," Satoshi interrupted my contemplation of the cage.

A younger Japanese lady, dressed in a seductive two-piece leather outfit with ankle boots and sheer stockings, approached us with a greeting.

"Kon'nichiwa, nani o nomitaidesu ka?" she asked, placing two drink coasters in front of us.

I think...she's asking us what we want to drink?

"Ichi highball-u," Satoshi quickly ordered.

Good guess, Mira. "And...a vodka ginger beer for me, please," I said.

The lady looked at me with a puzzled expression, slowly repeating my order in her thick Japanese accent. "Wodka... gingga...beer-u?" she confirmed.

"Yes," I replied firmly.

"Okay!" she exclaimed, striking a cute and kawaii pose as she winked and formed a ring shape with her thumb and index fingers.

Satoshi couldn't contain his grin, clearly delighted by my mesmerized state in the bar he had brought me to. It felt like he had just won some kind of bet. Sober as I was, I couldn't tear my eyes away from the surroundings, taking in every detail of the place.

Behind the bar stood the seven Japanese ladies, each possessing a unique look, age and body type. At the far end, there was a tall and slender woman with long dyed hair, donning a patent leather high-cut swimsuit-like one-piece outfit that flaunted an exposed silver zipper running down the front. Paired with knee-high leather boots and fishnet stockings, her attire accentuated her seductive appeal, revealing her hip bone and strong, lean legs. Her piercing yakuza-like stare seemed capable of killing. I could easily picture her in a *Kill Bill*-style bloody fight scene, using her legs to swiftly break an enemy's neck with a single twist.

In the middle of the bar stood a smaller yet curvier lady, blessed with luscious black curly locks and a commanding resting bitch face. She rocked a leather bodycon dress adorned with studded bra cups and a skirt slit that provocatively exposed her right hip. *Hot.*

Next to her was a lady straight out of a Japanese high school goth comic book. Sporting jet-black hair with a straight, blunt-cut full fringe, sharp cat eyeliners, dark lips and long black-painted nails; she gave me a sly wink and a peace sign when she noticed my gaze. Unfortunately, her intriguing outfit remained hidden under a cozy-looking, all-black zip-up hoodie. All I could glimpse were the fishnet stockings and platform boots, just like the other ladies.

As I admired their presence, I couldn't help but watch them move gracefully behind the bar, effortlessly communicating between the guests and the male patron who had greeted us earlier. It didn't take long for me to grasp the power dynamics at play in this establishment. The bosses were undoubtedly these badass femme fatale ladies, not the man up front. These ladies ruled the fucking place. And those intoxicated Japanese men? They were their devoted followers, there to worship those goddesses all night long.

The tall and formidable lady, whose looks and legs could easily strike down any opponent, approached us with our drinks. She immediately knew I wasn't Japanese. "Where are you from?" she inquired.

"I'm...from Indonesia..." I stumbled on my words, feeling nervous. Meanwhile, Satoshi was engrossed in conversation with the cute lady who had initially taken our drinks order.

"Do you live in Tokyo?" she continued her questioning.

"No, I'm just visiting for work, just for one week," I replied.

"Do you like Tokyo?"

"I *love* Tokyo!" How could I not? The city never failed to surprise me with each visit, and finding myself in this offbeat place called the Black Rose only added to my most unforgettable Tokyo experiences.

"Good," she said, offering a graceful smile as she lit a red candle on the bar.

There was something captivating about this lady. From her commanding presence, she seemed to be the most senior among them, not necessarily in age, but in experience. I couldn't help but feel entranced by her from the moment we started talking. She radiated a subtle but undeniably powerful allure. Calm and graceful, with a body that embodied fierceness.

"How long have you been here?" I asked.

"More than 10 years, from the start," she replied, confirming my suspicion that she was likely the queen of this establishment.

"I love all your outfits!" I said, maybe too excitedly.

"Thank you very much."

Wanting to share my love for dressing up, I took out my phone and began showing her some of my past Halloween costumes. First up was my portrayal of Cherry Darling from *Planet Terror*, complete with a gun as a makeshift prosthetic leg. That had definitely been my favorite Halloween costume ever. Next, I showed her my rendition of "Mira Wallace" from *Pulp Fiction*, donning a white shirt, a black bob wig and holding a cigarette with blood streaming from my nose.

"So, you like Tarantino?" she interrupted me just as I was about to show her my third Halloween photo as the Human Centipede.

"Yes! I absolutely love his films!"

"Tarantino comes here often when he's in Tokyo," she said, as if it were no big deal.

Whoa. Not only was I in Tokyo, but I was also in a Japanese bondage bar that Quentin *fucking* Tarantino himself frequented.

That night had just escalated from being incredibly random to downright *a-ma-zing*.

I looked at Satoshi, who was still engrossed in conversation with the cute kawaii lady, and felt bewildered disbelief

"I knew you'd like it here," he smirked, taking a big sip of his highball-u.

Before I could ask another curious question to "the Queen," she abruptly departed. I noticed the ladies exchange glances and nod in agreement, as if signaling that something significant was about to happen.

In an instant, their demeanor shifted. From casually standing next to each other behind the bar, they transformed into a structured formation. One lady positioned herself to the side, two stood strong, facing the back wall, while another entered the cage. The remaining three mysteriously disappeared below the bar, hidden from view.

"What's happening?" I grabbed Satoshi's shoulder, my fingers tightly gripping him. He smiled. And then, the lights went out.

In the pitch-black room, a familiar song began to play. A melodic synth keyboard resonated through the speakers, filling the space with a sense of anticipation. *Wait...I know this song.* Soon, a pulsating bassline reverberated, accompanied by the distinctive snare drum sound that characterized 80s glam rock music. It was Bon Jovi's "Livin' on a Prayer"!

The room was bathed in a sultry crimson glow as red lights illuminated the space behind the bar. It was as if a higher dominatrix goddess had given the command, and the ladies responded with mesmerizing synchronicity. They began to dance, their movements graceful and fluid, perfectly aligned with the rhythm of the drums. And just when I thought I couldn't be more astonished by the night, something incredible happened: the ladies were *lifted*. Yes, lifted. I couldn't believe my eyes. The entire area behind the bar revealed itself to be a hidden hydraulic stage, defying all expectations *Mindfuckingblown!* 🤯

What the hell is this place?!

From Tarantino to Bon Jovi and now a hydraulic stage? What other craziness will this night bring?

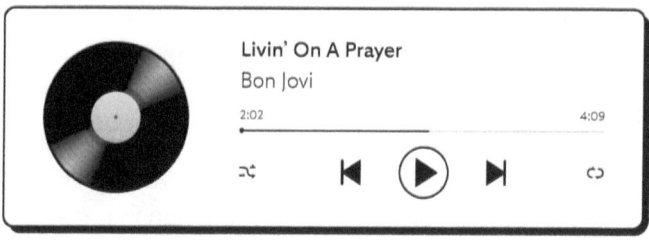

I was caught between confusion and exhilaration. Despite the taboo nature of such a place like the Black Rose, I couldn't deny that I was having the time of my life! If I were to confess to others that I had visited a bondage bar in Tokyo, I could already picture the raised eyebrows and moral judgments. Truth be told, I might have even judged such establishments myself if they were in a different country.

In the United States, I would probably be surrounded by a bunch of shady middle-aged white men and ladies with big fake tits. The girls would likely be sex workers, professional strippers or go-go dancers. The dark aesthetics of their outfits would probably scream Urban Outfitters rather than Rick Owens. And in that setting, I'd probably fear the constant unwanted advances from intoxicated men, hands attempting to grab at every opportunity.

If the same place existed in North Jakarta (a.k.a. Kota), I could envision girls flown in from Kazakhstan, Uzbekistan or other "exotic" Eastern European countries, serving as prostitutes while the notorious Chinese Mafia conducted their drug business on the side. It would certainly not be a safe place for a young woman like me to spend her Saturday night.

But that night in Tokyo, amidst all the craziness that was happening at the Black Rose, I experienced an inexplicable feeling of safety. Despite being the sole female guest that evening, I felt welcomed and protected by all the Japanese ladies behind the bar.

Moreover, there was a profound reversal of the traditional gender power dynamics at play at the Black Rose. Superficially, one might assume that such a place would degrade women, reducing them to objects of lust for the men's pleasure. Yet, to my surprise, I saw it in a completely different light.

These women worked for no one except themselves. They held all the control and power. The visiting men could only watch and converse, forbidden from touching the ladies. They also weren't allowed to engage in conversation with guests outside their group. When a tipsy Japanese man sitting beside me and Satoshi politely attempted to strike up a conversation with me, one of the ladies behind the bar swiftly pointed her whip at him, reminding him to behave and adhere to the rules, or face expulsion.

These ladies ruled the establishment. They established the boundaries and ensured complete obedience by their visiting patrons. They possessed an incredible (sexual) power and dominance over the enthralled Japanese men, who willingly submitted to their every command. To me, it felt like a realm of ultimate female emancipation.

And as if the hydraulic theater had just concluded Act No 69 with Bon Jovi, the establishment gradually returned to its "normal" state. The ladies gracefully resumed their positions behind the bar, effortlessly engaging with one customer after another. "The Queen" approached me once again, resuming our conversation. Her poise and unwavering composure were undeniably magnetic.

"Can I ask how old you are?" I had to know.

"Forty," she replied, leaving my jaw hanging in disbelief. I imagined all she must have seen during her time at the Black Rose.

Damn, she's in incredible shape for a 40-year-old!

"Would you like to change?" she suddenly asked, catching me off guard.

"What do you mean...change?"

"Change into one of these outfits," she said, gesturing towards the other ladies.

"I can do that?" I glanced at Satoshi, "I suppose... Why not?!"

"The Queen" called over one of the ladies behind the bar, pointing at me and giving instructions in Japanese. Then she motioned towards the entrance. The cute kawaii lady who received "the Queen's" instruction beckoned me to follow her, leading me back through the hallways I had entered from.

We passed the elevator I had taken to reach this place and continued walking until we reached the end of the corridor. There, in front of me, was the restroom door and on my left, a stretched metal clothes hanger displaying an array of bondage leather gear. *That's one impressive collection.*

The kawaii lady pressed her index finger to her lips, silently assessing my body from head to toe. With confidence, she plucked two items from the hanger. The first was a low-cut, studded leather vest with a diagonal silver zipper exposing a hint of skin. I hung the vest against my chest, feeling its cool texture against my fingertips. The size seemed just right. However, as I measured the high-waisted leather shorts she picked against my hips, it became clear that my butt and hips wouldn't fit.

"I think these are too small," I admitted, returning the tiny shorts to her.

She took another quick glance at my hips, surveyed the hanger and retrieved another bottom piece, handing it to me. This time, it was a pair of high-cut, low-rise, belted leather shorts.

I examined the shorts, gauging their size against my hips. They seemed more forgiving, offering a better chance of actually fitting. With a shrug, I nodded in approval. "Alright, these could work," I said, my voice filled with a mix of excitement and uncertainty.

"Okay!" she exclaimed, forming a circle with her left index finger and thumb before pushing open the door to the restroom.

I stepped into the dimly lit restroom, its ambiance cloaked in a deep raisin hue. The soft glow added an air of mystery to the space. A large mirror adorned one side of the wall, reflecting the dimly lit scene back at me. In stark contrast to the classic beige-colored Japanese Toto toilet, everything else within the restroom exuded a dark and on-brand Black Rose aesthetic.

The mirror before me beckoned, inviting me to explore my own reflection amidst this enigmatic setting. I hesitated for a second, staring at the image staring back at me, contemplating the choices that had led me to this moment. The vest and leather shorts I held in my hands seemed to pulsate with a unique energy, ready to transform me into someone new, someone daring.

Seriously, Mira, what the hell are you doing? As I stood there, clutching the low-cut, studded leather vest against my chest, doubts flooded my mind. Was I really going to do this? Change into a bondage outfit that screamed, "You must obey me now or face consequences!" And did I mention Satoshi was waiting for me out there?

But then again, I couldn't ignore the tingling sensation coursing through my veins. With a devilish grin, I shrugged off my apprehensions and stepped closer to the large mirror. I caught my own reflection, a mix of curiosity and trepidation dancing across my face. At that moment, I made up my mind. I muttered under my breath, a whisper filled with determination. *Fuck it. Why the hell not?*

***

I swung open the restroom door, ready to unveil my transformed self to the world. Before stepping out, I stole one last glance at my reflection in the mirror and a wide grin spread across my face. Damn, *I looked hot*. The sight of my black, cascading hair and the snug fit of the two-piece leather ensemble against my curves left me feeling like a completely different person. Gone was the familiar Mira; instead, a new side of me emerged—fierce, empowered and unapologetically confident. And I absolutely loved her.

As I made my way back into the bar, I was greeted by the presence of another Japanese lady, joining the kawaii one who had guided me earlier. Their eyes shimmered with excitement, and their faces lit up with delight. Instantly, they erupted into applause and repeated the word "Sugoi!" in unison. It was a resounding seal of approval, a chorus of admiration for my bold transformation.

"Please hit me," a drunken middle-aged Japanese man, fueled by liquid courage, pleaded with me as I made my way through the dimly lit space.

It was a surreal experience, to say the least. Sure, I had always been curious about BDSM, but actually being immersed in the midst of it all was an entirely different level of intensity. I couldn't deny the exhilaration as I began to realize that it's fundamentally about a mental power play.

It was as if a switch had been flipped in my mind. Observing the way those men looked at me, I realized it wasn't the degrading gaze of objectification. It was a complex mix of respect, adoration and fear. All intertwined into one captivating stare.

No longer were those grown-up dicks in control. It was *the women*, myself included, who held the reins of power. We possessed a potent sexual dominance over those men, and the sheer satisfaction it brought me was indescribable.

In many societies, women have long been depicted as being at the mercy of men's sexual desires. It's as if our pleasure and satisfaction are contingent upon their needs, while any discussion of a woman's own sexual desires and kinks is often deemed deviant and taboo. But inside the Black Rose, it was an entirely different story.

In this realm, boundaries were tested, desires were embraced and societal norms were challenged. It was an arena where power dynamics were inverted, and the intoxicating energy flowed through every interaction.

For that one unforgettable night, the tables had turned. I was the one calling the shots. I fucking ruled that place. So I nonchalantly disregarded the Japanese men's pleas for me to strike them, effortlessly walking past them and the curious onlookers, making a beeline towards Satoshi, who anxiously awaited my arrival.

As our eyes met, I could sense a mixture of surprise, intrigue and maybe even a hint of desire in his expression. It was as if he, too, recognized the shift in power dynamics that had taken place within me. In that moment, it became crystal clear that our "friendship" would be forever altered by what he was witnessing. Things would never be the same between us.

"You...look...*a-ma-zing*!" Satoshi exclaimed, his eyes wide with awe.

I couldn't help but bask in his compliment, feeling a surge of newfound confidence coursing through my veins. With a playful smile dancing on my lips, I coolly responded, "I know."

***

As I settled into the situation, each of the women behind the bar came over to me in turn, their approvals ringing out with a "Sugoi!" Suddenly, it felt like I had found my place there. I was one of *them*.

The Queen made her return. She signaled for Satoshi to rest his arms on the bar. He rolled his sleeves up and dutifully followed. Next, she handed me a fiery red candle, wax all teetering on the edge, ready to drip. A swift glance at Satoshi's upturned, bare arms and it clicked immediately what she was expecting me to do. And so, I began to drip the scorching wax onto his anticipative arms.

"Ooooohh...Ahhh..." Satoshi's moans echoed in my ears as the red wax dripped onto his bare arms. There was no denying the pain he was in. Yet, his eyes were on me, silently begging for more. So, I did what seemed natural at the time: I granted his unspoken wish. I guided the candle higher up his arm, pouring more of the molten wax onto the area I knew would cause the most discomfort—the tender, sensitive inside of his elbow.

"Ahhhhhhh..." A sharp cry escaped from his lips, biting down on them as his eyes slammed shut. I was the one responsible for his suffering, the architect of this agony and against all odds, I was enthralled by every second of it.

And in the midst of this odd enjoyment, questions started to bubble up in my mind. Was Black Rose, a BDSM bar, carving out a space for the ultimate gender equality? Or was it just an ironic jab at the fight for women's power elsewhere? Had these women, by owning their sexuality and harnessing the power that came along, carved their names into the bedrock of feminism? Or, when all was said and done, were they just another facet of men's desires? Could it be that this was a world where power and pain danced a provocative tango, drawn together by the bonds of mutual consent?

Yes, consent.

Everything unfolding within the walls of the Black Rose was a product of mutual agreement. And being inside there felt way safer than hitting up a club in North Jakarta, where my night would inevitably be plagued by annoying, lingering stares and uninvited advances from creepy old men who didn't understand the concept of personal space and boundaries.

As my mind drifted back to Satoshi, I stared into his eyes, my fingertips delicately tracing the contours of his arms as I peeled off the dried, hardened wax. I could feel the rhythmic thump of his pulse under my touch as I made my way towards his wrist. His heart was pounding like a drum, matching the electrifying beat of our little dance. With each last bit of wax I removed from his hand, one thought played on repeat in my head: *We are totally going to fuck tonight.*

I'm not gonna beat around the bush here. I was into him. And truth be told, I'd been feeling the pull of sexual intimacy for a bit, especially after wrapping up that whole saga with the Director. But I'd been keeping myself on a pretty tight leash when it came to spontaneous hook-ups because, let's face it, the emotional stakes are just too damn high. I couldn't risk making a blunder that would send my world into another tailspin. The thought of a Tinder meet-up for a no-strings-attached romp with a complete stranger was downright unappealing at that point. What I yearned for was intimacy that comes from familiarity and a touch of emotional connection. I was only prepared to bare my soul and body to someone I already knew...like Satoshi.

Biting my lip, I shot him a glance as I peeled off the last bit of wax from his hand. His eyes held the same spark of desire, mirroring my own. *Seems like he is on the same page.*

His arm was now wax-free, but I lingered, my hands remaining in contact with his skin. It was as if an invisible magnet pulled us in, our bodies subtly edging closer, inching towards that long-awaited kiss. His breath brushed against my face, an intimate whisper as we gravitated closer. Just as our lips were about to meet, a thunderous bang erupted from the stage, jolting us out of our little bubble.

We were drawn to the sudden noise, a jarring interruption in our private moment. It was as if a record had been abruptly scratched, halting the symphony of our shared anticipation. The sound reverberated throughout the room, commanding the attention of everyone present, pulling our focus towards the stage.

Caught in the spotlight was a topless Japanese man, stripped down to his underwear, crouching on all fours. The stinging crack of a whip against his back had him cringing like a scolded child on the cage's cold, hard floor. His face was buried down, submissive and contrite, as the curvy woman with untamed, curly hair towered over him, wielding her long leather whip with an air of authority. She was calling the shots, her words firing out in rapid Japanese. And he, like a child awaiting a spoonful of dinner, remained obediently in place, ready to heed her every command.

Then the counting began, her voice sharp and resonant, ringing out with each number in Japanese. Each count was accompanied by a fierce lash to his back. His reaction was a cacophony of screams and moans, a perverse blend of agony and ecstasy that held everyone's attention. This was his pain, his pleasure and we were all spectators in the theater of his unique performance. And I'll admit, a part of me was stirred by the spectacle. As bizarre as it was, there was something intriguing, something fascinating, something...fun about it.

Following the fourth crack of the whip, "the Queen" turned her attention to me. "Come, it's your turn now."

"Me?! On that stage?" I had to double-check, anxiety creeping into my voice as I pointed towards the looming platform.

"Yes, of course," she confirmed, stepping up onto the stage and extending an arm out to me in invitation. I cast a hesitant glance over at Satoshi, who responded with a reassuring nod of approval. Drawing a deep breath, I slid off my high chair, took the Queen's offered arm and gingerly placed one foot after another onto the circular stage, now feeling the intense energy of the human cage.

The half-naked Japanese man remained on the stage, still on all fours with his bare back vulnerably exposed to me. The curvy lady handed off her whip to me, its handle feeling surprisingly soft and reassuring in my grip. I began to slowly navigate the small space on stage, stepping in between the man's bent legs and positioning myself directly behind him.

Gripping the whip firmly, I allowed its leather tassels to slowly graze against his exposed back. He twitched in anticipation, primed for the forthcoming sting that he not only expected, but desired and it was all about to be delivered by my hand.

The surroundings, my outfit, the man in a submissive pose beneath me, all ready and waiting for my command—it was a thrill like no other. I was absolutely relishing this. Even if it was just for one night, I adored Dominatrix Mira.

"Are you ready?" I warned him. His eyes shut tight in response, bracing himself for the first...wuh-psss!

I couldn't deny it; my first crack of the whip was pitiful. Talk about being a noob! The leather just grazed his back lightly, barely leaving a trace. I'd always indulged in fantasies of being a dominatrix, but when reality was staring me in the face, I was a bundle of nerves.

Come on, Mira, you can do better than that.

I took a deep breath and swung again. *Wuh-Psssss!* This time, the whip's snap was followed by a potent, satisfied groan. It was a sort of "damn-that-hurt-but-I-want-more" kind of sound. His reaction was intoxicating.

"Give him 20," commanded the Queen. *Hell yes.* I bobbed my head in enthusiastic agreement, a wild grin tugging at the corners of my lips.

The man's body stiffened in response to the Queen's declaration. The anticipation of another 20 lashes was palpable. His back tensed, his head dipped lower and his eyes pressed shut. Part of me wanted to reassure him, tell him to relax, that it wouldn't hurt as much if he'd just let go. But truth be told, at that moment, I didn't give a damn. This was my domain, my stage and he was under my command.

"One..." *Wuh-Psssh!* "Two..." *Wuh-Psssh!* "Three..." *Wuh-Psssh!* With every count, the whip snapped loudly against his skin. His groans became a symphony to my ears. By the seventh count, his pain was the music to my power play. With each lash, my strokes grew bolder, the marks on his back, redder. His pleas grew louder, a desperate yet thrilling melody echoing throughout the bar.

But by the 12th lash, his strength seemed to falter. *Wuh-Psssh!* His frame gave out beneath the biting sting of the whip, and he crumbled onto the cold stage floor. His hands no longer propped him up, and he curled in on himself like a child retreating to the fetal position.

"Wait...wait...," he stammered out in broken English, gasping for breath.

It looked like someone needed a breather. Well, I wasn't about to let that slide. Not on my stage, not on my time. "Get up!" I ordered.

And just like that, as if my words held divine power, a commandment he dared not defy, he pushed himself back up. His trembling hands and knees supported his weight once more, contorting his body back into that all-fours stance. He was prepared, or as prepared as one could be, for the final, punishing lashes of the night.

"Eighteen…" *Wuh-Psssh!* "Nineteen…" *Wuh-Psssh!* "Twenty…" *Wuh-Psssshhhh!*

Whoa…that…was…absolutely…*whoa*.

My whole body was quivering by the time the session wrapped up. I handed the whip back to the Queen, its power lingering in the palm of my hand as I descended the stage, returning to my perch where Satoshi was waiting. He wore an amused, approving grin, a silent praise that echoed loudly in the space between us.

Settling back into my chair, I felt an undeniable change within me. I sat myself upright on the chair, my back erect in a display of confidence, my chest proudly outstretched. It was as though a hidden facet of my being had been jolted awake. The sorrow-laden part of me, which had been wallowing in self-pity for the past few months due to my broken heart, seemed to dissipate, making way for a reinvigorated Mira, radiating power and self-assuredness. This new version of me was absolutely determined not to let any man shatter my life ever again.

"Wow….," that's all Satoshi, who, under the intimate glow of the red light appeared irresistibly more charming than before, articulated.

In that exhilarating whirlwind of surprise and euphoria, our gazes once again intertwined. This time, the connection was much deeper, more intense. It felt as though we were picking up right where we left off. As we locked eyes, a silent understanding passed between us, an unspoken agreement that we both knew exactly what was about to unfold.

Our lips crashed together in a fiery, passionate kiss, a connection so intense it felt like a current of electricity was surging through my body. The world around us evaporated as Satoshi's arms instinctively wound around my waist, drawing me in even closer. My hand curled around his slightly chilled neck, the coolness contrasting the warm rush filling my senses. His lips tasted faintly of the whisky highball he'd been sipping throughout the evening.

As we surrendered to this unexpected, powerful pull between us, the world took on a dizzying quality. The bright red lights of Black Rose seemed to swirl into a whirlpool of color, as though Tokyo itself was spinning from our passionate exchange. Our combined breaths hitched and synchronized as we continued to push the boundaries of our old acquaintanceship, breaking into territories unknown.

Just as I was preparing to dive back into the embrace of his lips, Satoshi abruptly pulled away, leaving a lingering chill in the place where his warmth had been moments ago. "I'm sorry. But I can't do this," he blurted out, his voice filled with regret.

I was completely blindsided by his sudden shift. Confused and still slightly dazed from our passionate kiss, I stammered, "What... What do you mean?"

His face crumpled in a mixture of guilt and regret. "I'm really sorry...," he started, his voice shaky and the words stumbling out in an almost incoherent rush.

Panic began to swell inside me. I knew that look. With my heart pounding in my chest, I leaped to the worst conclusion I could imagine, hoping that it wouldn't be true. "Don't tell me you have a girlfriend?" I choked out the words, a desperate plea to the universe.

Satoshi swallowed hard, his gaze dropping to the bartop for a moment before meeting mine again, his usual confidence completely gone. "Actually...Yes, I do..."

His words landed like a gut punch. The echoes of our recent laughter and playful banter suddenly felt like a distant memory, replaced with a bitter taste of reality.

"You gotta be kidding, right?!" I exploded, my voice slicing through the midnight air. Sitting there in my risqué BDSM getup, I felt both vulnerable and livid. Our recent kiss, the intoxication from the night, my increasing desire to take Satoshi to bed—everything added fuel to the anger raging inside me. And there he was, casually dropping a girlfriend grenade into the mix like it was no big deal. "Then why did you ask me out this weekend?! Why the fuck did you bring me here, of all places?!"

"But I didn't plan for any of this to happen," he slurred, the alcohol in his system making his response even less convincing. "I genuinely just wanted to see you and catch up on life with you."

What a fucking plot twist. I felt like I was in the middle of some messed-up rom-com. "Dude," I started, aiming to defuse the tension with a casual bro-talk vibe, though my frustration still managed to seep through. "If you told me you have a girlfriend, I would not do any of this. I wouldn't have come here with you, I wouldn't have flirted with you, and most certainly wouldn't kiss you wearing all this!"

"I'm sorry...," he mumbled, guilt evident in his eyes.

"I mean sure, I can be a bit crazy sometimes. But I do have morals, you know. And there are certain lines that I simply do not cross." I made my stance clear. "And getting in the middle of someone else's relationship drama is really the last thing I needed right now." I sighed.

I felt blindsided by someone I thought I knew. Someone who I thought was safe. I mentally shook myself, thinking, *alright, girl, time to sober up and hit the brakes,* because there was no way I was letting this situation spiral further.

"It's really not cool what you're doing," I expressed my lingering displeasure. My expectations for a night of passion had been abruptly derailed. Seemed like I was destined for a case of blue pussy. Sigh.

"I'm really sorry," Satoshi repeated. "I should have told you I have a girlfriend. But it's complicated," he added, his attempt at an explanation. "I guess we just got carried away."

"Yeah, right," I responded, taking a generous sip of the ice-cold water on the table. It was a dual attempt to process the recent events and to regain some semblance of sobriety. "Save the whole 'it's complicated' bullshit for yourself. I am not getting involved in that," I declared, giving him a serious look. The night might have taken an unexpected turn, but I wasn't about to let it spiral into unnecessary complications.

Okay, calm down, Mira. No harm has been done.

It was just one harmless kiss between two highly intoxicated adults. It happens.

I know you're horny, but get it together, girl.

Fuck, I should have masturbated before the night started to release some steam.

"Okay, it's all good," I told him, exhaling deeply into my seat, trying to shrug off all the disappointment. "I mean, I hate you for this, but it's fine. It happens, I guess," I continued, trying to downplay the awkwardness of the situation. "But you should know, I would never ever do this with you had I known you have a girlfriend!" I defended my moral compass once again.

"I had fun though," he said, flashing a cheeky smile.

"Yeah, me too," I reluctantly agreed. "It's been a really fun weekend," I added, trying to focus on the positive aspects. "Let's just forget about the kiss, then. Let's just pretend it never happened," I proposed.

"Deal," he said. We sat there in reflective silence for one long minute before Satoshi, breaking the quietness, suggested, "Shall we get one last drink before calling it a night?"

"Hmm...Not sure if that's the best idea now. I'm pretty tipsy already." I hesitated. "But, okay sure," I finally gave in.

We spent the last 25 minutes finishing our last drink and continued our chat as if the kiss never happened. We quickly transitioned from two flirting people back to becoming two good drinking buddies, recounting the last two days we spent together. From the techno night at Circus to the unconventional fun at Black Rose. We did a lot! And we weren't going to let an honest mistake of a kiss ruin our memory. The reunion weekend had been amazing, and I wanted to remember it as that.

***

The clock struck 2:15 in the morning, and we found ourselves back at the street corner just outside of Black Rose. I had changed back into my normal outfit from the start of the evening, feeling a bit tipsy and ready to hit the bed. After a few attempts, a cab finally stopped.

"That was fun. Crazy night," I remarked.

"Yeah, tell me about it," he replied, opening the taxi door for me.

"Thanks for the weekend. I had a lot of fun," I said, placing my hand on his shoulder.

"Pleasure is all mine! I had a blast too," he grinned.

"See you next time in Jakarta? I'll return the favor and take you around on a cultural tour of my city."

"That sounds great!" We hugged and exchanged our goodbyes.

I slid into the backseat of the cab, ready to close the door, when Satoshi put his hand on it, holding it open. Suddenly, he slid into the cab, prompting me to scoot over to the right.

"Uhm, what are you doing?" I looked at him with disbelief.

"Let me drop you back at your hotel," he said, with a slight drunken slur.

Oookaayyy...I don't think this is a good idea.

After everything we discussed and agreed upon inside the bar, I was perplexed by his sudden decision to join me in the cab. But on second thought, maybe I was just drunk and overthinking it. Satoshi was probably just being nice, wanting to make sure I arrived safely back at my hotel. Plus, I was well beyond just a tipsy state at that point to argue, so I figured it was fine.

The taxi pulled over at the empty Ritz-Carlton lobby. The front desk concierge, surprisingly as friendly at the wee hours as in daylight, stood there ready to open the taxi door for me. I reached inside my purse to find a 100-yen coin to give to Satoshi. Now that he had made sure I made it safely back to my hotel, I assumed he would continue his journey home with the same cab.

He hesitated, looking from me to the hotel entrance and back again, like he was arguing with himself. Finally, almost reluctantly, he asked, "Can I join you upstairs? Just...to talk a bit more?"

"Dude. Seriously?!" I looked at him with disbelief, squinting my eyes as Satoshi fixedly gazed into mine. We exchanged silent stares and deep breaths, engaging in a long internal battle of consciousness before I finally gave in. "Fine."

I handed the cab driver the money and quickly made my way out of the cab, heading straight into the lobby, with Satoshi following close behind. My tipsy inability to refuse him made me regret that one last drink I had.

We rode the lift up to the 56th floor in near silence. Thank God for elevator music. In my somewhat inebriated state, I knew that, upon reaching the room, my priority should be downing an entire bottle of cold mineral water to sober up. I needed to ensure that nothing beyond that point happened between us that night. However, I was also so tipsy that my moral compass felt temporarily compromised, and I found myself caring less about the potential consequences of the night.

In my defense, I didn't want him there, but he insisted! So, if anything, he was the one who decided to come up to my hotel room with me. After everything that had happened in the past couple of months, maybe I deserve some fun? Even if, for just one night, it meant going against all of my own moral principles.

"Just so we're clear...We are only going to hang out and talk. Nothing more. And you, my friend, will leave in 30 minutes." I warned him before I opened my door.

He nodded and walked into my room.

***

Perched on the bay window in my room, I took in the sprawling Tokyo night beneath me, a mesmerizing tapestry of lights. From my vantage point, the city looked like a tranquil miniature, with tiny beacons emanating from the windows below. Each lit window felt like a gateway to an undiscovered world, a silent narrator of untold stories. The complexity of the city unfolded before me. I seized a cold water bottle from the minibar, downing it with haste as my gaze lingered on the Tokyo night. Yeah, that liquid refreshment set me back eight dollars, but whatever. I needed it, a swift attempt to regain some sobriety. No chance was I stepping out to the 7-11 across the street just for a more budget-friendly option.

As I sat there, my eyes met Satoshi's slightly intoxicated gaze from across the room. Perhaps it was the lingering effects of alcohol combined with that peculiar *Lost in Translation* ambiance of the Ritz Carlton again. In that moment, I felt an overwhelming desire for intimacy, for the warmth of touch, for closeness with someone familiar and trustworthy. This longing reached a peak, transforming into a physical ache in my stomach. The intensity was particularly painful because, for a brief moment, I believed I could satisfy that yearning with Satoshi that night. Everything seemed within reach yet painfully out of grasp. *If only he didn't have a girlfriend.*

"Are you okay?" Satoshi inquired as he settled at the opposite end of the bay window, maintaining a cautious distance.

"Yeah, I guess so," I replied hesitantly, taking a long, deep breath. "I just love sitting up here, staring at the world down there." The mood of our night had shifted. The soundtrack, once filled with the thunderous beats of Bon Jovi at Black Rose, had transformed into the melodic tones of Jesus and Mary Chain, accompanied by a lingering sense of sadness in the riffs.

"Are you thinking about your ex?" Satoshi gently inquired.

"Not really," I said. "Well, of course, sometimes I think about what could have been between us if we went ahead with the wedding," I paused.

"I'm sorry." He looked at me gently.

"Don't be, it's all good. The breakup was really for the best. Still, it doesn't make it any easier."

"I'm sure it's not," replied Satoshi.

"I thought I would be in a much better place by now. It's been almost half a year, you know."

"Hey, don't be too hard on yourself. There's no set timeline for these things," he replied as he rested his head by the window.

"Thanks for that," I took another sip of my water.

"And I'm sorry for earlier. Seeing you again tonight...it brought back a lot of our past moments." Satoshi admitted.

"It's okay. It happens."

"Can I have some of your water?" he asked as he came closer to my side.

"Sure, here you go," I handed him the bottle.

Satoshi drank two large gulps of the water before putting the bottle down on the small wooden table next to the bay window. He shifted a little closer as he came right next to me. Our hands nearly touched. As we both looked deeply into each other's eyes, we both knew we were at a critical crossing point of the night.

In a movie, this would be the moment where the most important decision that could lead the protagonist to avoid an unprecedented disaster would need to be made. It's a make-or-break point. The point of no return. The point for me to call it a night and ask him to leave before anything regrettable in the future happens or...and before I even finished contemplating in my own head, he came forward and kissed me. His lips locked mine deep with a one passionate, heavy kiss. I wanted to pull away but...I didn't.

As his lips tenderly met mine, a warm embrace enveloped me, fulfilling a yearning that had lingered for far too long. The closeness I deeply craved manifested in that fleeting moment. I was acutely aware that this was a forbidden kiss—a conscious choice we both made, aware of its potential consequences. While guilt should have flooded my senses, in that selfish moment, I convinced myself that after enduring the trials and tribulations of the past, I deserved that kiss. I deserved to feel wanted. I deserved to feel desired. And I deserved to feel loved. Succumbing to the intoxicating allure of the kiss, I placed my hands on his face and pulled him closer.

As the cool touch of that refreshing bottle of water began to have its sobering effect, a sense of clarity gradually returned to my mind. It marked the commencement of the first round in the internal battle of morality that was about to unfold in my head:

WTF, Mira. Stop it! He has a girlfriend!

Why are you doing this to yourself? You're going to regret this.

Imagine if YOU were the girlfriend.

I know you're craving for intimacy, but this is not the way to go.

You're better than this.

The conflicting voices in my head continued their debate:

But...Why not? He chose to be here. It's not my problem if he decides to cheat on his girlfriend right?!

I just want to enjoy a bit of romance. Is that too much to ask? I've been through shit this year. Don't I deserve a bit of this?

You do. But not like this. Not this way.

In the midst of my internal struggle, it was evident from Satoshi's demeanor that he, too, was wrestling with his own moral dilemmas.

"I think we should stop," I declared, seizing a fleeting moment of sobriety.

"Yeah, you're right. I think that's a good idea," Satoshi concurred, leaning back against the window, creating a deliberate distance as if attempting to extinguish the flames between us.

As if drawn by an irresistible magnetic force, we found ourselves entwined once more. His lips met mine, his warm body pressed against mine and his hands tenderly caressed my hair while mine rested on his neck. Each interval of moral clarity was short-lived as we instinctively pulled away. Yet, with each separation, the gravitational pull intensified, drawing us into deeper, more intense embraces. We had transitioned from the window to the bed. With him now above me, our passionate kisses escalated, a tacit acknowledgement of the impending consensual act of adultery.

"Dude, you have a girlfriend," I made a final attempt to inject some sense into the situation.

"It's...complicated between us. We're figuring things out," he bargained.

Another round of "it's complicated" nonsense. Honestly, at that moment, I felt like I had exhausted my efforts. Still a bit tipsy, I reached a point where I simply didn't care anymore. So, I thought, screw it.

***

A high-pitched ring jolted me awake. Confused, I fumbled to make sense of my surroundings in the pitch-black room. *Where am I again?* It took me a few moments to gather my thoughts.

As the bedside phone persisted in its insistent ringing, I laboriously crawled to the opposite end of the plush king-size mattress to grasp the receiver.

"Good morning, Miss Sumanti. This is your wake-up call," the soft-spoken Japanese lady on the other end announced. *Ah, right, the concierge. So, I'm still at the hotel. What a relief.* I reached for the bedside drawer, pressing the button to open the curtains, allowing a sliver of light to reveal the aftermath of the night.

As my eyes gradually adapted to the increased brightness of the room, a sharp, familiar pain throbbed in my head. I hoisted myself up to assess the aftermath more thoroughly. *What a mess.* My dress and underwear from the previous night were scattered across the floor. A champagne bottle, likely emptied, two champagne glasses and a half-full glass of what appeared to be cola were left on the desk. I took a whiff. *Uff, that's a lot of vodka.* That must have been the culprit of my headache, a.k.a. Hangover. Not far from the edge of the bed, I noticed two used condoms thrown to the floor.

SHIT.
We had sex.
Ugh, WHYYYYY?
So much for a moral compass.

I disposed of the dried-up condoms with a tissue, grabbed my clothes from the floor and tossed them into my open suitcase. Still naked, I began to feel the nausea from all the alcohol the night before. I made my way slowly to the bathroom and stepped into the shower for the much-needed refreshment to wake myself up.

As the checkout time approached, I brushed my teeth and organized all my travel-sized toiletries into my pouch. I noticed an open hotel toothbrush set next to my own Oral-B toothpaste. *Did he crash here last night? When did he leave?* I can't seem to remember much.

Dropping my toiletries into my suitcase, I reached for the little pink box of emergency—a.k.a. morning-after pill hidden in the side pouch. A NorLevo 1.5 mg tablet. I knew I saw condoms, but my memories of the previous night were choppy, so I wasn't going to take any chances. The last thing I wanted from last night was a souvenir for life in the form of a baby.

I opened the minibar and grabbed the first bottle of orange juice, once again without checking the price. It was the Ritz, so it was bound to be another ridiculously overpriced OJ. *Whatever, I'm putting it under work expenses.* I took the pill and chugged the whole bottle in a flash.

I grabbed my phone to check the time. I had 20 minutes left before I had to checkout of the room. I sat down on the messy bed to catch my breath for a bit after rushing to pack my suitcase. The realization of what happened the night before slowly started to sink in, and the emotional aftermath of the night. I hesitantly began to type a message to Satoshi.

"Dude," I paused for a while as the morning-after guilt consumed me. "Last night was a mistake." *He* was The Mistake.

"Hey," read his reply. "Yeah…" He continued, "How's your hangover? My head hurts so bad." Obviously, avoiding the real matter at hand.

"Dude!" I needed him to focus. "It really shouldn't have happened. I'm not that kind of person!" I attempted to defend myself, feeling the weight of my actions.

"I know," he replied. "It just...happened. It is what it is. Can we blame the alcohol?" He tried to justify.

Sure, alcohol played a huge part in clouding our judgment last night. But honestly, blaming everything on it felt like an easy way out. We had a lot of moments of full consciousness, yet we still decided to go against what was right.

Even as things unfolded in the night, I had a feeling the emotional fallout from committing adultery would be brutal. But in the moment, I just wanted to drown everything out, numb the guilt and silence the voice in my head telling me this was wrong. So I used alcohol to escape, to allow myself one night of reckless fun.

But of course, the morning arrived, the alcohol faded and reality came crashing down: that I knowingly slept with someone who had a girlfriend. And that fact left me with a massive regret, a terrible hangover and a feeling that all the breakup recovery progress I had been making with my therapist went straight down the drain.

**

If anything, this whole mess with The Mistake taught me one thing: never skip The List. The List, my friends, is basically your date-vetting cheat sheet. It's designed to prevent awkward misunderstandings and save you from full-blown relationship drama or heartbreak. Ask it early, during the first drink, not the fifth, before things get hazy.

Here's a sneak peek: if your date answers *yes* to any of the questions, *walk away*. Trust me, you'll thank me later. Unless, of course, you're a drama queen who thrives on chaos in your love life.

The List

Things you need to ask when you go for your first drink together:

1. Do you have a girlfriend?
2. Are you seeing someone?
3. Are you married?
4. Do you have any kids?
5. Are you gay?
6. Ehmm...Really?
7. Are you 31? (they are weird at that age)
8. Do you know more than 10 people I work with?

If there's a YES to ANY of those questions, give him 2 dollars for your beer and WALK AWAY

IMAGE 22: *The List that thou shall never forget*

***

"Would you like another glass of champagne?" The flight attendant came over with a bottle of Moet.

I was still hungover from the night before. "Sure, why not?" I gave her my glass to refill.

As the plane soared through the clouds on my journey from Tokyo to Jakarta, the plush surroundings of the business class cabin cocooned me in comfort. The distant hum of the engines and the subtle clinking of glasses from the attentive flight attendants created a soothing ambiance to reflect on my trip.

Taking a delicate sip of the freshly poured champagne, I couldn't help but let my thoughts wander. The effervescence of the bubbles mirrored the swirl of reflections in my mind. Another failed attempt at romance. Another city left behind. Another failed chapter of my love life that left me wondering what the hell am I doing? And then, it hit me. *Why do I rely on these men to make me feel better?*

With the city lights below casting a gentle glow, I reached into my bag. My fingers brushed against the cool surface of a new item I just got before I left Tokyo—a lipstick-shaped rubbery item. I still couldn't believe how small and cute it was. As it clicked open, it revealed not a lipstick but a discreet vibrator. A knowing smile played on my lips.

I stretched my legs out on the flatbed, covering them with a soft blanket. Slipping on my eye mask, I feigned sleep, all the while discreetly placing my hand and the even more discreet companion inside. With a subtle buzz that blended seamlessly with the ambient hum of the cabin, it began its gentle rhythm.

As the plane gracefully cut through the night sky, the soothing sound of the engines provided a backdrop for my introspection and my own enjoyment. In the serene luxury of the cabin, my thoughts soared and a newfound sense of empowerment emerged, gently replacing the turbulence of my past relationships.

Taking control of my own pleasure, I made a silent pact with myself. From that moment forward, reliance on myself was the plan, a foolproof strategy to steer clear of any potential drama with men.

Chapter 5

THE PORNSTAR

Six months after the breakup, I found myself tangled in a different kind of toxic relationship—with Tinder. I'd swipe mindlessly, chasing that fleeting dopamine hit of validation. Then, in a burst of clarity, I'd delete the app for a few days, temporarily escaping its grip. But despite my best efforts, I kept falling back into the cycle: relapsing, redownloading, swiping, questioning and eventually deleting again.

Eventually, I hit a small but meaningful milestone: I managed to keep the app off my phone for over two weeks, a personal victory worth celebrating. During that time, I started to reflect. The Director made me realize that I wasn't ready for a relationship, and The Mistake had shown me how the wrong people, sometimes even the ones I trusted, could shake my peace of mind. Slowly but surely, I began to accept that, for now, avoiding men and their drama was probably the healthiest option.

And when the urge to relapse crept in? My reliable companion (read: vibrator) came to the rescue, reminding me that I was perfectly capable of meeting my own needs. Each moment of pleasure was like a grounding ritual—a message to my restless body to chill out and let my rational brain steer the ship. I redirected that energy toward the one thing that wouldn't betray me or derail my sanity: my work.

Every day after work, I'd either sweat it out in a grueling 90-minute hot yoga session at the Senayan Arcadia studio or hit the pavement with the G-Runners crew, clocking a solid 5K around the national stadium just a stone's throw from the office. After these calorie-torching sessions, I'd shower, grab a quick bite at Plaza Senayan, usually at the low-key Japanese spot tucked away in the basement and then head back to the office to power through another two hours of work. By 10:30 pm, I'd hop into a trusty Blue Bird taxi and finally make my way home. Rinse and repeat, day in and day out.

Weekends were reserved for cutting loose and diving headfirst into Jakarta's nightlife. I'd start the night with pleasure at the smoke-free Curtain Club, a rare oasis in a city where cigarette smoke clings to everything, before making my way to Colosseum in Kota for the surreal, sensory overload of Enter The Void. Fridays and Saturdays blurred into booze-fueled adventures, while Sunday mornings were spent sweating out the excess at the gym. It was my version of a well-balanced life.

My routine felt bulletproof. I filled every waking hour with motion, with noise, with purpose, leaving no space for breakdowns or tears. I'd had enough of those, thank you very much. I was done looking back. I was moving forward, full steam ahead. And damn, it felt good to be in control again.

***

This worked until it didn't. By the time December rolled around, I was exhausted, teetering on the brink of physical burnout. For months, I'd been pushing myself to the limit in an effort to move forward, running on fumes and sheer willpower. There was no time to wallow, but also no time to rest. My days blurred into nights as I powered through, fueled by little more than adrenaline and determination.

Despite my best efforts, sleep remained elusive. Insomnia plagued my nights, punctuated by restless tosses and turns. I knew I was running on borrowed time, riding the adrenaline that kept me going. But even the mightiest rush of adrenaline eventually ebbs away, leaving exhaustion in its wake.

As the days passed, each morning seemed to weigh heavier on my shoulders, burdened by intermittent bouts of depression that crept in uninvited. I was determined to shake off the darkness, believing that the key lay in drowning myself in physical exertion. So, I ramped up my exercise regimen, adding more miles to my weekly runs, sweating it out in spin classes and immersing myself in the heat of hot yoga sessions. But instead of feeling stronger, I found myself shedding pounds at an alarming rate.

And when the endorphin rush from sweaty workouts failed to lift my spirits, I turned to a familiar coping mechanism: alcohol. My consumption soared, and what had once been occasional blackouts soon became a weekly occurrence. I justified my escalating intake, telling myself that as long as I made it home in one piece (albeit often collapsed on the sofa, fully clothed), I was still in control.

My mom lived just a stone's throw away, yet our visits were sparse, limited to obligatory dinners every other week. I avoided family gatherings like the plague; I couldn't bear the thought of fielding questions about my nonexistent love life or enduring concerned comments about my shrinking figure.

Amidst my own personal turmoil, the world seemed to spiral into chaos that year. While it might not have reached the apocalyptic levels of 2020 in hindsight, it was still a tough one, possibly one of the roughest we'd collectively faced up until then. Before COVID cast its long shadow, 2016 served up a grim buffet of global crises. The war in Syria raged on, senseless shootings rocked France, Brexit loomed ominously on the horizon and to top it all off, the unthinkable happened: Trump snagged the presidency. As if that wasn't enough, we bid farewell to a slew of icons, from the incomparable David Bowie to the beloved Snape (Alan Rickman) of *Harry Potter* fame and the mighty Muhammad Ali. It was a year that felt like a relentless onslaught of bad news, leaving everyone feeling utterly spent. And like everyone else, I was *done*.

I was back on the express Shinkansen train to destruction. The only thing tethering me to some semblance of sanity was this desperate need to prove to my ex that I was doing just fine. That I was moving on, living my best life and absolutely killing it at work.

But the reality couldn't have been more distant from the facade I'd crafted for myself. That $10 million budget boost we received almost half a year ago initially felt like a godsend for my professional trajectory. But slowly, insidiously, it morphed into a double-edged sword, slicing into my personal life. The injection kept me perpetually occupied, whisking me off on whirlwind tours across Indonesia for campaigns and on-ground activations. Deep down, I knew I was just another cog in the corporate machine, sacrificing my waking hours at the altar of work. In return, I received a fleeting sense of productivity and a temporary escape from the misery of my single life.

Night after night, I wrestled with the urge to re-download Tinder, but I resisted, knowing full well the potential consequences it could have on the fragile stability I'd maintained over the past few months. With early December already upon me, and the impending exodus of colleagues by mid-month, I had less than two-and-a-half weeks of work left. I reminded myself to hold it together, just a little while longer.

"Just one more work trip," I repeated to myself, "and just five more on-ground brand activations to oversee." *Keep it together, Mira. Just a little while longer, and then you can finally crash...all on your own.*

***

"Will you come with me to Lombok, please?" I pleaded with my sister over the phone.

"Why don't you go with Andara and Tia?" she suggested, referring to my usual travel companions.

"They decided not to go anywhere this year," I explained. "Please join me. I'll pay for your ticket," I tempted her.

"You've been traveling a lot this year. Why don't you just rest at home during the break?"

"No, I don't think I can do that. Being home will drive me crazy. I don't want to spend alone time in my apartment for that long. It will remind me of everything that happened this year. I need to go somewhere. Please come with me?"

"Why Lombok, though?" she asked.

"I don't know. I shot a campaign there last quarter with my agency, and we stayed at this really cute surf bungalow. I just want to go back there. It seemed very peaceful."

"When are you going again?"

"I should be there around Christmas. I'm going to Lombok straight from my last work trip. Are you free already?" I asked.

"No. Idris is coming to Jakarta around that time. The earliest I can join you might be around the 30th."

"That's fine. I can go first and spend time by myself, and then we can go and disappear somewhere for the New Year. What do you think? I promise it will be a chill one; I don't want to party or anything. I just want to disappear a bit for the New Year, write down resolutions and read a book or two or something."

"That doesn't sound like you," she observed.

"Yeah, I know, right? I don't know if it's the breakup or what, but I definitely feel more introverted now. Too many people are draining me."

"Welcome to my world," she said.

"But seriously, I get it now! I get what you mean when you say people-ing is tiring."

"It is! Took you long enough to finally get it," she teased. We'd always had very different social batteries.

"Okay, you just let me know when you want to fly, and I'll book your ticket. I'll cover our hotel and everything, too. I found this cool glamping resort in the far east of Lombok. Google it, it's called Jeeva Beloam. It looks really remote, and everything is inclusive including food. Seems like a perfect place to disappear for New Year's Eve. You can just bring your books and stuff."

"Okay, fine," my sister reluctantly agreed.

"Yay! Thank you!"

I felt relieved knowing that I wouldn't be facing the end of the year alone. And what made it even better was that I'd have my dear sister by my side. She's laid-back, not one for too many activities and just having her around would ensure that I didn't get caught up in any romantic entanglements. Plus, if I were to have a breakdown during the trip, she'd handle it with ease. Traveling with her meant a drama-free adventure, and that was exactly what I needed.

The last holiday I had was with the Director. And that ended... how it ended. Then came my trip to Bhutan, touted as the happiest place on earth. I had hoped it would lift me out of my depression slump, but it turned out to be a letdown. When I signed up for the volunteer trip, I envisioned a cathartic, soul-fulfilling experience—something rough and gritty, like building a house for the poor with my bare hands. Something to jolt me out of my usual world. Instead, I found myself assigned to teach professors how to use Google Workspace for their teaching. I mean, sure, it was probably meaningful for the university, but it felt too close to my day-to-day work.

I had imagined my mornings in Bhutan filled with happiness and gratitude as I sipped tea overlooking the country's breathtaking landscape. Instead, I woke up in tears every morning. The peace and quiet of the setting only emphasized the turmoil in my heart. Bhutan, with all its beauty, provided the perfect backdrop for solitude. But solitude was the last thing I wanted. It offered me a quiet space to confront my inner turmoil, but I wasn't ready. It was all too overwhelming, too raw, too soon.

So when neither of those trips lived up to the *Eat Pray Love* promise of post-breakup rediscovery and happiness found in a foreign land, I cursed Elizabeth Gilbert for giving us brokenhearted girls such high expectations from our travels. For making us believe that happiness could be found in far-off places rather than within ourselves.

And now, another trip. If there was one year where I really, really did not want to spend New Year's by myself, it was *that* year. My ex had always been a part of my most memorable New Year's celebrations. We spent one turn of the year staring at stars over the Sahara Desert in Morocco (magical!), and another experiencing a New Year's sunrise on the top of Mount Merapi in Yogyakarta (absolutely breathtaking!). And to top it all off, we got engaged on another New Year's in Amsterdam. He went down on one knee in the presence of our nearest and dearest friends, right before the clock struck midnight. I said yes. And the rest was history.

Whatever we did for New Year's, our principle had always been the same: New Year's Eve isn't for partying. Because, well,

New Year's Eve parties are almost always disappointing. From the mad traffic in the city to the rush to get wasted as fast as possible before midnight and the exorbitant entrance fees for subpar club programming that simply never deliver on the promise of a great party night to usher in the New Year. So, we preferred to save the partying for all the other nights throughout the year and use the New Year's break to go somewhere random, disappear and reflect on the passing year.

But I knew that the breakup year was different. There were still a lot of emotions that I hadn't—and didn't want to—process from the year. The thought of being alone with my own thoughts absolutely terrified me. That's why I did everything I could to convince my sister to join me. I also couldn't just stay in Jakarta and risk having yet another mental breakdown. Nope, no way. What if my ex found out that I was all alone on New Year's while he was maybe out partying in Amsterdam or Bali? Hell no. It would have felt like I lost. And that he had won the "who ended up better at the end of the breakup year" game. No, I couldn't allow that. Not a chance.

* * *

I landed in Lombok on December 25—a date that never meant much to me growing up Muslim. I don't celebrate Christmas in the traditional sense, but I've always enjoyed the twinkly lights, the festive playlists and the excuse to gather with people you love (or at least like enough to share dessert with). Unlike Bali, with its strong Hindu influence, Lombok is a predominantly Muslim island, so traveling on Christmas Day didn't feel like missing out. If anything, it felt like a smart move; I skipped the holiday chaos and scored a cheaper ticket.

Pak Indar, a cheerful local driver whose contact I received from one of the crew members from my previous campaign shoot, was waiting for me at the airport. His warm smile and easy-going demeanor instantly put me at ease.

"Halo, mbak Mira, how are you?" he asked as he helped me with my luggage.

"I'm good, Pak, thank you. How about you?"

"Alhamdulillah, I'm also good, mbak," he responded. "Are you traveling alone? Where is your husband?" My solo travel must have struck him as odd, or at least a little out of the ordinary.

"Uhm, I'm not married, Pak. So yeah, no husband. I'm just traveling by myself," I explained with a smile.

"Oh, okay. You're really brave, traveling alone."

While I appreciated his friendly banter, I couldn't help but chuckle inwardly at the typical assumption that a woman my age should be accompanied by a spouse. It's a cultural norm that I've grown accustomed to.

"Where are you staying this time?" Pak Indar asked.

"At Drop Inn, Pak. That surf bungalow where we shot our advertisement last time. Do you remember?"

"Ah, yes, yes, the one near Kuta." he put the key in and started the car engine. "Okay, mbak."

"How long does it take to get there from here?"

"Just around 30 minutes. Not far," he assured me.

"Perfect," I said with a sigh of relief, ready to unwind and embrace this break.

Despite its close proximity and similar land size, Lombok remains markedly different from Bali. While Bali bustles with traffic jams and ongoing development projects, Lombok, situated to the east, seems to operate at a more leisurely pace. For every 20 new villa or resort developments in Bali, Lombok boasts just one. Apart from the Senggigi area in the west and the three Gili Islands, reachable by a short ferry ride from the main island, much of Lombok retains its raw and underdeveloped charm.

As the car carried me from the airport to the Drop Inn, I couldn't resist rolling down the window and letting the wind tousle my hair. The winding roads revealed lush jungle and the occasional sight of farm animals roaming freely in the wild. With every passing mile, the tranquility of nature eased the weight of the year I was about to leave behind.

This journey marked my very first solo trip. Excitement and nervousness intertwined as I contemplated the days ahead. With five days and zero plans before my sister's arrival, I was embarking on an adventure of uncertainty. After spending one and a half years meticulously planning a wedding that never came to fruition, I vowed to embrace spontaneity. This time, I was going to let life lead me.

***

Drop Inn's accommodations were simple yet stylish, offering a unique kind of luxury—the luxury of seclusion and tranquility. Tucked away from the noise of busy streets, the only soundtrack here was the melodic chirping of birds and the laughter of children playing in the nearby village. Stepping through the entrance, I found myself in a spacious, single-story building with an open-plan layout, adorned with what appeared to be a quaint little café at the front. Soon after I entered, a friendly woman, sporting blonde hair and appearing to be in her early forties, emerged from a room on the right.

"You must be Mira," she greeted me, evidently anticipating my arrival.

"Yes, that's me," I confirmed with a smile.

"Great. Welcome to Drop Inn. How was your travel? Is that all your luggage?" she inquired, gesturing towards my trusty red suitcase, which Pak Indar was lugging inside.

"My flight went smoothly, thanks. And yes, that's all I brought."

"Perfect. Well, your bungalow is all set. It's Number 3, right in the middle." I followed her lead through the inner courtyard.

"So, Mira, where are you from? And if I may ask, how did you find out about us?" she asked as we strolled past the inviting round pool nestled at the center of the garden, heading towards a row of charming huts crafted from bamboo and wood, topped with thatched roofs.

"I'm actually Indonesian, but I live in Jakarta. And I was here a few months back for a shoot. I think I remember seeing you around."

"Oh, were you part of the Google shoot?"

"Yeah, that's the one."

"Are you part of the production company?" she probed further.

"Nope, I'm the client." I smiled.

"How cool. Well, thanks for choosing our place for the shoot."

"Your place is really lovely. That's why I wanted to come back and actually stay here this time!"

"Thank you. Good to have you back then!" she replied warmly. "And is the film done? Can I see it somewhere?"

"Yeah, it is. It actually aired on TV nationwide for a couple of weeks. It's also on the Google Indonesia YouTube channel. Let me find it and show it to you later."

"That would be great!" She halted and placed my luggage down on the porch. "Welcome to your bungalow!" She handed me the key.

"How lovely," I remarked, stepping inside.

"If you need anything, just knock on my door there. My name is Angela."

"Thank you, Angela." I waved at her as she walked away.

I settled into my bungalow, placed my suitcase inside and switched on the AC to cool down the room. After kicking off my traveling sneakers, my trusted Adidas, I began to walk barefoot on the patio toward the hammock swaying gently at the far end of the porch. With a light leap, I settled into the hammock, feeling the gentle sway beneath me. I then texted Pak Indar to head home, took a moment to capture the serene scene with a photo of my feet against the backdrop of lush greenery and made a compulsory arrival post on Instagram: "Home for the next five days 🌴🌴."

***

I woke up naturally in the morning, untethered to the shrill ring of an alarm clock and made my way to the café for breakfast. As I savored my açai bowl paired with toast and a refreshing glass of green detox juice, I contemplated how to spend the day ahead.

A quick Google search offered up a few ideas: a beach on the southern coast promising spectacular sunsets, or a handful of scenic spots perfect for aimless wandering. But the thought of navigating it all alone gave me pause. It was only my first full day in Lombok, after all. There was no need to rush into exploration. So I stayed in, nestled into the quiet corners of the Drop Inn with a book in hand.

Armed with four books to stave off any potential boredom, I was determined to stick to my plan of complete relaxation and spontaneity. However, it didn't take long for anxiety to sneak in. Instead of fully embracing the freedom of being on holiday, I found myself plagued by feelings of guilt for simply lounging around and not filling every moment with activity. I couldn't shake off the nagging sensation that I was somehow wasting precious time.

I yearned for solitude to contemplate the ups and downs of my tumultuous year. But paradoxically, after just an hour or two, I found myself glued to Instagram and WhatsApp, refreshing them every few minutes in search of some distraction, any distraction. My posts painted a picture of sunlight, smoothies and pool views, but behind the curated frames, my mind buzzed with unease.

I paced restlessly from the terrace of my bungalow to a lounge chair by the pool and back again, as if a better seat might quiet my thoughts. I wanted to lose myself in a book, to relax, to be present, but instead, I was locked in a slow, silent wrestle with my own loneliness. I wasn't used to this much stillness. I wanted the day to end. More than anything, I wished for my sister to arrive sooner, just so I wouldn't have to be so alone.

***

The next morning, I woke up dreading the prospect of facing another day all by myself. If you planned on having no plan, did that still count as having a plan? Just one-and-a-half days into this solo adventure, and my brain was already spinning. Eventually, I dragged myself out of bed, went for breakfast and asked myself the same question: *What should I do today?*

Maybe another day holed up in my bungalow, trying to get through a few chapters of my book? Or maybe more shots for Instagram, pretending I was living my best life and finding deep meaning in all this alone time? Or...should I actually leave the bungalow? I could handle a solo meal, but the thought of being out and about all day in Lombok on my own felt a bit much. Plus, there wasn't anything within walking distance. If my ex were here, he would've rented a scooter and we'd be zipping around to the beach and all over the island. But alas, he wasn't there, and I had zero clue how to ride a scooter.

I slammed the book shut, a sudden jolt of "you only live once" energy revving me up. Who cared if I was alone? Who cared if I didn't know how to ride a scooter? I could learn, right? Then I could go to the beach for sunset. And I knew the bungalow had scooter rentals. So I jumped up and headed straight for the reception. Now I just had to figure out if there was someone there who could teach this total noob (me).

***

"Have you ridden a motorbike before?" Gusti, the young boy manning the scooter rental at the bungalow, asked me.

"Um, only on the back with someone else driving," I said, trying to sound confident. I was worried he wouldn't let me rent the scooter.

"Don't worry. I can teach you! It's easy," he said.

"And I don't need to have a license to ride, right?" I asked.

"Nah...no need," he replied, grabbing a yellow Scoopy scooter from the parking lot.

What a cute scooter.

"Okay, let's go to the field over there." He motioned with one hand while dragging the scooter with the other.

I was anxious. I kept remembering what my ex always said:

"Babe, your cycling skills are terrible.

"You're going to get hit if you keep on cycling like that."

"Mira, watch out!"

His words played over and over again in my head. Being Dutch, he and all the other Dutch kids were practically born on a bicycle. From a working mother in heels and a suit driving a bakfiets with two kids, to a student expertly maneuvering his luggage with one hand, to pregnant ladies in boots cycling in the snow—you have to hand it to the Dutch; they *know* how to cycle. So when my ex told me I sucked at cycling, I believed him. Plus, growing up in Jakarta, my mom would never let me hop on the back of an *ojek*, or a motorcycle taxi, for obvious safety reasons.

"Don't worry. This area is the best place to drive motorbikes," Gusti said, maybe reading my anxiety. "There are barely any cars around, so you should be okay."

What a relief.

"But the roads are just a bit bumpy and at night there's not much light."

"Right..." *That's not helping.*

"Here's how you turn on the bike," Gusti said, inserting the key and turning it on. "Here's your gas, and here's your brake." He showed me while sitting on the bike. He turned the gas handle, and the bike moved forward slowly. "Just keep your hand on the brake and release slowly to speed up."

"Okay." It seemed simple enough.

"Now you try."

Shit, it's my time already?

I put on my helmet before hopping on the yellow bike. "To be safe, you know, in case I fall."

With my helmet properly on, I sat on the bike and put both of my hands on the handlebars. *Brake with the left and gas with the right,* I reminded myself. "Okay, let's do this!" I held the brake all the way down first, then turned the gas. The bike didn't move.

"Release the brake!" he said.

The bike's sudden forward movement caught me by surprise, and my reflexes made me hit the brake again to stop. Realizing I was at a standstill again, I released the brake while still holding the gas at the same position. The bike moved forward. This kept happening over and over until I was moving and stopping every two seconds. I must have looked like an idiot.

"Just release the brake, it's okay." Gusti directed me calmly.

And so I did. And I was finally cruising along the field. *That was not as bad as I thought!* The field was spacious, giving me plenty of room to practice turns and maneuvers. With each loop, I felt more in tune with the bike, more confident in my abilities. The initial jerks and stops were gone, replaced by smooth, fluid movements. As I continued to ride along the field, the sensation of freedom grew stronger. The wind blew against my face, whipping my hair back. It was like the world had suddenly opened up, offering endless possibilities just waiting to be discovered.

Gusti watched from the sidelines, and a grin spread across his face. He gave me a thumbs-up, and I responded with an enthusiastic wave. Without his help, I might never have had the courage to try. I took a deep breath, savoring the taste of the salty air. This was it. This was what I had been missing. The sense of liberation, the thrill of the unknown. Riding a motorbike wasn't just about getting from one place to another.

I felt proud as I slowed down and brought the bike to a stop. I had done it. I faced my fears and came out stronger on the other side. I turned off the engine and dismounted, my legs slightly wobbly but my spirit soaring, excited about all the places I could explore on the island.

Gusti walked over, clapping his hands. "You did great. See? I told you it was easy."

***

Day three felt like a rebirth. With the taste of freedom and the rumble of the motorbike engine echoing in my ears, I woke up grinning like a Cheshire cat.

Not only had I conquered the art of motorbike riding the day before (insert a mental high five here), but I had also spent the afternoon channeling my inner Easy Rider, cruising around Lombok on my trusty Scoopy. The destination? Tanjung Aan beach, where I witnessed a sunset that could've given a Pantone color swatch a run for its money.

As I lay in bed, scrolling through photos on my phone (knowing full well they couldn't do that sunset justice), I yearned to share my badassery with someone. I wanted to shout from the rooftops about my accomplishment, to have someone cheer me on and join me.

I had banished Tinder, that digital wasteland of shirtless gym selfies and cheesy pickup lines, from my phone weeks ago. But in this moment, I thought, *screw it*. After all, if I could navigate the winding roads of Lombok, I could surely handle a few more awkward first dates. With a mischievous grin, I redownloaded the app, ready to swipe right on whatever (or whoever) came my way.

The next morning, as I sipped my morning tea, a notification popped up: a match with a cute Brazilian guy from Melbourne, also exploring Lombok solo. Without missing a beat, we decided to meet for lunch and see where the day would take us.

***

True to my "minimize the risk of a bad coffee date" philosophy, I'd strategically picked the Drop Inn's café as our meeting spot, just a two-minute stroll from my bungalow. The place had an easy charm to it: mismatched wooden chairs painted in cheerful colors scattered across an open-air patio, practically begging you to linger over a cup of locally roasted coffee and a conversation with potential.

If sparks flew, we could always wander down to the beach together. If not, I had an easy out, a polite goodbye, then a quiet return to my bungalow or some solo beach time. Either way, I'd win. It was a low-stakes setup disguised as casual spontaneity. Foolproof.

As I waited, a message popped up on my Tinder app. "I'm here," it read. We hadn't exchanged WhatsApp digits yet at that point.

"I'm at the back," I replied.

"Cool, I'll find you in a minute."

As he walked into the café, I spotted him easily from a distance. He not only looked like his photos but was also the only guy entering the café. The other people were mostly German girls in their mid-20s.

"Hi!" I blurted out as he sat down, my mind drawing a blank. "How do I say your name again?" He kindly corrected my bad pronunciation, a small smile gracing his lips.

I found myself staring at him a beat too long, an odd sense of familiarity washing over me. My mind raced, trying to place him. Have we met before? No, that couldn't be possible. Yet, the feeling persisted, a nagging whisper of recognition.

"Get the quinoa chicken wrap," I suggested as he scanned the menu. "I had it yesterday with a watermelon juice, and it was delicious."

"Sounds good," he replied, jotting down his order on the slip of paper the waiter had provided.

"Make that two," I chimed in.

"So, where should we start?" I asked, taking the lead. "Tell me what brought you here."

"I'm just here for my New Year holiday. I've been in Lombok for three days and will be here for another week and a half."

"And you're here on your own?"

"Yeah, I like to travel solo sometimes and take photos of the people I meet. How about you? How long are you here for?"

"I arrived three days ago and will head to East Lombok for a few days for New Year's Eve once my sister arrives in a few days."

"What's in the East?" he asked, curiosity piqued.

"To be honest, I don't know. I've never been. I'm just going to this supposedly secluded beach resort with no TV or internet. Gonna disappear for a bit with my sister for the New Year."

"Sounds nice, actually," he said.

"Yeah, looking forward to it," I replied. "So...what's your story?" I wanted to cut through the small talk. Tell me how you've been hurt in love, and I'll gauge whether our vibes align.

"You mean why am I on Tinder?" he clarified.

"Yeah."

He paused, a flicker of hesitation in his eyes. "Well, let's just say my last relationship didn't end well," he admitted. "It was a classic case of 'right person, wrong time,' but it still left a mark." He took a sip of his water, the ice clinking gently against the glass. "Honestly, I'm just here trying to figure my life out," he said with a half-smile. "And hey—if Tinder helps me find someone who actually gets the importance of a good playlist, that's a bonus."

"A good playlist is crucial." I agreed, leaning in with a conspiratorial whisper, "So, tell me. What went down with your last relationship? If I may ask, of course."

He took a breath. "We were together for a while," he began. "Ever since we both lived in Valencia, a lifetime ago, it seems. We even got engaged and moved to Melbourne, her hometown." His voice trailed off, the weight of the past evident in his tone. "One thing led to another, and we ended up calling off the engagement."

"No way. You also had a broken engagement?" I paused, letting the reality of the coincidental situation sink in. "How long ago was this?"

"About three years ago. Did you have a canceled engagement too?"

I nodded. "Yeah, it kind of just imploded earlier this year. The whole thing was a Taylor Swift song waiting to happen."

"I'm not really a big fan of Taylor Swift, but I get your point." He tried to make a joke, but quickly moved on. "Anyway, I'm so sorry to hear that. That's rough, no matter how long ago it happened." He paused, searching my face. "How are you now?"

"Not great, to be honest," I confessed, feeling vulnerable. "But I guess that's also why I'm on Tinder. Trying to put the pieces back together, one swipe at a time."

He chuckled. "It's been three years for me, and I still haven't figured it all out. The scars fade, but they never truly disappear."

My heart sank a little. "Nooo...Please tell me something more optimistic," I pleaded desperately. "I really hope I will have recovered from this in three years!"

He raised his eyebrows. "Do you know when your Saturn return is?"

I blinked, utterly bewildered. "My what? No." My astrological knowledge was limited to my star sign. "All I know is I'm an Aquarius."

"Your Saturn returns," he repeated, like it should've been common knowledge, "is an astrological transit that happens when Saturn returns to the same place in the sky as when you were born. It's this phase in your late twenties when everything kinda gets shaken up—career, relationships, life stuff. Total cosmic reset."

I shook my head, still lost. "Nope, never heard of it."

He raised an eyebrow, a knowing smirk playing on his lips. "How old were you when your engagement ended?"

"Twenty-nine," I replied.

"Me too," he said.

"No way." A chill ran through me.

"Your canceled engagement must have been during your Saturn return. It's a notorious period for relationship breakdowns."

I stared at him, a mix of astonishment and intrigue swirling within me. Could it be possible that the stars had played a role in the tumultuous events of my past? And was this chance encounter with a stranger who supposedly also experienced a Saturn return-induced canceled engagement just a coincidence? Or was it something more?

Here I was, thousands of miles from home, on a supposedly healing holiday, and I had happened upon someone who shared a similar wound. It was a crazy coincidence, yes, but it also felt like a cosmic wink, a sign that maybe opening up to this stranger wasn't such a bad idea after all. After all, he understood the pain of a love lost, the feeling of having your world turned upside down just as you thought you had it all figured out.

The air between us shifted, charged with understanding. It was like we'd stumbled upon a secret language, spoken only by those who had survived the wreckage of a love gone wrong.

People who've weathered similar storms tend to offer a kind of empathy that's hard to find elsewhere. And most of the time, that's all I need. I don't want to be judged for swiping right; I just want to lay my cards on the table—the almost-married, ex-fiancé-fled-the-country-in-a-mental-breakdown card—and skip straight to the good stuff, like planning a spontaneous beach trip.

"So, tell me more about this beach you mentioned. Is it scooter-accessible?" I asked.

"Yeah," he replied, completely oblivious to my not-so-hidden agenda. "It's just about a 15-minute drive from here."

"Shall we go?"

"Sure. Do you have a bike?"

"Of course!" I said. The fact that I had just mastered the art of scooter-ing yesterday remained a secret.

***

"Two chairs and two coconuts, right, boss?" the beach vendor confirmed as we settled into our bamboo lounge chairs on the serene Tanjung Aan beach.

Ah, Tanjung Aan, my happy place in southern Lombok. The beach sprawled out before us, a wide expanse of white sand kissed by crystal clear water, dramatically divided by a rugged cliff. This raw, unspoiled beauty was a far cry from the bustling energy of Bali. Sure, Bali's got it all, but Lombok's untouched charm is like a breath of fresh air, just what this city girl needed.

"So, who called off the engagement, if I may ask?" I ventured, sipping my coconut water.

"After living in Valencia for a couple of years, she wanted to move back to Australia," he explained. "I joined her and when we got engaged, it made sense for me to be under her dependent visa. But I guess once we moved, she changed her mind."

I nodded, knowingly. "Big international moves can be tough on any couple. My fiancé's move to Jakarta was the beginning of the end of my relationship, too."

"Yeah...And she also fell in love with this jerk from her office."

"Ouch," I winced, not wanting to pry too deeply into painful territory. "And are they together now?"

"Nope, they broke up."

"I'm so sorry about all of that."

"It's okay," he said, with a soft smile. "I'm in a better place now."

"You seem like it! So, what helped you recover from this whole thing?" I asked, leaning in with genuine curiosity. "I'm taking notes for myself, of course."

"Well, my ayahuasca retreat helped a lot."

My eyes widened. "Oh wow, you've done ayahuasca? What was that like?"

"It was actually quite tough," he admitted. "I went to some dark places. But in the end, it was good."

"What does it feel like?" I pressed, my curiosity now bordering on obsession.

"It felt like I died. Not me personally, but my ego died and then was brought back to life," he replied, a faraway look in his eyes.

"Wow. That's a bit scary but so deep. I'd love to try it one day," I confessed, feeling a mix of excitement and trepidation at the thought of venturing into the unknown depths of my own consciousness.

"Yeah, you should," he encouraged. "I think you'll enjoy it, and I'm sure it will give you some answers to your questions."

"Will you do it again?" I asked.

"Actually, I have another retreat booked next month after I come back from this trip."

"Oh, nice. Please keep me posted on it. I'd love to hear more about it."

"Okay, sure," he agreed. "Then let's keep in touch after this trip," he suggested.

"That sounds good," I replied, feeling a spark of connection ignite between us.

"Shall we jump into the water?"

"Yeah, let's!" I exclaimed, springing up from my chair.

As we walked toward the water, a herd of cows ambled past, guided by a local farmer. Their hooves left imprints in the pristine sand. On the other side of the beach, a group of children from the nearby village frolicked, their colorful kites dancing in the sky like vibrant birds. The scene was a perfect postcard from rural Lombok, a world away from the hustle and bustle of everyday life.

We tiptoed into the water, the gentle waves lapping at our ankles like playful puppies. As we ventured deeper, the cool water enveloped our legs, offering a refreshing respite from the warm sun.

"So," I asked, once we were waist-deep in the turquoise embrace of the ocean, "what do you do back in Australia?"

"I'm a photographer," he replied, a touch of pride in his voice.

"What kind of photography do you do?"

"Mainly portrait and travel," he replied, his eyes scanning the horizon as if framing a potential shot. "I love capturing the beauty of the places I visit."

"That's amazing," I said, genuinely impressed. "I work in marketing," I shared, hoping my profession didn't sound too mundane in comparison. "It's not quite as artistic as photographing exotic landscapes, but it has its moments."

"I'm sure it does. Maybe you could help me market my photos someday."

I laughed, splashing him playfully. "Maybe I could," I said, feeling our sense of camaraderie growing.

"So, before Australia, you were in Valencia?" I prodded, trying to piece together the whirlwind adventure that had landed this Brazilian in my corner of the world.

"Yup," he confirmed.

"And before that?" I pressed.

"London."

"Ah, cool. For your studies?" I ventured, assuming the obvious.

"Yeah, I studied there...and I also did some porn," he added nonchalantly, as if casually mentioning what he had for breakfast.

"You did what?" I nearly choked on the seawater. "Porn? As in like porn films?"

"Well, I never had sex on screen, but I was naked in those films."

"And what did you do then? What was the story?" My curiosity was palpable.

"Well I had to masturbate on screen. The story was about this lady who owns a car repair garage that's going through some financial troubles," he started.

"Okay." I listened attentively.

"There were seven mechanics at the garage, and she had to fire someone to save money. So we all had to line up naked and jerk off. The last person to cum gets fired."

"And did you...?"

"Of course I did," he answered casually with a wink.

I instinctively darted my eyes down to his board shorts, trying to gauge the size of his private parts, my mind racing with the absurdity of it all.

"Do you still have the film?" I had to know.

"No, I don't," he replied, sounding genuinely disappointed. "I've been looking for it too," he said. "But I have some photos from the set," he added, a glimmer of hope returning to his eyes.

"Can I see?" I pressed, eager to catch a glimpse of this cinematic treasure.

"Sure, I'll show you later," he promised with a playful grin, before turning and swimming back toward the beach.

A Tinder match with a broken engagement and a past life as a pornstar? I was completely floored by the absurdity of it all. I mean, I thought I'd seen it all, but this? This was a plot twist I never saw coming.

As we relaxed back into our bamboo chairs, the coconut lady's timing was impeccable. "Another two, please," I chirped, already feeling the tropical vibes.

"And a bottle of mineral water," the Pornstar chimed in.

Our comfortable silence was broken only by the gentle sound of the sea. But my mind was racing. "This whole thing is so surreal," I blurted out, my thoughts tumbling out like a Jenga tower collapsing.

He turned to face me, his curiosity piqued. "What do you mean?"

"The whole Saturn return thing," I began, gesturing vaguely towards the sky. "You, also having a canceled engagement, your pornstar past..." I laughed nervously, wondering what other plot twists the universe had in store.

He leaned forward. I could practically see the gears turning in his head.

"What's on your mind?" I asked.

He took a deep breath, his eyes searching mine. "Can I kiss you?"

The question hung in the air with a mix of vulnerability and boldness. I was caught off guard; my heart skipped a beat. But as I looked into his eyes, I knew the answer. I smiled and leaned in to meet him halfway.

***

Picture this: a sun-drenched beach, an epic sunset, a scooter adventure around the island and a romantic dinner on the hill. The spark between us was undeniable, and by the end of the day, we decided to spend the next few days together until I had to head to East Lombok for New Year's Eve with my sister.

Our days blurred into nights, a stolen slice of paradise before real life came knocking. Knowing that we had to say goodbye so soon, we decided to squeeze every ounce of joy out of our remaining time. We both knew what we signed up for—a holiday fling, a whirlwind romance with a built-in expiration date.

The island became our playground as we zipped around on a scooter, my confidence soaring with each twist and turn. By day,

I felt like a seasoned pro, my hair whipping in the wind. But as darkness fell, a hint of trepidation crept in. My grip tightened on the handlebars, my speed reduced to a crawl, as I navigated the island's unpaved roads with the caution of a first-time driver.

Selong Belanak beach, a surfer's paradise, beckoned us with its gentle waves and sandy shores. We rented boards and took turns conquering the surf, each wipeout met with laughter and encouragement. As he emerged from the water, board in hand, dripping with saltwater and that irresistible surfer charm, a thought struck me like a rogue wave.

"Am I in *Eat Pray Love*?!" I exclaimed, my voice a mix of amusement and disbelief. The parallels were uncanny: Elizabeth Gilbert met a Brazilian guy at the end of her trip in Bali, and there I was, on my own soul-searching journey, falling for a Brazilian hottie with a heart of gold. Coincidence? Or maybe Elizabeth Gilbert knew what she was talking about, after all.

On our last day together, the Pornstar and I perched atop the cliffs overlooking Tanjung Aan beach once more, our eyes glued to the horizon as the sun descended. Lombok's sunsets were pure magic, a kaleidoscope that painted the sky with every shade of pink, orange and gold. From our clifftop perch, the world stretched out in a panoramic masterpiece, a 360-degree canvas of natural wonder. In that moment, we were high on life, on the sheer beauty of it all. I felt grateful.

***

My phone buzzed. It was a text from my sister. I held my breath as I read the words: "I got typhoid."

"What do you mean you got typhoid? You're supposed to come to Lombok tomorrow," I typed back, my fingers flying across the screen. I selfishly clung to our New Year's Eve plans.

"I'm in the hospital."

My heart sank. "Oh no, it's that serious? What happened?" I asked, now more worried.

Her reply came quickly: "I think I got it from some bad food, when I was stressed from a lot of work too."

"Are you okay now?"

"The doctor said I'll be fine. But I need to stay at the hospital for a few days, so I can't come to Lombok anymore." My sister delivered the bad news.

As I processed the news, my mind spiraled into a vortex of uncertainty. The prospect of spending New Year's Eve alone in a secluded corner of Lombok felt like a scene from a horror movie, a stark contrast to the romantic comedy I'd been living in just moments before.

I considered cutting the trip short and flying back to Jakarta. Or...*should I invite the Pornstar?* With a mix of hesitation and hope, I opened our chat and typed: "Hey, any chance you want to head east with me for New Year's?"

His response was swift, "Oh, I thought you were going with your sister?"

"Unfortunately, she got ill," I replied. "She's hospitalized with typhoid."

"So sorry to hear that," he said. "Is she okay?"

"Yeah, she'll be fine. It's not her first rodeo with typhoid,"

"Oh, I see." He paused.

"I went for it. "I know we said our goodbyes already. But, well, I wasn't expecting my sister to get sick either."

"It's okay. I really enjoyed our time together. And I was planning on spending NYE by myself anyway. So maybe we can simply postpone our goodbye until after the new year?"

"Is that a yes then?" I couldn't help but press, my hopes rising.

"Let me check if I can cancel my New Year accommodations. Give me a min."

The suspense was agonizing. I waited, my fingers tapping a nervous rhythm on the table.

Finally, his message came through. "Okay, sure. I'm down. So where are we heading tomorrow?"

"Yay!" I squealed, a giddy smile spreading across my face. Maybe it was the start of a whole new adventure, a sequel even better than the original.

***

"How much longer?" I asked Pak Indar. The further we ventured, the more remote and untouched the landscape became. The bumpy road seemed to stretch on forever, a testament to Lombok's untamed beauty.

"Just another 30 minutes," Pak Indar assured us.

The Pornstar, ever observant, chimed in, "I wonder why they wouldn't build this road."

Pak Indar chuckled, "The local government purposely doesn't want to."

"How come?" I asked.

"They're worried that if they build the road, foreign investors will buy up all the land," Pak Indar explained. "Too much development would ruin the island."

I nodded in agreement. "Smart. I wouldn't want Lombok to lose its raw beauty either."

The anticipation for New Year's Eve bubbled up, and I turned to him with a smile. "So, what should we do for NYE tomorrow? The resort mentioned a BBQ."

"That sounds fun," he replied. "We should definitely join. What do you usually do for New Year's?"

"I'm not really into the whole drinking and partying scene on New Year's," I confessed. "I prefer to wake up sober and reflect on the past year. Usually, I spend the morning writing down my resolutions."

"That's actually really good." He nodded thoughtfully. "I'm not a big fan of the NYE party scene either. It's always a bit of a letdown."

"Exactly!" I exclaimed, feeling a sense of connection. "I much prefer a quiet dinner with close friends."

A mischievous glint appeared in his eyes. "What about doing some shrooms for NYE?"

My eyebrows shot up in surprise. "Wait, you have some?"

"Yeah," he grinned. "I picked some up from the reggae bar near my bungalow this morning."

"Wow," I said, curious and hesitant at the same time.

"You've done it before, right?" he asked.

"Yeah," I admitted.

The idea hung in the air, thick with possibility and a hint of apprehension. The Pornstar, with his sun-kissed skin and easy charm, was already an unexpected detour. Now, with the prospect of shrooms adding a twist to our New Year's Eve escapade, it felt like we were crossing a line. As the van bumped along the dirt road, I couldn't help but wonder if this New Year's Eve was about to take a different kind of turn. Buckle up, Mira, I told myself, this trip is about to veer into the unknown.

***

We arrived at Jeeva Beloam, a haven of glamping luxury. Ten lodges, in the shape of traditional Sasak fishing huts, reinvented with sustainable materials, dotted the landscape, their alang-alang (or thatched) roofs blending seamlessly with the lush greenery.

"This feels like a place where someone would go for a honeymoon," the Pornstar remarked, his eyes scanning the idyllic surroundings.

"Yeah, you're right," I agreed, smiling. "This isn't going to be weird, is it?"

He winked. "We can always pretend we're husband and wife."

"Oh, and we're celebrating our anniversary," I added.

"Yes. And we left the kids with the grandparents." We laughed loudly together, and it felt good.

"So, no Wi-Fi here, right?" the Pornstar asked. His voice echoed in the bamboo-framed lodge as he unpacked his minimalist gear. Just a backpack and a duffel bag—the man traveled light.

"Nope," I replied, tossing my phone onto the woven bedspread. "And zero bars of service for me."

"Yeah, me too," he chuckled. "It's like a digital detox retreat, whether we signed up for it or not."

"Honestly, it's kind of refreshing. I don't even have to wish people a happy New Year tomorrow, simply because I can't!"

"True," he agreed. "We'll be blissfully ignorant of the world until we re-enter civilization after the New Year."

I laughed. "We could be missing out on the passing of someone famous, or even the apocalypse and we wouldn't have a clue!"

Suddenly, the Pornstar wrapped his arms around me, pulling me close. "So, my dear wife," he whispered playfully in my ear, his voice a low rumble that made me shiver with excitement. "How do you want to spend the rest of this glorious afternoon?"

I leaned into his embrace, a warmth spreading through me like a shot of whisky on a cold night. "Well, dear husband," I purred, "I think it's time we explored this paradise we've found ourselves in."

He nodded towards the inviting king-sized bed draped in mosquito netting. "Should we start with the bed?" I returned his smile, my heart pounding with anticipation.

"That sounds like a great place to start."

As our bodies intertwined, the sound of the ocean waves outside seemed to fade into the distance. The afternoon sun cast dappled patterns on our skin and created a kaleidoscope of light and shadow. Every touch, every whisper, felt like a stolen moment in time, a testament to the unexpected connection we had found. The "honeymoon" resort, it turned out, was the perfect setting for our impromptu celebration of love and lust.

Each touch, each kiss, was a balm to my wounded heart, soothing the ache of past betrayals and reawakening a sense of hope. As I lost myself in the depths of his eyes, a realization dawned on me: this was more than just a holiday fling. This was a healing touch, a chance to rediscover the joy of intimacy and vulnerability. And as we drifted off to sleep, tangled in each other's arms, a single thought echoed in my mind: *Damn, Tinder, you've really outdone yourself this time.*

* * *

"You're number 111," he announced as I emerged from the bathroom, towel-clad and hair dripping wet.

"Number 111?" I repeated, bewildered, taking a seat on the bed to dry my hair.

"On my list," he clarified.

"Your list of...what?" I asked, still confused. Then...*No way.* "Wait a minute. Are you talking about the number of people you've slept with?!"

"Yes," he replied, nonchalantly tilting his laptop screen toward me. "Do you want to see?"

Still a bit stunned, I managed a hesitant, "Uhm. Yeah, sure?"

And there it was, his list. The little black book, the catalog of conquests, immortalized in a Notepad file on his laptop. He'd meticulously recorded all the pertinent details:

- Name (first name only)
- Age (of the women when sex happened)
- Race (white, Asian, Black, others)
- Nationality
- Meeting (where they met)
- Squirt (Y/N)
- Anal (Y/N)
- Alive (Y/N), one, apparently, had passed away

And at the very end, there I was: Mira / 29 / Asian / Indonesian / Tinder / Squirt Y / Anal N / Alive Y.

I stared at the screen for a moment. Logically, I should have been disgusted, offended even, at being reduced to a line item on someone's sex list. But, surprisingly, my first reaction was: "You know that you are sitting on a lot of data, right?"

He looked at me, puzzled.

"You should totally move all that data into Google Sheets and create charts from it. So you could easily visualize it all!"

"How do I do that?" he asked.

"Don't worry, I'll make you the template," I offered excitedly. "All you have to do is transfer your data. This is going to be really interesting!" In my mind, I was already picturing the possibilities: pie charts breaking down the nationalities, bar graphs showing the age distribution...it was strangely thrilling.

If someone I was seriously dating had shown me their list, I probably would have walked out the door. Even though you know there were others before you, seeing your exact number is a bit jarring. But there I was, with this charming, open-hearted Pornstar, enjoying a holiday fling. He had been nothing but respectful and kind, so there was no reason to feel jealous or weird about his past. We were two consenting adults having a fantastic time.

"I like your list. It's very thorough," I admitted. "My list only has names. I think I'm going to follow your lead and expand the data on mine," I added. "Oh, and in case you're wondering," I said with a wink, "you're lucky number 13."

***

Just before escaping to Lombok, I'd wrapped up one last project at Google: creating the 2016 Year in Search list and localizing the global video for Indonesia. It was always a bittersweet task, a reminder of the year's highs and lows, the moments that made us laugh, cry and everything in between. But 2016's video hit differently. It acknowledged the darkness, the fear, the uncertainty, but it also celebrated the resilience of the human spirit. The closing line, a twist on the classic Google tagline, resonated deep within me: "Love is out there. Search on."

With those words echoing in my mind, on the last afternoon of 2016, I stepped out of my cabin and strolled towards the main restaurant. The warm Lombok air caressed my skin, carrying the scent of the ocean and the promise of a new beginning. I took a deep breath, letting the moment wash over me. No matter what 2017 has in store, I was ready. I had survived 2016, and that in itself was a victory.

"Ready?" The Pornstar's voice startled me out of my thoughts.

"More than ready," I replied. "Let's bid farewell to this crazy year and see what adventures await us in the next."

He grinned, his eyes sparkling with mischief. "You know, someone famous could be dying right now, and we simply wouldn't know."

I laughed, the sound echoing through the twilight. "Oh my god, you're right! Just when we thought the Grim Reaper was taking a break, Carrie Fisher passed away after Christmas!"

"Maybe Phil Collins is next," he joked. "Or Cher!"

"Oh god, not Cher!" I playfully clutched my chest in mock horror. "We won't know until we're back in the land of Wi-Fi."

"True," he said, "but for now, let's just focus on the present. Let's make this New Year's Eve one to remember."

"Agreed," I said, taking his hand. "Let's get this trip started."

We headed towards the restaurant, ready to embrace the unknown with open hearts and a touch of psychedelic wonder.

The familiar face of our waiter greeted us as we entered the restaurant. He flashed a knowing smile, as if he'd been expecting us.

"Can you whip up two magical concoctions with these, Pak?" the Pornstar asked, handing over the black plastic bags filled with six smaller, mysterious pouches. "Something fruity and refreshing to fuel our New Year's Eve."

He peeked inside the bag, then shot us a suspicious glance, back to the bag and finally said: "Pineapple, okay?"

"Pineapple is perfect," I replied.

Ten minutes later, our waiter emerged with two tall glasses filled with the thick, dark yellow concoction. A perfectly placed pineapple wedge perched on the rim for the illusion of an innocent tropical drink.

"Are we really doing this?" I asked. The reality of our New Year's Eve plan was starting to sink in.

"I guess there's no turning back now," the Pornstar replied. He raised the glass that had just been set down in front of him. "Cheers to the unknown!"

We clinked glasses and took tentative sips. The taste was surprisingly pleasant, a tropical sweetness masking the earthy undertones of the shrooms. "It tastes alright," I said.

"Yeah, not too bad," he agreed.

Just as we were finishing our first round, our waiter reappeared with another glass, three-quarters full. "Here's the leftover," he said with a smile.

We exchanged glances, a silent conversation passing between us. Should we push our luck and finish the rest? A sense of adventure, fueled by the impending trip, took over. "Sure, why not?" we said in unison, reaching for the shared glass. As we sipped the remaining potion, my sense of anticipation grew.

"Time check," I said, glancing at my watch.

"It's 4:15. We probably won't feel anything until around five."

"True, but let's head to that spot under the roof structure at the end of the beach. It's close to our lodge, in case we need a quick bathroom break."

"Good idea," he said, grabbing his backpack. "I'll grab my music and meet you there." He pointed towards the bamboo structure with the inviting bean bags nestled beneath it.

With a shared smile and a flutter of excitement, we parted ways, each of us preparing for the psychedelic experience.

A small part of me, a worry I couldn't quite shake, whispered, *But he's a stranger, a match from Tinder I just met a couple of days ago.* But as I made my way towards our designated spot, my nerves were quelled. What would this New Year's Eve bring? What hidden depths would the shrooms reveal? I was ready to embrace them all.

***

The time was probably around 4:25, a rough estimate since I'd intentionally left my phone back in the cabin. I adjusted my sunglasses, nestled into the plush beanbag and took a deep breath of the salty air. "Let The Trip begin," I whispered to myself.

Moments later, the Pornstar arrived. I was happy to see him. He carried two bottles of water, a thoughtful gesture that spoke volumes about his preparedness. "Here," he said, handing me one. "Hydration is key."

"Thanks," I replied, burying the bottle in the cool sand beside me. He was definitely the responsible one in this duo, a welcome balance to my impulsive nature.

He settled into the beanbag next to mine, adjusting it with a few practiced movements. With a final sip of water and a downward tug of his sunglasses, he turned to me and nodded. "Ready?"

"Yeah." I gazed out at the view, the private beach stretching out before us like a scene from a postcard. "This spot is incredible," I breathed.

"It's perfect," he agreed, his eyes mirroring my own sense of wonder. The vastness of the ocean, the rugged cliffs, the endless sky—it was a canvas waiting to be painted with the colors of our trip. "And just imagine the sunset," he added, his voice filled with a mix of awe and anticipation. "It's going to be epic."

After a while, the world around me started to shift. At first, subtly. Colors became more vibrant, and sounds took on a new depth. My body felt warm and light, as if gravity had loosened its grip. I pushed my sunglasses up, curious to see how my vision was playing tricks on me. Time seemed to stretch and bend, each moment lingering just a little longer than usual.

"I'm definitely feeling it," I said in a hushed voice. The world was starting to shimmer and pulse, the boundaries between reality and dreamscape blurring. I took a deep breath, trying to ground myself amid the sensations.

"Me too," he murmured, his gaze fixed on the horizon. Though his voice remained calm, I could sense a flicker of apprehension beneath the surface.

The hill before us was morphing, the patches of green grass melting into the brown rocks like a Salvador Dalí painting coming to life. It was as if the earth itself was breathing, its surface undulating in a slow, hypnotic rhythm.

My gaze drifted upwards, towards the sky ablaze with the setting sun. The colors were otherworldly, a palette of fiery oranges and vibrant pinks that danced and swirled before my eyes. "Okay," I breathed, my voice barely above a whisper, "this is intense." The sheer beauty of it all was almost overwhelming, a sensory overload that left me breathless.

"It's getting pretty intense for me, too," he admitted. We sat in companionable silence, each of us lost in our own psychedelic reverie while the world around us transformed into a breathtaking spectacle of light and color.

The sand beneath my fingertips felt both impossibly soft and strangely textured, as if each grain had come alive. The crash of the ocean intensified, the crashing waves enveloping me in a surround sound experience that vibrated through my very core.

He squeezed my hand, his touch a reassuring anchor in the midst of the psychedelic storm. "Maybe we should have skipped that last glass," he said.

The realization hit me like a tidal wave. We were in deep, far deeper than any of my previous trips.

I took a deep breath, surrendering to the unknown. "Well," I said, a nervous laugh escaping my lips, "I guess we're in this together." I chose to trust in the connection we had forged and prepared to face whatever the universe had planned for us.

When I closed my eyes, instead of the usual darkness, I got transported into a bright psychedelic world that pulsed and moved with the beat of my heart. The shapes were organic, fluid and so bright they practically glowed in the dark. The more I tried to fight the effect, the heavier it felt, the more vivid the shapes and colors became.

When my eyes opened again, it was as if someone had thrown acid all over my vision, melting the beach, the ocean and the hills into another trippy Salvador Dalí painting. The colors were stunning, but so bright. Maybe even too bright.

After a few moments of emotional turbulence, I just decided to let go. All of a sudden, the mood shifted. I felt euphoric. "This is so fucking crazy!" I screamed at the top of my lungs. The Pornstar, gripping my hand a little tighter, agreed.

I was tempted to look over and see how he was handling this wild ride, but I couldn't. It felt like my body was melting into the bean bag, stuck in place. I couldn't even move my hand. My sense of time, space and gravity got all mushed together like a melted ice cream sundae. I remember thinking that if a tsunami hit right then and there, and we got swept away in a massive swirl I'd probably die happy.

I closed my eyes again, feeling the warm air on my face. Behind my eyelids, it was like stepping into a personal IMAX theater of the mind, playing the highlights reel of my life from 2016 on fast-forward. The New Year's volcano hike with my ex-fiancé, those steamy nights on the Jakarta apartment sofa, the glass I threw at him in a fit of rage, the day he walked out, the bittersweet "wedding cancellation" party, the new job I'd thrown myself into, the icy emails about splitting the wedding costs, the unexpected apology from his mom, the late nights with the Director, boozy Tokyo nights with The Mistake, the carefree scooter rides in Lombok. Until there I was, tripping on shrooms with a Tinder match to usher in a New Year.

Each memory flashed by in a split second, but still, the emotional weight hit me with full force. It was like reliving every single high and low in vivid Technicolor. When I arrived back in the present moment, it felt like my body was being ripped from the earth and sucked into the cosmos. Lombok shrank beneath me, then Java, then all of Indonesia—all dwindled until I was staring at the whole world, a tiny blue marble hanging in the void.

Our whole solar system appeared before me, a celestial mobile hanging in the blackness. The planets were now just nine tiny stars. And then, one last cosmic tug: The entire universe stretched out before me, a breathtaking tapestry of galaxies and nebulae. I was floating in space, a peaceful observer in the grander scheme. It was like Neo finally seeing the Matrix for what it was. All the heartbreak and drama that had consumed my year—the breakup, the canceled wedding, the career roller coaster—it all seemed so trivial now.

I had zoomed out on Google Earth and watched my entire life shrink down to a pinprick on a map, then a speck on a globe, then a grain of sand in a vast cosmic desert. Life on planet Earth, with its endless dance of joy and sorrow, birth and death, continued its relentless rhythm. I was just a tiny blip, and everything that had happened to me were ripples in a vast ocean.

Gratitude enveloped me. Having been shown that cosmic perspective, it was like finally coming up for air after being held underwater for too long. I was finally liberated from the emotional shackles of my year. And it was so damn good to be alive.

Belinda Carlisle's "Heaven is a Place on Earth" started playing in my mind, and warmth spread through my chest. Not only was I alive, which in and of itself felt like a miracle after the dumpster fire that was 2016, but I also had so much to be grateful for. My family, my friends—they'd been my rock, my lifeline through it all. I'd managed to turn a potential wedding disaster into the party of the year, and my career was taking off.

Ooh, heaven is a place on earth. The lyrics echoed in my mind. *In this world we're just beginning / To understand the miracle of living.* The song continued, and I felt a sense of peace settle over me. *Baby, I was afraid before / But I'm not afraid anymore.* With a deep breath, I squeezed the Pornstar's hand a little tighter, grateful for this moment, for this connection.

"Here, listen to this," he offered, extending one earbud towards me.

"Who is it?" I asked, curious.

"Just listen....," he replied with a mysterious smile.

The music was...delightful and happy! It instantly lifted my spirits and kept me in a good place, miles away from any bad trip territory. "This music is so nice!" I exclaimed, grinning.

"It's Pogo," he replied.

The Pornstar had impeccable taste in music! Not a single track that came from his playlist failed to produce fascinating visuals. And they kept me away from any dark corners of my mind.

Just a few hours ago, we were practically strangers who had only spent a few days together. Now, as the sun began to set, after a journey to the cosmos and back, it felt like I'd known the Pornstar my entire life. *Well done, Tinder. You've truly outdone yourself this time. I don't know how you'll ever top this match.*

***

As the sun dipped below the horizon, the magic mushroom's effects started to fade like a Polaroid picture developing in reverse. The once-vibrant visuals softened, and the darkness of the night subdued the dazzling lights. The moon cast a silvery glow on the ocean, and with my head resting on the beanbag I got hit with exhaustion. I removed the headphones, allowing the soothing sound of the waves to fill my ears. It was like someone had turned down the volume on a surround sound system, still crystal clear, like listening to Funktion-One speakers on a beach but less overwhelming.

"How long was that?" I asked, trying to gauge how long we'd been out there, lost in the psychedelic world, as we stepped into the cool air of our bungalow, realizing we'd forgotten to turn off the AC.

"It's nine," he replied. "We've been tripping for four hours."

"That's it?!" I exclaimed, shocked. "It felt like days, like we journeyed through countless lifetimes!"

"Yeah. It felt the same for me."

The bungalow, once a cozy haven, now felt like a foreign land. The shadows played tricks on my eyes, and the familiar furniture seemed to warp and shift. But the most profound transformation was in the way I perceived the Pornstar. His face, once merely attractive, now held a depth and familiarity that startled me.

His eyes, once sparkling with playful curiosity, now seemed to hold the weight of shared experiences, unspoken secrets and a connection that transcended the boundaries of time and space. It was as if we'd shared countless lifetimes, traversed galaxies together and witnessed the birth and death of the stars in each other's company.

***

We showered back at our hut, washing away the sand and any remains of our cosmic journey.[8] The phone rang, and the Pornstar answered. "They want to know if we still want to have dinner," he said, holding the phone. "They kept the food from the BBQ for us."

"Right, dinner," I said, stepping out of the shower. "I almost forgot. But yeah, sure." I wasn't particularly hungry, but I knew we should eat something.

"Yes, we'll come down to the restaurant," the Pornstar confirmed on the phone.

By the time we finally made it to the restaurant, it was almost 11 pm and the dining room was deserted. We settled into a cozy two-seater by the window, and a familiar face emerged with a carafe of water.

"Good?" the waiter asked with a knowing smirk.

---

[8] Disclaimer: For the record, since I used the term "cosmic journey," I should clarify. This book does not condone the use of shrooms for self-medication or any purported therapeutic benefit. My actions took place in a bubble of ignorance, and I now understand that spontaneous decisions involving psychedelics come with real-world legal risks—so, maybe don't do that.

"Yeah, really good," the Pornstar replied, his voice a mix of exhaustion and elation.

The food arrived, a massive plate piled high with shrimp, meat and chicken for each of us. As we gazed at the feast, we burst into giggles, the absurdity of the past few hours hitting us again. "Can't believe we missed the whole BBQ," he chuckled. "They must have been looking for us."

"And can you believe it's not even New Year's yet?" I asked, shaking my head in disbelief. Time had warped and stretched during our trip, making it feel like we'd lived a lifetime in just a few hours.

After dinner, we ventured out to the outdoor fireplace, drawn by its warm glow and the promise of a gathering spot as midnight approached. We exchanged greetings with a few other guests, the shared anticipation of the New Year hanging in the air. Glimpses of fire dancers practicing their moves and the telltale signs of mini fireworks being set up added to the growing excitement.

I longed to crawl into bed, but the New Year was fast approaching, and it felt wrong to miss the countdown. So, I curled up against the Pornstar on the big lounge sofa, his chest a comforting anchor in the aftermath of our psychedelic odyssey. His embrace felt different now, a warmth radiating from him. The awkwardness of those first Tinder dates had vanished, replaced by a sense of deep connection. I still couldn't believe this was happening, especially with just 10 minutes left until midnight. It was a surreal, magical way to welcome a new beginning.

"Let's not meet again after this trip. We should say our proper goodbyes," I said, the words heavy but necessary.

He looked at me, surprised. "What do you mean?" he asked.

"I mean, this...all of this has been truly amazing. And I just feel like nothing can top it, even if we try. The coincidences have been insane."

"You're right," he conceded, a little sadly. "This was a Tinder jackpot."

"Ya right?!"

I knew a relationship with the Pornstar wasn't in the cards. The list of reasons why it wouldn't work was endless: the distance, our families, our religious differences, his porn-filled resume... But at that moment, none of that mattered.

I needed to rediscover physical intimacy, to shed the layers of fear and hurt that had built up over the past year. And even though our connection was temporary, it didn't make it any less special. In fact, it made it even more so. Our memories wouldn't be tarnished by the mundane realities of long-distance or the inevitable challenges of cohabitation. Our connection felt like destiny, a fleeting gift from the universe and I wanted to preserve its magic.

As he wrapped his arms around me, his playlist humming softly in the background, I felt supported. I allowed myself to melt into his embrace, to feel the full spectrum of emotions that had been bottled up for so long. The Pornstar wasn't Mr. Right, but he was undeniably Mr. Right Now.

And then, with a burst of light and color, the fireworks erupted, painting the night sky with a symphony of sparkling hues. "Happy New Year!" we shouted, our voices joining the chorus of cheers that echoed across the beach.

With the echoes of celebration still ringing, we retreated to our bungalow. The remnants of the cosmic journey painted a dreamlike quality over everything, amplifying the raw emotions that coursed through us. We made love with the passion and intensity of two souls who had just glimpsed the vastness of the universe and returned, forever changed. It was a celebration of life, of connection, of the fleeting beauty of the present moment. And as we drifted off to sleep, wrapped up in each other and naked, the rhythmic lullaby of the ocean carried us into a peaceful slumber.

We'd made it through the night, through the year and no one else had died, at least not that we knew of. And in the aftermath of this extraordinary encounter, one thing was clear: Google's Year in Search message was right. Love is out there. Search on.

Chapter 6

THE WEDDING

"I have something to share," my sister announced.

"Tell me," I replied, slurping up the delicious soup from my xiao long bao at Paradise Dynasty.

It had been almost a year since the breakup. And ever since my sister returned to Jakarta after finishing her master's degree in construction management from the Netherlands (yes, she's the brainy engineer one), our midweek sister dinners had become a sacred ritual, a lifeline in the turbulent sea of post-breakup life.

"So, Idris and I have decided to get married," she said, her voice carefully measured.

My stomach lurched. "Oh, wow," I managed, forcing a smile. "That's...great!" *Seriously?! Fuck my life!*

"Did he propose? Have you told Mom? What's the plan?" I tried hard to keep my composure despite the inner turmoil. My own wedding had been canceled last year, and now my younger sister was getting hitched. A plot twist I wasn't expecting.

"No, he didn't propose," she explained. "We just sort of decided together. And no, we haven't told Mom yet. I wanted to tell you first because, well..."

"Well, this is big news," I said, trying to sound enthusiastic. "I'm happy for you!" But I wasn't. I knew I *should* be happy for her, but at that moment, all I could feel was a crushing sense of failure.

Being 30 and single is already a societal taboo in Indonesia, but having your younger sibling marry before you adds another layer of shame and superstition. It's seen as a disruption of the natural order, a sign that something is amiss with the older sibling's love life. There's even a special tradition called "langkahan" to address this awkward situation.

"Langkahan" literally means "stepping over," and since being metaphorically stepped over by your younger sibling in the marriage department is pretty crappy, our culture has devised a way to soften the blow. The younger sibling must ask permission from the older one and offer a "consolation" gift, all in the name of seeking blessings and fostering acceptance. In my case, that meant my older brother, also still perpetually single at that time, and I were both entitled to a little something for our troubles.

"Tell me what you want for the langkahan gift," my sister said.

"I don't know yet," I replied, my mind already racing. "I'll think about it." And I was going to think *hard*. At the very least, I was going to claim my consolation prize, and it better be good.

A full day of pampering at the Four Seasons? A timeless Rick Owens leather jacket? A plane ticket to a far-off destination, away from this reality? The possibilities were endless.

"How does it usually work?" I asked, trying to gauge the appropriate level of extravagance. "Is there a budget for these langkahan gifts?"

"To be honest, I'm not sure," she admitted. "But please don't go too crazy. We need to save for the wedding."

"Fine. I'll let you know when I decide."

"Okay. Well, would you like to be involved in..."

"Nope," I cut her off, anticipating the request for wedding planning assistance. I loved my sister dearly, and I was genuinely trying to be happy for her but the sting of my own canceled wedding was still too fresh. I couldn't bear to immerse myself in another person's happily ever after just yet.

"What about just doing some food tasting with me?"

"Nope," I repeated.

"Okay...," she sighed, giving in.

***

My brother, another brainy engineer in the family, was single too (busy distracting himself with cosplay and Wikipedia entries). I was reeling from a canceled wedding from the past year, and suddenly, my younger sister was the one taking the plunge. It felt like she'd jumped the queue, leaving me and my brother stranded.

Her wedding plan, coming in hot a year after my own wedding was canceled, shifted the focus at family gatherings. The pitying glances and hushed whispers about my misfortune were quickly replaced by the excited chatter of another grand wedding in the works. My sadness, it seemed, had a short shelf life.

Every time an aunt gushed over my sister's upcoming nuptials, I felt a pang. The thought of her wedding filled me with dread. The *pelaminan*, the traditional wedding dais where the family takes photos with the bride and groom, loomed large in my mind. It's a public display of family unity, a celebration of couples. And there we'd be, my brother and I, conspicuously alone.

I could avoid wedding talk with everyone else, but it was impossible to do with my own sister. Having gone through wedding planning myself, even though mine never came to fruition, she naturally looked to me for logistical advice. Each time she called, eager to discuss her hair, the catering, the venue, the guest list, I'd offer only a few minutes of polite conversation (*basa basi*) before claiming I was too busy with work. Her excitement felt like a constant reminder of what I'd lost, and I just didn't have the strength to face it. I desperately wanted to escape.

***

My acceptance into the Marketing Academy, a two-week, Google-sponsored, executive education program at the esteemed Wharton Business School, came just in time. It gave me a legitimate reason to create distance between myself and the escalating pressure of my sister's wedding.

To capitalize on the opportunity further, I decided to extend my travels and embark on a summer holiday throughout Europe (paid for by my sister, of course, as her "langkahan" gift. Double win!). New York, Berlin, Amsterdam—the perfect itinerary for a girl who needed a serious dose of "me time" (and maybe a little international romance).

This extended US-Europe escapade was also a strategic retreat from the impending familial pressure cooker. I knew that as my sister's wedding day inched closer, her stress levels would reach DEFCON 1 and our family would be sucked into the inevitable vortex of wedding-related chaos. My mission? Evasion.

I was selfish. I knew it. Since my trip landed right in the peak of summer travel season, the flight extension my sister had to cover wasn't cheap. I did feel a bit of guilt asking her to pay for it, especially with all the wedding expenses she was already juggling. But when I learned what my brother requested for his langkahan gift—a subsidy for his Kamen Rider cosplay outfit that also set her back about $500—I felt a bit better. I guess we all cope with being the "leftover" siblings in our own unique ways.

Enter Tinder Passport, my new travel BFF. I pre-swiped, pre-matched and pre-arranged a date for my first night in New York City. First up? A techno-loving artist who was down to accompany me to a techno party in Brooklyn.

Berlin called for a different vibe. Instead of diving headfirst into another dating whirlwind, I opted for a reunion with my Berlin bestie from my Bali days. Familiar faces, good vibes and zero pressure—exactly what I needed. And as for Amsterdam? Well, with my squad already there, I vowed to give Tinder a time-out. It was time to trade wedding bells for wanderlust.

The view from Output's rooftop that night was just breathtaking. Manhattan's skyline glittered across the river—the Empire State Building, the Chrysler Building, even the new World Trade Center—putting on a light show just for me. And to my right, Brooklyn stretched out in all its gritty glory, a patchwork of warehouses, brownstones and graffiti-covered walls. I heard the distant rumble of traffic, the chatter of voices from the bars below and the pulsating beat of the music spilling out from Output's open rooftop all as one city sound.

I took a deep, long breath as I soaked in the view. My breath melted away the last vestiges of jet lag and replaced them with a sense of calm euphoria. I leaned against the railing, feeling the cool night air on my skin and the vibrations of the music through my feet.

It was hard to believe I'd landed in New York barely 12 hours earlier. I'd checked into my hotel, The Standard in the Lower East Side, and gone for a quick wander around the neighborhood to stretch my legs after that long flight from Jakarta. A disco nap (that essential snooze before a party and to combat jet lag) and a quick shower later, I was Brooklyn-bound, ready to meet my pre-arranged Tinder date at Output.

My Marketing Academy training in Philly was starting in less than 24 hours, but damn, I was determined to squeeze in a proper New York night out. And not just any night out—this was Output, with the queen, Nicole Moudaber, herself, on the decks. It was the perfect way to kick off my adventure.

"Thank you. Tonight is exactly what I needed," I said. My soul was craving this—the energy of a city I adored, the anonymity of a crowded dance floor.

"My pleasure," my Tinder date replied, taking a long drag of his cigarette and sending a plume of smoke into the night sky.

"Thank you for being a great dance partner," I continued, "and for agreeing weeks ago to this random night out with someone you hadn't even met!"

"It's been a fun, random night!" he said with a grin.

"It has!" I agreed. "If we hadn't planned this, I probably would have crashed in my hotel room and spent the next week battling jet lag. Partying on the first night is like a hard reset for my body clock. And the music...," I paused, searching for the right words. "That set earlier by Nicole was unreal. She was like a goddess commanding the dance floor. So hypnotizing."

"Yeah, that was a magical set! One of the best I've seen of her," he agreed, carefully stubbing out his cigarette.

I turned and leaned against the railing, gazing out at the other partygoers taking a breather from the dance floor. The rooftop was buzzing with a feel-good energy, even at 2:30 am. Fairy lights twinkled, casting a warm glow on the scene. Couples flirted, friends chatted and solo dancers swayed to the distant music, each lost in their own little world.

Turning back to my Tinder date, I took a deep breath and decided to go with my gut. "You know," I began, "I know the typical next step of the night would be to head back to your place or mine to have sex." I paused. "But honestly, I've had such an amazing night already. I don't think we need to take it any further."

He looked a little surprised, but not in a bad way. It was more like a flicker of curiosity, a hint of respect. "You're right," he said with a smile. "Why don't we just meet for brunch tomorrow before you head out? I know a great vegan spot nearby."

"Sounds like a plan," I replied, feeling relieved. It was liberating to acknowledge my own needs and desires, to set boundaries without apology.

This trip, I was determined to make conscious, deliberate choices, to break free from the impulsive patterns that had sometimes led me astray in the past. Standing on that rooftop, bathed in the city lights, I felt a surge of pride.

"Shall we go dance a little more before calling it a night?" he asked, extending his hand.

"Yeah, let's do that," I said, taking his hand and feeling a genuine smile spread across my face.

***

I woke to a message notification pinging on my phone. It was my sister, and judging by the time stamp, it was almost midnight back in Jakarta. Apparently, the wedding-related anxieties didn't adhere to any respectable sleep schedule. I checked the time: 11 am in NYC. Ha! Seemed like that all-nighter at Output had magically cured my jet lag. Who needs melatonin when you have Nicole Moudaber?

"What do you think of this makeup?" her message read, accompanied by a selfie that made me want to reach through the screen and surgically remove those eyebrows.

It seemed like many makeup artists (MUA) in Jakarta had taken the "natural brow" trend and morphed it into some kind of bizarre stenciling experiment. My sister's brows looked like they'd been drawn on with a Sharpie, two thick, identical caterpillars perched precariously above her eyes. It was the kind of makeup that screamed, "I spent way too much money on this," and whispered, "I'm secretly terrified of looking like myself on my wedding day."

It's horrible. "It's...nice." I typed back, laying the sarcasm on thick. It was her third MUA trial, and while the previous two hadn't been much better, I was trying to be supportive. "But the makeup is more fitting for an evening event," I added, hoping she'd pick up on my subtle hint that this look was a tad too extra. "Is this for your daytime *akad* or your evening ceremony?"

"It's for my *akad*," she replied, confirming my suspicions.

"Yeah, it's too much for that," I said, finally giving in to honesty. "You should ask her to tone down the eyebrows."

I tossed back the covers and opened the curtains, letting the sunlight flood the room. It was a glorious New York summer day, the kind that begged to be spent wandering aimlessly through Central Park or sipping iced coffee on a sidewalk patio. Unfortunately, my time in the city was rapidly dwindling. In a few hours, I'd be packing my bags, meeting the Tinder date for that promised vegan brunch before hopping on the train straight to Philly.

***

Wharton was a whirlwind. Between intensive lectures on consumer behavior and dissecting case studies of marketing triumphs and failures, my brain felt like it was doing bicep curls with a textbook. But even amidst the academic intensity, my sister's wedding drama managed to penetrate the hallowed halls of the business school.

One afternoon, in the middle of a particularly dry lecture on market segmentation (apparently, dividing potential customers into groups based on their love for pumpkin spice lattes was a legitimate strategy), my phone buzzed with another frantic message from my sister. This time, it was about her kebaya for the *akad* ceremony. It wasn't just any kebaya[9]; it was *the* kebaya, the one she'd painstakingly designed and commissioned months ago.

"They ruined it! It doesn't fit!" she wailed, attaching a picture of her in a kebaya that looked like it was trying to stage a daring escape from her body. "What am I going to do?"

"Wait, I thought you had it made from scratch?" I typed back, my fingers flying across the keyboard. A wave of disbelief washed over me. A custom-made kebaya ordered a few months ago, and it still didn't fit? How was that even possible?

"I did!" she wailed, her words practically vibrating with panic. "But I don't know what these idiots did. It doesn't fit! And they can't undo it! And now it's too late to make a new one. My wedding is next month!!" Her message was punctuated by a string of crying emojis.

Something shifted within me. A softening, a letting go of my own self-absorption. Maybe it was the lingering effects of Professor Davies's lecture earlier on empathy, or maybe it was a reminder from Lombok that my canceled wedding was just a blip in the grand chaos of the universe. Whatever it was, I felt a pull. A desire to show up, to be present. To finally become the supportive older sister I should've been all along.

"Don't panic," I typed back, pushing aside my textbook and summoning my inner fixer. "Let's figure this out."

I called my sister, her voice trembling as she recounted the disastrous fitting. I listened patiently, and then I got to work. I messaged friends who worked in the Jakarta fashion scene, seeking recommendations for kebaya rental vendors with

---

[9] A traditional garment often worn by Indonesian woman for weddings

extensive catalogs and lightning-fast tailoring services. I navigated a labyrinth of miscommunications, soothed frayed nerves and finally managed to secure an appointment for my sister to visit a rental boutique the next day.

When the kebaya crisis settled, a quiet warmth spread through me. Not the kind of pride that demands a spotlight, but the quieter kind that whispers: *You showed up. You did good.* Maybe this was what actually mattered—not just nailing presentations or chasing promotions but being there for your people, for your family, even when your own life felt like a work in progress.

Later, as we gathered for a final group photo in front of the Penn University campus, I felt something shift again, a sense of clarity. I didn't need to prove myself in a classroom to know I had something to offer. The real world had been teaching me all along.

Still, I couldn't help but notice how Western the curriculum remained—how often we dissected US case studies while overlooking the seismic shifts happening across Asia. Alibaba, Bytedance, Gojek, Grab—these were the real disruptors reshaping the future, right here in Asia, my own region.

The Google Marketing Academy had been a milestone, but now, I was ready to carry what I'd learned out into the world, into the chaos, into the unknown. And as I walked away from that Ivy League institution, I felt grounded, not lost. The world was changing fast. And I was more than ready to meet it.

"Let's set you up here." Mouna, with an air mattress tucked under her arm, ushered me into the study room in her Berlin apartment.

"How can I help?" I asked, genuinely eager to lend a hand so we could relax and catch up. It felt like forever since our last reunion in Bali.

"Just move your suitcase over here so I can lay your mattress on that side," she instructed, her focus shifting between the mattress and the task at hand.

We made ourselves comfortable and dove into an overdue catch-up. We talked about her boyfriend, recent travel, our families, work, people we knew in common and the night out we were planning for ourselves.

"We're going to Berghain this weekend, yeah?" she confirmed.

"Yeah, I've got you, me and Linda on the Optimo guest list," I said.

"Sweet! They're the ones who were supposed to DJ at your wedding, right?"

"Yeah! I love them so much! More than anything, I was probably more bummed by the fact that I had to cancel on them than the wedding cancellation itself. And I haven't seen them play again since. So it's such a perfect coincidence that they are playing this weekend!"

"Are you in touch with your ex after the whole thing?" Mouna asked carefully.

"Nope, no contact whatsoever. He tried to reach out to talk, but I refused. There's really nothing to talk about. We both have a different truth of what happened, and that's just what it is."

"Fair enough," Mouna said, shrugging. "He still lives in Bali, right?"

"Yeah, I think so. In Ubud."

"I think he met up with Michael not so long ago in Amsterdam,"

"Oh, how was he?" I asked, my interest momentarily piqued.

"Not sure," Mouna replied, slowly. "But Michael seemed to think he's changed a lot. You know his hair is now long, yeah?"

"Yeah, someone actually showed me a recent photo of him. It feels like he's become this full-on hippie. Maybe he's taken up meditation and only eats organic mangoes now."

Mouna burst out laughing. "Well, I didn't want to say that, but you said it, haha!" She took a sip of her tea, her eyes twinkling. "Look at what you did to him, Mira!"

"Hey! Don't blame it on me!" We both laughed. I felt happy to be with friends and not to be breaking down over the mention of my ex. I felt ready to dance and shed any residue of the past.

***

"Selamat Lebaran, nak," my mom's text flashed on my phone screen, a stark contrast to the dimly lit dance floor of Berghain. It was 7 am, a time when most of the world was just waking up, but here in this Berlin techno haven, the party was in full swing. The bass reverberating from the Funktion-One speakers pulsed, a rhythm that drowned out the noise of the outside world, the world where I was supposed to be celebrating Eid with my family.

Yep, it was Eid, the Muslims' biggest celebration day of the year. Last year's Eid, with the fresh wounds of my canceled wedding, was enough to scar me for life. This year, I craved a different kind of celebration, one where I wasn't the subject of pitying glances and intrusive questions. Berghain, with its pulsating energy and anonymous faces, was the perfect alternative.

Berghain was more than just a club. A concrete behemoth of hedonism best described as a present-day Sodom and Gomorrah, it held a mythical status in the realm of techno music. Rumours swirled about its infamously strict door policy (Sven Marquardt, the legendary bouncer, could sniff out a poser from a mile away), a topic so widely discussed it even warranted a dedicated thread on Reddit where hopeful partygoers strategized their chances of getting past the snake. Its labyrinthine interior was a legend in itself—getting lost in Berghain was practically a rite of passage. And the debauchery that unfolded within its walls? Let's just say that because of its strictly no-photo policy, what happened in Berghain stayed in Berghain, fueling whispered tales of ecstasy and excess. It was a place where the lines between reality and fantasy blurred, where inhibitions were shed like cheap sequins and where the only rule seemed to be to let go completely.

Split across two main levels, Berghain was a playground for the senses. The ground floor, a cavernous space with towering ceilings and a sound system that could make your internal organs vibrate, was the domain of hardcore techno. The air thrummed with a raw energy, a potent cocktail of sweat, pulsating basslines and the lingering scent of something that might have been amyl nitrite, or perhaps just the byproduct of pure human excess. The crowd was a glorious mashup of subcultures, sexualities, ages and states of undress. Think Berlin art students rubbing shoulders with leather-clad daddies, all moving to the same relentless beat. It was a scene that could make even the most seasoned club kid raise an eyebrow.

Upstairs, the Panorama Bar offered a slightly more subdued atmosphere, with its focus on house music and those legendary ceiling-height windows that liked to tease the crowd with glimpses of daylight. It was a cruel but beautiful game they played, those windows. After hours of dancing in the dark abyss of Berghain, a sliver of sunlight felt like a divine revelation, a reminder that the outside world still existed. The effect was almost biblical, like Moses parting the Red Sea, but instead of escaping slavery, the ravers were being offered a glimpse of salvation in the form of glorious, life-giving sun rays.

Ignoring the insistent buzzing of my phone, I dove back into the sonic embrace of Optimo with my two besties, Mouna and Linda, flanking me like guardian angels of rave. Optimo's set started subtly, seductively, like a siren's song luring us deeper into the night. JD Twitch and JG Wilkes, the Scottish duo behind the decks, were masters of their craft, weaving a sonic tapestry that spanned decades and genres. They began with a playful blend of old-school acid house and disco, a nostalgic nod to the early days of rave culture. The familiar melodies and infectious beats were like a warm embrace, a comforting reminder of simpler times.

They were supposed to be playing at my wedding, a night of champagne wishes and tropical dreams, with Mouna as my maid of honor and Linda by my side, clinking glasses and celebrating my "happily ever after." Instead, there we were, bathed in the sweat and strobe lights of Berghain for Optimo's 20-year anniversary party, dancing our asses off to the music that was meant for a very different kind of celebration.

As the six-hour-long set went on, the tempo increased, the basslines deepened and the energy intensified. The music evolved into a hypnotic dance between synth-wave classics, heavy industrial techno and even the occasional unexpected curveball, like a Prodigy remix thrown in for good measure.

As I moved my whole body on the dance floor, I felt a sense of closure, a knot in my chest slowly unraveling. It was as if the universe, in its infinite wisdom (or perhaps just a cosmic coincidence), had brought me to this moment, to this place, to heal and reclaim my power. Berghain, with my friends sweating by my side, was exactly what I needed. By the end of the night, we were three slightly disheveled women, perched on a giant metal swing in the middle of Berlin's most notorious techno club. Mouna, ever the comedian, started mimicking the dramatic swaying of a heartbroken Disney princess, which sent us into peals of laughter.

The swing creaked gently as we continued to chat, our voices mingling with the ambient hum of the club. We talked about everything and nothing, our laughter echoing through the space. The cathartic dance to Optimo had been a turning point. At that moment, surrounded by the comforting presence of my friends and the music of my favorite artist, I felt like I could face anything. Even my sister's wedding.

"Shall we go dancing again?" Linda asked, her eyes sparkling with the unyielding energy of a rave bunny on a triple espresso.

"I think I'm going home," I said. 12 hours in Berghain was my personal record, and I felt like a champion marathon runner crossing the finish line.

"Yeah, me too," Mouna chimed in, her voice slightly hoarse from all the yelling over the music. "Shall we just head back to my place and order some pizza?"

Linda let out a dramatic groan. "Come on, you're no fun," she sighed. "Okay, but what about we come back again later tonight?"

"Oh no, no. I'm done. Come on, Linda, let's go home," I pleaded. "Let's all just chill." The thought of greasy pizza and a Netflix marathon was suddenly very appealing.

Linda finally gave in, with a final sigh of defeat. "Okay, fine," she mumbled, but we all knew she'd love the cozy pajama after-party.

✵✵✵

Before heading back to Jakarta to face the ultimate test, attending my own sister's wedding, I'd arranged one last dinner with my friends in Amsterdam. Before bracing myself for the inevitable barrage of family inquiries about my nonexistent love life, I craved the comfort of my other friends who were there at Morabito: Boy, Lieke and Marieke. They were my people, the ones who knew my story, who'd witnessed the train wreck that was my last relationship.

We'd chosen the restaurant at De School, that temporary club in the west, as the venue for my farewell dinner. The space was as if a Wes Anderson film set had a baby with a Berlin techno club. It was all exposed brick, mismatched vintage furniture and that effortlessly cool vibe that Amsterdam just exudes.

"Are you ready for your sister's wedding?" Boy asked over dinner.

"Honestly? Not sure," I admitted. "I mean, I'll be there, obviously. Can't exactly skip my own sister's wedding."

"Wait, how many people are we talking about?" Lieke asked.

"About 500."

"Holy moly, that must be expensive," Lieke said.

"Yeah, but there's no alcohol, and it's basically an all-night buffet so the cost per person isn't too insane, probably less than 50 euros," I explained.

"No alcohol?" Marieke gasped. "That's brutal. Watching tipsy relatives make fools of themselves tumbling around at weddings is half the fun!"

Boy chimed in, "Speaking of tumbling around…do you guys remember Michael at Morabito? He really couldn't handle the concoction he took and started stumbling around, holding onto the ground."

Marieke laughed. "And he started speaking German to all of us!"

I chuckled. "Yeah, and you started speaking Dutch to me!"

She nodded. "When I'm high, I sometimes get this urge to speak in Dutch. English is too hard."

I understood completely. I felt the same way about Bahasa Indonesia, my native language.

Lieke, ever the stoic one, said, "I've never had that."

Marieke changed the subject. "Mira, do you remember those lights out at sea?"

"Yeah! I still can't figure out what they were."

"They must be fishermen's boats on the water."

Marieke shook her head. "To be honest, I don't know. They kept disappearing and reappearing at odd timings."

I smiled. "But those lights gave me such a feeling of peace."

"You kept staring at them, Mira!"

I nodded. "When the world around me was chaos, with Michael stumbling and everyone speaking Dutch, I could just look at those lights and they gave me a sense of calmness. They were like my anchor."

Lieke smirked, a hint of irony in her voice, and said, "Oh wow, that's deep, haha. We were definitely high."

Marieke laughed. "Haha yeah, definitely. It was a good one, though!"

Boy nodded. "Yeah, the right portion for most of us. Except for Michael."

I was curious and asked, "What happened to him in the end?"

"I think he had a bad trip and puked it all out," Boy explained. "It was maybe too much for him."

"Was it his first time?" I asked.

"Not sure," Boy replied, "but it sounded like it."

Marieke sighed contentedly. "Ahh, good times."

"Yeah, thank you all for being there at Morabito with me," I said, my voice thick with emotion. "It really means a lot."

"You're welcome," Lieke said. "We all had a really good time, too."

"And I'm glad you broke up with your ex!" Boy added.

"Oh, me too!" I exclaimed.

Marieke nodded in agreement. "Yeah, if not, Morabito would never have happened."

"Everything happens for a reason," I mused. "Can you imagine if we had gone through with the wedding? We probably would have divorced by now."

Lieke's eyes twinkled. "But are you dating someone at the moment?" she asked.

"Nope," I declared proudly.

"Are you sleeping with anyone at the moment?" she pressed.

"Nope!" I said, feeling prouder still. "This trip has been clean! I can't afford to have any men drama before my sister's wedding!"

Lieke's eyebrows shot up in surprise. "Oh wow, well done!"

Yeah, well done me.

***

Bittersweet flashes of the life I once shared with my ex drifted back as I walked home through De Pijp after that final Amsterdam dinner. The memories arrived quietly, uninvited but not unwelcome. I saw us sprawled on a picnic mat at Sarphatipark, sunlight warming our faces, an open bottle of wine between us, sharing a single pair of headphones—as if the music was our lifeline, tethering us to something deeper than words.

The city felt familiar, yet distant. It was like an old friend I hadn't seen in years—still warm, still kind but holding parts of me I no longer carried. Pieces of my past were scattered like breadcrumbs along its canals and cobbled streets.

I passed the corner where we used to line up late into the night for our favorite soto soup at the tiny Surinamese joint. I could almost taste the broth, feel the warmth cutting through the chill and hear the echo of our laughter still suspended in the air.

As I kept walking, more memories flickered to life—nights spent biking home after parties at Trouw, tipsy and glowing, weaving through traffic with flushed cheeks and full hearts, trying to match each other's rhythm beneath the hush of Amsterdam's streetlights.

I turned a corner and passed Mouna and Boy's old building, the place where we rang in the New Year together. That was the year he proposed, just after Google had relocated me to Jakarta. It wasn't just a proposal, it was a promise. His vow to build something new with me in my hometown, to start fresh together.

Things shifted after the move. The fights, the shouting, the pressure—we were both unraveling, but too deep in it to see clearly. The city overwhelmed us. Maybe it amplified what was already broken. Or maybe our love needed Amsterdam's calm to survive—its bike rides and still canals, not Jakarta's gridlock and grit.

But life is hard sometimes—brutal, even. And being a couple means learning how to weather that together, to face the noise without turning on each other. We should've been able to hold each other up the way people in Jakarta hold steady through the floodwaters and the endless honking. But we didn't. We collapsed under the pressure, and neither of us knew how to rebuild. Sometimes I wondered if we'd still be together had I said no to that Google job. But maybe it was never about the city. Maybe it was always going to end this way.

Amsterdam held the ghosts of who we were before. And as I breathed in the soft ache of it all, I realized I didn't feel bitter, just tender. And somewhere beneath the ache, beneath the silence and the space between then and now, I found myself hoping... that he was well. And that I, too, was on the right path to healing.

※※※

My sister looked resplendent in her traditional wedding attire. They decided to honor the groom's side of the family by going with the Padang custom for their wedding. The intricate white kebaya, adorned with delicate embroidery, shimmered under the soft lights. Atop her head, the quintessential Padang headpiece, a towering structure of gold and jewels, resembled a majestic crown. She was the epitome of a Padang princess, radiating an ethereal beauty that would make any royal envious.

"How are you feeling?" I asked, noticing nervousness behind her smile.

"I don't know," she confessed, her voice trembling a little. "I'm worried about what Bangdo will say."

Bangdo, short for Bang Dody (a.k.a. brother Dody), our eldest brother, had been bestowed with the honor of officiating the wedding, a role traditionally reserved for our father, who was no longer with us. My sister's concern was palpable. Bangdo, bless his heart, had a knack for saying the most unexpected things, often at the most inopportune moments. It was like he channeled a blend of Mr. Bean's awkwardness and Chandler Bing's sarcasm, creating a unique brand of unpredictable humor that could either charm or disconcert an audience.

"I'm sure he will behave," I reassured her, my eyes drawn to the mesmerizing gleam of her golden headpiece. "Is that thing heavy?"

"I have a headache already. I think they put it on too tight."

My heart went out to her. It was like trying to balance the Leaning Tower of Pisa on your head. "Let's get them to loosen it up!" I suggested.

"No, no. There's no time. I spent five hours on hair and makeup already."

"Yeah, but you're going to wear this thing until the evening! You'd better be comfortable. People can wait another 20 minutes," I insisted.

"Okay, okay, you're right."

"Which one was the hair lady?" I scanned the room, searching for the culprit behind my sister's discomfort.

"That one." she pointed towards a woman meticulously sorting through hair equipment on the sofa.

"Mbak, can you loosen my sister's headpiece? It's too tight."

"I'm nervous," my sister admitted.

"I can tell. Also, can I be honest about something?"

"What? What did you do?"

"Don't worry; I didn't do anything. But last night, I was this close to going out for a party and going drinking with Natasha," I confessed.

"What?" she gasped.

"Don't worry, I ended up staying home, so I'm not hungover at your wedding," I joked. "And see, I'm here on time!" My sister rolled her eyes.

The night before, when Natasha's invitation to an art event with her DJ husband landed on my phone, it felt like the universe was tempting me with a decadent chocolate cake while I was on a juice cleanse. Dancing and drinking away my pre-wedding jitters seemed like the perfect escape. I envisioned myself gliding through my sister's wedding day in a blissful, zombie-like hangover state, immune to the probing questions from nosy relatives about my own perpetually single status. It would be like attending the wedding in an emotional hazmat suit, shielded from any potential awkwardness.

After all, I'd once conquered a high stakes work presentation with a hangover. Surely, I could handle my sister's wedding with a little residual vodka cola courage coursing through my veins.

But as I nearly made it out the door, the guilt hit me. My sister, God willing, would only experience this momentous wedding occasion once. And as her big sister, I owed her my full presence, not a watered-down, hungover version of myself, even if it meant confronting my own messy emotions. So, with a sigh of resignation, I texted Natasha my regrets and traded my dancing shoes for a pair of bedroom slippers and headed to bed early.

***

I held my sister's arm, the door of the holding room looming before us like the entrance to another dimension.

"Ready?" the wedding organizer's voice chirped, breaking the tension.

Turning to my sister, I mirrored the question, "Are you ready?"

"Yes," she replied.

"Cue walking music," the organizer instructed her audio team, and the first notes of a familiar melody filled the air.

We began our walk towards the main reception hall, my sister's hand gripping mine tightly. "You look absolutely stunning," I told her, hoping to offer some reassurance.

"Shhh," she hissed, her anxiety bubbling to the surface. She'd always been terrible at taking compliments.

"Walk slowly," I reminded her, feeling her pace quicken as the nerves started to take over. It was like she was trying to get the whole thing over with as quickly as possible.

"Okay, okay," she mumbled, trying to rein in her steps.

As we entered the reception room, a grand ballroom bathed in a warm, creamy hue, her worries shifted. "Is Bangdo there?" she whispered, her voice filled with concern about our eccentric brother. She kept her head down, eyes glued to the floor, making sure she didn't trip on her kebaya. It was almost comical, my sister's way of making sure our brother hadn't decided to pull a disappearing act on the most important day of her life.

"Yes, he's there," I assured her. "Idris is already at the table, too."

I escorted her to the akad table, the epicenter of the upcoming ceremony. In Muslim tradition, the akad is the main event, the moment when the marriage becomes officially recognized. It's a beautiful, sacred ritual, steeped in tradition and respect for elders. The father of the bride typically leads the akad, handing over his daughter to the groom, who in turn asks for permission to marry her and presents a dowry. But our father had passed away, so my brother, Bangdo, was stepping in to fulfill this important duty.

After the akad is done, there's the wedding reception. But for Indonesian Muslims, the akad is the actual wedding. It's when things become official, in front of the legal system and in front of God. And the most nerve-wracking part of it? The time when the groom has to declare his acceptance of the marriage while mentioning the bride's full maiden name, the bride's father's full name and the value of the dowry on offer in a single, uninterrupted breath. If he stumbles or hesitates, he has to start again. It's a tradition that puts the groom's confidence and commitment to the test.

As we walked down the aisle, my sister veiled and her steps measured. I knew she was worried about two things: what Bangdo would say during the ceremony and how well Idris would handle his lines.

"We're almost there," I whispered as we approached the akad table, adorned with beautiful purple floral arrangements. I could see Bangdo's smirk, a clear indication that he was relishing the task ahead of him. Our two uncles, one from each side of the family, sat ready to witness the occasion. Idris's expression, facing forward, was a mystery.

"Bangdo is smiling," I noted, trying to keep my voice light.

"Why is he smiling?" my sister fretted.

"It's okay. Better he's smiling than being too serious. That would be weird."

As we neared the table, I saw our mom in the front row, beaming with pride. I was secretly relieved that the spotlight was on my sister, hoping it would deflect any attention from my own single status.

"Okay, let me pull your chair out," I said, helping her navigate the delicate task of sitting gracefully in her kebaya and Padang headpiece.

My most important duty of the day was complete. I'd successfully walked her down the aisle to her akad. I made my way back to the empty seat next to our mom.

Of course, she didn't miss a beat. "I'm going to pray that you're next," my mom whispered, her voice laced with the familiar hint that my single status was not exactly something to celebrate.

"Mom." I looked her in the eye. "Today is about Farhana." I wanted her to focus on the beautiful ceremony unfolding before us, not on my lack of a love life.

"It's okay, I will still pray for you," she insisted.

"Okay, Mom, thank you." I took a deep breath and settled into my chair as the ceremony began.

The MC's voice echoed through the hall, "Ladies and gentlemen, the akad ceremony is about to start. We ask you to take your seat and put your phones on silent."

A hush fell over the room as the imam began. "Assalamualaikum warrahmatullahi wabarakatuh. Let's begin this ceremony with a prayer by reciting the surah Al Fatihah."

Everyone raised their hands to their chests, palms turned upwards and recited the surah in unison. A collective "Amin" echoed as the imam wiped his face with his hands.

"Today we are gathered here to witness the Akad Nikah of Gina Farhana binti Budiharto and Idris Firmansyah binti Zulkarnain," the imam announced, "that will be witnessed by Bapak Indra Sahnun Lubis and Bapak Zulkarnain."

The witnesses nodded in acknowledgement.

"Farhana, did you come here voluntarily at your own accord?" the imam asked, following the traditional formality.

"Yes," my sister replied, her voice steady.

My brother, ever the comedian, couldn't resist a joke, whispering to our uncle, "She was forced here."

I couldn't see Farhana's face, but I imagined her shooting him a death stare.

"Idris, did you come here voluntarily at your own accord?" the imam asked the groom.

"Yes," he answered.

"Good. I will now pass the mic on to Dody, the brother of Farhana, to proceed with the akad ceremony," the imam declared.

My brother, channeling his inner Mr. Bean, feigned ignorance. "Oh, now what do I need to do?"

We all knew he was just messing with Farhana, who was already a bundle of nerves. The imam played along. "You just need to read that paper that you have already."

"Ah, this one!" my brother exclaimed. "Ah, okay, this is easy."

"But do you want to say a few words first?" the imam asked.

No, just go straight to the main ceremony, please, I thought, worried about what other antics he might pull.

"Hmm...okay, ya, why not," Dody said.

"Test test..." My brother tapped the mic. "Is this thing working?" He fumbled with the switch. "Ah, yes, it is."

Come on, hurry up, I thought, don't joke around anymore.

Suddenly, my brother's cheeky smile vanished, replaced by a sombre expression. "I'm only sitting on this chair because our father is no longer here with us."

My chest tightened at the mention of our late father.

"So I will only say things that I think our father would say had he been here on this chair," my brother continued, his voice thick with emotion. "My dad once told me that before you get married you need to open your eyes and know everything about your partner, all the good and the bad." He paused, wiping a tear. "But once you have decided to marry, you need to be ready to close your eyes on all the bad from the past and accept your partner as they are."

Farhana, Dody and I all broke down in tears. It was as if our father, a man of few words, was speaking through my brother, sharing his wisdom from beyond.

My brother's words struck a chord deep within me. They made me reflect on my own past relationships and the reasons they ended. Had I been unable to accept my partners' flaws and all? Maybe if I had been more accepting, we would have been okay? But more than anything, his words made me miss our dad terribly.

"So Farhana...are you ready to accept Idris as he is?" Dody asked, his voice gentle.

"Yes, I am," Farhana replied, wiping away her tears.

I rushed to the front, tissues in hand, knowing Farhana needed them. As I headed back to my seat, I locked eyes with Dody and gave him a nod of approval. Despite his earlier antics, he'd really stepped up and taken the role seriously. He was doing a damn good job.

Dody began the ijab kabul, the sacred vows that would bind my sister and Idris together. "Idris Firmansyah, son of Mr. Zulkarnain, do you take Gina Farhana, daughter of Budiharto, with the agreed dowry?"

A hush fell over the room as Idris prepared to utter the most important sentence of his life, the one that would forever change his status. He took a deep breath, the air thick with anticipation.

"I accept marrying Gina Farhana, daughter of Budiharto, with the dowry of 50 grams of gold paid in cash," he declared in one breath, his voice strong and steady.

A collective sigh of relief swept through the room. The tension that had hung in the air dissipated, replaced by a wave of joy.

"Okay, sah!" Dody announced with a broad smile as the room erupted in applause.

I heard my aunt whisper "alhamdulillah," a prayer of gratitude that everything went well.

Then, her voice took on a teasing tone, "Mira, you're next, ya." She poked me playfully. *Come on, not again. Focus on Farhana, people!*

It was my sister's day, and I wasn't about to let anyone steal her spotlight, not even with a well-meaning joke about my love life.

***

I had been dreading the reception that night, specifically the inevitable barrage of questions. But with each awkward conversation, the weight on my chest seemed to lessen. It was like the wedding reception was this bizarre form of exposure therapy.

"Nope, he's not here."

"We broke up."

"I don't know where he is now. Probably still in Bali."

"I'm fine, thank you. No, I don't have a boyfriend."

"I need to get married, Auntie? Well, I've tried. Didn't exactly work out, did it?"

"When am I getting married? Uhm, how about we discuss the weather instead?"

As I stood in line for a second helping of *kambing guling* (because, let's be honest, no Indonesian wedding is complete without it), two of my nephews, Hazel and Nathan, materialized beside me. I recognized them instantly from Instagram. Hazel, the elder brother, was already in university, while Nathan was still navigating the treacherous waters of high school.

"Auntie Mira!" Hazel greeted me with a grin, followed closely by Nathan.

"Oh, hey, guys!" I gave them both a hug, feeling a surge of affection. "Where's your mom? Is she here with your dad?" I asked, referring to my cousin who lived in Medan, our hometown.

"Yeah, she's probably hanging out with the other uncles," Hazel replied.

"How are you guys doing?" I asked, genuinely interested.

"Good! But I have exams next week," Nathan shared, his face falling slightly. "School sucks!" he added with the dramatic flair only a teenager can muster.

"How was your trip to Berlin and Amsterdam?" Nathan asked, his eyes wide with curiosity. I hadn't spoken to them directly about my summer adventures, but they had obviously been keeping tabs on my Instagram feed.

"Amsterdam looks so cool! I'd love to go there someday!" Hazel chimed in, echoing his brother's sentiment.

"Yeah, it's definitely worth a visit," I agreed, flashing back to those hazy, canal-filled days.

"And you worked at the Google office there too?" Hazel continued, his fascination evident. It was official: These boys were my biggest Instagram stalkers.

"I did," I confirmed. "We can basically work from anywhere as long as we have our trusty office badge."

"Whoa, that's so cool! Can we visit you at the office sometime?" he asked, his eyes sparkling with excitement.

"Sure, why not! How long are you in Jakarta for?" I asked, already planning their visit in my head.

"Until next Tuesday," they replied in unison.

"Well then, how about you come by on Monday for lunch?" I offered.

"OMG, yes please!" they both exclaimed, their faces lighting up.

"Your life is so cool, Auntie Mira! I wanna be like you when I grow up," Nathan declared.

And then it hit me. I had been avoiding family gatherings because I felt like a complete failure in life. But here were these two amazing young nephews, completely unfazed by my marital status or my less-than-stellar track record with relationships. They saw me as the cool aunt with the cool job and the enviable Instagram feed. And in that moment, I realized that maybe, just maybe, I wasn't such a failure after all.

"Auntie," Hazel began, "Can you take me out clubbing? I see you always go to those cool parties."

I was taken aback. "Err...sure," I stammered, "But is it okay with your mom? I'll need to ask her first."

"Yes, please ask my mom," he said, his eyes pleading.

"How old are you now? Are you even allowed to drink?" I tried to sound responsible.

"I'm 20," he replied with a hint of pride. "And I've already tried beer with my dad!"

"Okay, alright. Not bad," I said. I quickly texted my cousin to get her permission.

"It's so bitter, though," he added, wrinkling his nose at the memory.

"Yeah, I'm not a big fan of beer either," I admitted. "Oh, look! Your mom says it's okay. But you need to be home by 2 am."

"Yay! Thank you, Auntie! Where are we going?" he asked, his excitement bubbling over.

"I'll take you to Jenja tonight," I said, already picturing the pulsating lights and the thumping bass. "My friend, this awesome Japanese DJ called DJ Apsara, is playing there!"

"Jenja? Awesome!" he exclaimed. "We're staying at the hotel next door."

"Perfect! Be ready by 11 pm, okay? I'll pick you up."

**

Jenja was pulsating at midnight on that Saturday. The place was packed, a sea of bodies moving to the music. This club, with its sister location in Bali, was my go-to for a healthy dose of electronic beats and good vibes in Jakarta. I'd arrived straight from the wedding, still sporting full makeup and an intricate hairdo, but I'd thankfully ditched the kebaya for my trusty black jeans and tank top. Hazel, bless him, had gotten the memo and was sporting a black t-shirt himself. Despite being of legal drinking age, his baby face practically screamed "underage." Knowing we'd get carded for sure, I took charge and headed straight to the bar—vodka with Coke for me, Heineken for him.

"Three beers max, okay?" I said, handing him his drink with a playful wink.

"Okay, Auntie!" he agreed, beaming. He was clearly just happy to be there, soaking in the atmosphere. "So, who's playing again?" he shouted over the music.

"A friend of mine," I yelled back. "Her real name is Mari, but her DJ name is Apsara."

"She's good!" Hazel shouted, nodding his head to the melodic techno set.

"She is," I agreed, proud of my friend's talent. We started to navigate our way through the dancing crowd, aiming for the front of the DJ booth.

As we pushed through the throngs of people, a familiar voice cut through the noise. "Mira!"

I turned to see Rio, Mari's husband and biggest fan, grinning at me. Rio was a fixture at her gigs, always there to support her.

"Rio, this is my nephew, Hazel," I said, pulling him closer. "We came straight from my sister's wedding."

"Wow, that's cool! Taking your nephew clubbing!" he observed, impressed.

"Auntie Mira is the coolest auntie! She's the best!" Hazel piped up, making me blush.

As I danced the night away, keeping a watchful eye on Hazel, I came to accept that maybe I would be that aunt who marries later in life, but I would definitely have the best stories to tell

Chapter 7

THE ONE

"Congratulations on your promotion!" Veronica announced during our year-end one-on-one. I was floored. "You're ending the year with a 'Strongly Exceeds Expectations' this time around."

My jaw hit the floor. "Thank you so much! I seriously did not expect it!" I stammered, feeling like I was in a dream.

How was this even possible? For the past 18 months, I'd had to navigate the aftermath of a canceled wedding. At work, I'd been juggling the largest budget of my career, navigating the complexities of my first national TV campaign with every media touchpoint imaginable and traveling like a madwoman. *And I... pulled it off?* Oh, the wonders of a breakup.

But impostor syndrome reared its ugly head. What did this mean for my future? Did I need to perform at an even higher level now? What if I couldn't keep up? What if I had another emotional breakdown, and they regretted their decision?

Growing up with Asian Tiger Parents who constantly compared my achievements to others, even when I proudly brought home a nine in math (not good enough because it was not a perfect 10), had instilled a deep-seated sense of inadequacy. While this constant pressure had fueled my drive, the lack of acknowledgement had left me perpetually doubting myself.

Maybe I should channel my confident inner white male and brag a little: *I am simply good at my job.*

***

Fresh from my year-end chat with Veronica, a bouquet of flowers in one hand and a bottle of champagne in the other, I grabbed a colleague for the obligatory Instagram photo op. Priorities, right? Social media fame before family updates.

That night, crammed in the back of a Blue Bird taxi inching through Jakarta traffic, I couldn't help but reflect on the whirlwind that had led to my promotion. Was it luck? Timing? Or maybe the breakup had been an unexpected catalyst, freeing me to pour every waking moment into work. Whatever the reason, I knew I had a solid support system to thank—my family, friends and incredibly understanding colleagues. I thought about Veronica, who juggled two boys, a chef husband, a burgeoning cooking school business and her role as the family breadwinner with the grace of a seasoned circus performer.

And there I was, living the solo life by choice, with the freedom to be as selfish as I pleased. I had no one to answer to, no mouths to feed, no need to justify a spontaneous splurge on Alexander Wang shoes or a $500-a-night escape to Potato Head's Oceanfront suite in Bali.

So why was the single life, with all its supposed freedom and flexibility, feeling like such an uphill battle? Was it the pressure to "have it all" without the traditional support system? Or was there something more profound at play, a deeper yearning for connection and purpose beyond the material comforts of my independent existence?

A good chunk of my Amsterdam crew had pressed pause on their seemingly perfect lives, opting for soul-searching sabbaticals. The pattern was eerily similar: good job, thriving social life, living the dream in your 20s and then...*Bam!* Thirty arrives. Suddenly, everyone around you, especially in Jakarta, is married with kids, or already navigating divorce from their first marriage. It was like a 30-year-old crisis epidemic, and yet, no one seemed to be talking about it. Was it because society expected us to have it all figured out by this age?

I imagined those judgmental glances from the younger generation, thinking, *Wow, she's 30; she must have life on lock. So wise, so successful.* And then there were the late 30s. Thirty somethings, looking down their noses at us with a *what's with all the whining, you entitled millennials? Sabbatical to "find yourself?" Seriously?* Caught in this crossfire of expectations, I felt utterly lost. The truth was, I was winging it, just like everyone else. Since you've made it this far in my story, you would know I'm far from having my shit together.

In the midst of all this I recalled Veronica's comment about juggling work as a working mother during a one-on-one earlier in the year: "Even if I have the shittiest day at work, I can come home and I know I have two boys that adore me. And everything will be okay." It was like a lightbulb moment. Maybe the chaos of family life, despite its challenges, provided a sense of purpose and much needed balance that my solo, independent existence lacked.

I joked with fellow single friends that maybe having a kid was the go-to solution for a 30-year-old life crisis (disclaimer: terrible idea, do not recommend). A friend once compared having kids to taking drugs. You know the comedown is going to be rough, but the high is so euphoric, so connection-fueled, that you'd willingly endure the crash over and over again. That's what those guaranteed highs of unconditional love, of tiny arms wrapped around you, felt like, apparently.

So, my breakup survival story wasn't exactly a happily ever after just yet. Emerging from the wreckage of heartbreak, I walked straight into a 30-year-old life crisis, amplified by my own sister's wedding. The existential questions bombarded me:

Will I ever find someone?

Do I even need a man?

Should I give up on marriage and just adopt a kid?

What am I doing with my life?

Why am I pouring all my energy into work? I had survived the year and got a promotion along the way but true happiness felt like a distant mirage.

Also, I wasn't sure yet what kind of partner I needed to thrive in my career in the long run. At that moment, I was single, and ironically, my career seemed to be taking off. I knew I didn't want a traditional partner who would expect me to stay home and raise kids while he brings home the bacon. But the idea of having someone to share life with, to come home to and swap stories with, to bring a sense of balance—I had a deep yearning for it.

Despite the euphoria of my recent promotion, I couldn't ignore the glaring imbalance in my life. I needed to diversify my portfolio of purpose, to find joy and meaning beyond the spreadsheets and presentations. Long-term survival in the corporate world required balance, a yin-yang of professional drive and personal fulfillment. It was high time I started to work on it.

***

I threw my own Tinder rulebook out the window the moment I swiped right on the Banker. His profile was a desolate wasteland of information—no witty bio (lazy!), a stuffy suit in his main photo (boring banker alert!) and aside from his age (38, hinting at either divorcée status or some other mysterious baggage), there wasn't a single clue to his identity. No company name, no alma mater, nothing I could plug into Google to stalk him with even a modicum of finesse.

So why did I swipe right? Well, I was bored during a work trip to Singapore. Also, blame it on the name. It was a unique twist on an otherwise common moniker, and it just so happened to be identical to that of my beloved BFF from Amsterdam, who's Turkish and Swedish. Consider this right swipe a tribute to nostalgia.

Oh, it's actually a match.

***

"Have you been married?" I asked, casually tossing the question into our Tinder chat like it was just another Tuesday.

"Yes," he replied. Short and sweet.

"When did you get divorced?" I pressed, inner detective already on the case.

"Five years ago," he responded. Now, the million-dollar question—the dealbreaker or dealmaker, depending on your life stage and baggage allowance.

"Kids?

"I have a son."

Whoa.

Okay, this was uncharted territory. Divorce was one thing, but divorced with a kid? That was a whole different ball game. My only experience dating a single parent was KDY, a.k.a. Best Rebound

Ever, and he had been exactly that—a rebound. Temporary, no strings attached.

"And you're from Turkey?" I tried to guess his nationality.

"Yes."

"And what do you do?" I typed, continuing my interrogation and already bracing for the answer.

"I work for a bank," he replied.

Aaaand there it was—Banker—just as I'd pictured. My mind conjured up images of pinstripe suits, boring conversations about interest rates and zero common ground.

The easiest option would have been to ghost him, to disappear back into the Tinder void and move on to the next profile. It was exactly what the old Mira would have done, but the past year and a half had taught me that I didn't know myself as well as I thought I did. Hell, the man I almost married, the one I shared everything with, had turned out to be a complete disaster. So who was I to be so high and mighty about my judgments?

And hey, a divorced dad? He probably had some wisdom to share, some battle scars that could teach me a thing or two about navigating the minefield of relationships. "That's the spirit, Mira," I muttered to myself. A flicker of curiosity reignited within me as I continued my chat.

"Do you have any photos where you're not in a suit?" I asked, curious to see a different side of him, the off-duty version. The thing about suits is, anyone can look sharp in one as long as it fits well. But the real test is how someone dresses when they're not in their work "uniform." That's when you get a glimpse of their true style.

"Yes, of course," he replied, and after a few moments of anticipation, two photos arrived on my WhatsApp. The first one was a black and white shot of him on a rugged beach, looking like he belonged in a Nirvana music video. With a black hoodie pulled over his head, sunglasses hiding his eyes and a graphic tee peeking out, he was giving off the "startup founder" vibe. It was a far cry from the buttoned-up Banker I had initially pictured, and I have to admit, I was intrigued. If he had been born a few years later, he would have been a Fintech founder (way cooler) instead of a banker for an old-school financial institution.

"You look much younger there," I commented. "You should dress like that more often. Ditch the suit," I added, throwing in my two cents about his fashion.

"And the other one is with my son," he said, and my heart melted a little as I saw a photo of him with a young boy, around six or seven years old, beaming in front of a massive Transformers statue. It was like a scene straight out of a heartwarming family movie.

"Is that at Universal Studios?" I asked, recognizing the iconic backdrop.

"Yes," he replied. "He visited me last month with my parents."

"Oh, nice," I said, picturing them all having a blast at the theme park. "Did he like Singapore? Was it his first time?" I inquired, remembering how excited I was on my first trip to a new country.

"Yes, they all loved Singapore. It's very safe here," he said, echoing a sentiment I had heard many times before.

"Yeah, too safe sometimes," I joked, thinking about how Singapore is often called the "Disneyland of Asia."

"You should come visit."

"I go there quite often for work," I replied, thinking about all the times I had been to the Google Singapore headquarters for training and meetings. "I'll let you know when I'm there next."

"Looking forward to it," he said, and I couldn't help but feel a little flutter of excitement. Maybe this banker was more than just a guy in a suit after all.

***

"I'm going to Jakarta this weekend," the Banker announced after we'd been chatting for over a month. To my surprise, our conversations had been far from the dry, predictable exchanges I'd anticipated.

Over those four weeks of virtual pen-palling, I discovered he'd recently relocated to Singapore from his hometown of Istanbul for a major career move. He'd landed a fancy global role with an international bank, heading up operations in 33 countries. It sounded demanding, requiring a ton of travel. "Smart, but a workaholic" was my initial impression.

"Are you coming to Jakarta for work?" I asked, curious about his sudden travel plans.

"No, I'm coming to see you," he replied, sending a flutter of excitement through me. No one had ever flown to another country just to meet me for a first Tinder date. This was definitely a new one, and one for the books.

"Oh, okay," I responded, trying to maintain my composure. "Sure, I'm around this weekend." I added a casual winky face emoji, hoping to convey a sense of nonchalance. "You know Jakarta has a lot of traffic, yeah?" I tried to set his expectations of my city.

"I'm from Istanbul; don't worry," he said.

Was flying over to meet someone for the first time a bit too much? The pressure was on—he was making a grand gesture, and I didn't want to disappoint. Should I play the role of tour guide and hostess for the entire weekend? What if we had zero chemistry in person? I couldn't just ghost him after he'd flown all this way. Maybe he was just a big personality, prone to grand gestures. Was I overthinking things? It wasn't like he was flying across continents; it was only a one-and-a-half-hour flight from Singapore.

Despite my worries, I tried to give him the benefit of the doubt. Maybe this is what mature, secure people did. Besides, if things didn't work out, we could always just be a LinkedIn connection.

His divorced status oddly gave me a sense of reassurance. After going through my own canceled wedding, I found myself instinctively drawn to people who had survived a major heartbreak, whether a divorce or breakup that had shaken them to their core. Some saw that as a red flag, assuming that past relationship failures meant that someone was "bad" at love, but I saw it differently. If they'd truly faced their ending—grieved it, learned from it—I figured they'd likely come out the other side with more clarity, self-awareness and a deeper understanding of what they wanted in a partner. And let's be honest—I had my own emotional carry-ons. If I couldn't hold space for someone else's story, how could I expect anyone to hold space for mine?

My own breakup had taught me a lot about who I was and what I needed. I was still a work in progress when it came to love—*who wasn't?*—but I'd come out of it with a clearer sense of my boundaries, my deal-breakers and the kind of connection I wanted. And oddly enough, it was the aftermath of my sister's wedding that helped crystallize those realizations.

Watching my sister and her husband settle into married life was unexpectedly emotional. It wasn't all romance and fairy lights—they were quick to admit they'd had a post-wedding spat on their very first night. Turns out, sharing a bed for the first time revealed just how differently they liked to sleep. She ran cold, he ran hot. There were disagreements over duvet thickness and AC temperature. Neither had ever lived with a partner before (they were good Indonesian Muslim kids, after all). So, cohabitation was a whole new frontier—one that required patience, negotiation and more than a few middle-of-the-night compromises.

Still, even with the bumps, I found myself quietly envious. Their honeymoon took them from Ubud to, of all places, Russia. They returned with stories, inside jokes and a growing list of shared dreams. They talked about kids—not if, but when and how many. They were already apartment hunting, saving for a place they could call their own. They were building a life together, one decision at a time. And beneath my cool, single auntie exterior, I longed for that too. I wanted something real. I wanted to co-build, co-dream, co-struggle—with someone who chose me back.

Maybe it was time to be more open. Maybe I didn't need perfection. Maybe I just needed someone who was willing to try. Relationship experience—even the messy, painful kind—wasn't something to be feared. It was something to be honored.

So, I gave the divorced Banker a chance.

***

The Banker and I ended up at Loewy for brunch, the same spot I'd taken the Neuroscientist. Now, before you jump to conclusions, I'm not one of those people who has a "go-to" first date restaurant. Jakarta traffic is a beast, and after a long week of commuting, the last thing I wanted was to spend my weekend stuck in another car. Loewy was simply a practical choice.

Our first date felt like a job interview. At one point, I actually caught myself wondering, *Is he taking notes?* He fired off questions with laser-like precision, eyes sharp behind his horn-rimmed glasses. There was an intensity to him like Steve Jobs in those old Apple keynotes: equal parts focused and intimidating.

He'd married young, divorced by his early 30s and since then had poured himself into his career—you could tell. He was the kind of man who wore a Rolex without looking at it and carried a Montblanc pen like it was an extension of his hand. On paper, he was wildly impressive. But when it came to matters of the heart, it felt like he was a vintage car that hadn't been driven in years—polished, well-maintained, but a little rusty when you tried to take it out for a spin.

I'd dated older men before, but there was something different about him. Most of the older guys I'd gone out with had a youthful streak—still blasting Radiohead, rocking worn-in Converse, staying up late to talk about everything and nothing. With them, the age gap felt irrelevant. We were on the same wavelength.

But the Banker was different. Even though he was only in his late 30s, he gave off a solid mid-50s energy. There was a steadiness to him, almost paternal—not in a creepy way, but in that comforting, old-soul kind of way. I could picture him savoring a glass of scotch with a hardback novel in hand rather than enduring the chaos of a club on a Saturday night. He wasn't just older in years—he carried a different kind of weight, a stillness that made me curious and cautious at the same time.

I also noticed a trace of sadness in his face; a shadow tucked behind his eyes. It didn't feel fresh—more like an old scar that had long since healed but never fully disappeared. It softened the edges of his confidence, gave him depth. He was an unexpected mix of energies, and I found myself drawn in. I wanted to understand him better.

"So...what happened with your marriage?" I asked, casually slicing into my chicken and waffles.

"I guess we wanted different things," the Banker sighed, leaned back in his chair and continued. "We met at university. She was a couple of years older, and she wanted to have kids at a certain age. I wasn't there yet." He paused, swirling the lukewarm coffee in his mug. "The pregnancy was...unexpected. A beautiful surprise, don't get me wrong. We tried to make it work, for our son's sake. We really did. But the truth was, we were just going through the motions."

"I see," I said softly, nodding as I took a sip of tea.

"The divorce was a slow burn," he continued, his voice low. "By the time our son turned one, we were basically strangers sharing the same space. The legal part was just a formality by then." He looked up at me, and for a moment, I caught a flicker of something raw in his eyes. "So, yeah...my son's kind of used to me not being there."

"I'm sorry. It must not have been easy," I said, feeling a pang of sympathy for him. "How are you now?" I asked.

"It's okay," he said, his voice steady. "I went through a midlife crisis already in my early 30s. Got myself a Porsche and all that," he said with a hint of pride in his tone.

Since he was from Turkey, I was curious about his religious beliefs. Were we both Muslim? But I didn't want to dive into that on a first date. It felt too heavy, too loaded. Like I was already fast-tracking him through the "meet-my-mom" checklist. So instead, I played it cool.

"Where's the Porsche now?" I asked, feigning interest.

"I left it back in Turkey," he said with a shrug. "Have you been there?"

"Not yet, but it's definitely on my list," I replied. "I would like to see the Hagia Sophia," I added casually, referencing Istanbul's iconic grand mosque—half-curious about the architecture, half-fishing for clues about his faith.

"You should go," he said, eyes lighting up. "It's beautiful."

For the next half hour, we drifted through conversation—Turkey, travel, yoga. It all started to feel surprisingly easy, the kind of flow you hope for on a first date. I was beginning to lose track of time...until his phone rang.

"I'm sorry, do you mind if I take this call?" he asked apologetically. "It's my boss."

"Sure, go ahead," I replied.

He talked for a couple of minutes in a serious tone. When he hung up, he said, "Sorry about that. My boss doesn't take days off. And it seems like I need to go to Dubai now on Monday."

"As in this coming Monday? Your work schedule sounds intense," I said, realizing the kind of high-pressure world he lived in.

He nodded. "I'm sorry, M, but I do need to head back to my hotel now to work on this thing. But where are we going for dinner?"

"Um...to be honest, I haven't thought about dinner," I admitted. I wanted to see how our brunch went first before planning anything else. But now that our brunch had been cut short by his work, *I guess we are going for dinner?* "You know what? Leave it with me," I said, taking charge. "I'll figure out a place and let you know where."

"You're the best!" he exclaimed.

I smiled. "Do you want me to drop you at your hotel? I came with my driver."

"Sure, if you don't mind," he said, grateful.

"No problem at all, let's go," I said, waving my hand to ask for the bill.

As we left the restaurant, I couldn't help but wonder if this whirlwind date was a sign of things to come. Was this the kind of relationship I wanted—one where work always came first?

***

I arrived at Potato Head's Kaum restaurant, a favorite for Indonesian cuisine and trendy ambiance, about 15 minutes late.

"Sorry, traffic," I explained, offering the Banker a hug and a cheek rub as I joined him.

"It's okay," he said, gesturing towards the live acoustic band. "I've been enjoying the music."

"How did you get here?" I inquired.

"Oh, I just walked. It was very close," he replied.

"Ah yes, you're right. Mandarin Oriental is just around the corner." I remembered. "So anyway, did you manage to finish your work?"

"Yes, I did," he confirmed.

"Your boss happy?" I probed playfully.

"Well, if he calls me again tonight, I won't be surprised," he said with a hint of resignation.

"Your work is a bit nuts, huh?" I commented.

"The company has bought my soul," he joked, his humor a welcome surprise.

"I hope they at least pay you enough for your soul," I quipped back, keeping the lighthearted banter going.

"Yeah, they do," he admitted, "but sometimes, I don't know if it's worth it."

"Well, then quit," I said, feeling a surge of boldness. "I'm sure you've made enough money in your life to take a break."

He chuckled wryly. "Not enough yet. We're all going to live till 90 or 100, you know. I still need to work more to save up for retirement."

"Depends on where you live, I guess," I pointed out. "I'm sure Turkey isn't as expensive as Singapore."

His eyes widened. "Singapore is crazy! The other day I bought some grapes at the supermarket, and they cost me $15. Can you believe it?"

I laughed, shaking my head in disbelief. "So tell me," I pressed, "What's the main driver for you then, if you don't want to quit just yet? Is it the money? Is it your passion for the industry? Or the position?"

He paused, taking a sip of his drink. "Hmm...maybe it's a mix of all that," he admitted. "You know, M, my life is 95 percent my job and 5 percent my son." He sighed, a hint of sadness in his eyes. "So I can't quit."

I understood the impulse; when there's no one waiting for you at home, it's easy to lose yourself in your career. I'd been there myself.

"Do you even have time for a relationship?" I asked, wondering where things might go if we hit it off.

He looked at me intently. "I have time for you," he said, his voice low and sincere.

His words hung in the air, charged with a meaning that went beyond the casual atmosphere of our date. A warmth spread through me. Was this a declaration? A promise? Or just a well-placed line? I decided to play it cool.

"Well, that's good to know," I said, taking another sip of my wine. "Plus, you gotta have some fun besides work, right?"

He nodded in agreement. Then, out of the blue, he asked, "Tell me about your mother."

"Oh, well—I would say that she is quite a character!"

"In what way?" he questioned, his interest piqued.

"Well, she's a lawyer," I began, "and she heads up this lawyer organization in Indonesia. But all the lawyers under her organization aren't the white-collar, corporate lawyer type. I like to joke and say that they're the mafia lawyer type."

His eyes widened in surprise. "Oh wow, powerful lady," he said in admiration.

"Yeah, they are all so gangster," I continued, "and my mom is basically their leader." I felt so proud talking about her.

The Banker then asked about my siblings, and I found it so natural to share their idiosyncrasies and the layers to our dynamics—my brother's obsession with cosplay and Wikipedia editing and my sister's comparative traditionality.

"Growing up, my brother was the smart, diligent one, I was a rebel goth with way too much eyeliner and my sister decided she could never compete with either of us so she just wanted to be normal. She even wears the hijab!"

"Oh, wow. And what about your mom? Does she wear it?" he asked, his eyes widening.

"Nope, she doesn't wear a hijab, just my sister." I took a bite of my rendang, savoring the rich flavors. It felt like the right moment to bring up religion. "Are you Muslim, by any chance?"

"Yes, I am," he said. "But, well, I drink." He took a sip of his wine, as if to demonstrate his point.

"Me too," I said. It had been a while since I'd met or dated a Muslim guy, let alone someone who might share my moderate views. "Do you pray five times a day?" I asked, curious about his level of religious observance.

"Not really," he admitted. "Maybe I'll go to the mosque for Eid."

"Ha, same!" I said, feeling a connection. "I'll do Ramadan, but I'll drink and do other stuff. My family is also pretty moderate, I'd say." Knowing that we not only shared the same faith but also the same way of practicing it, the Banker suddenly became a whole lot more attractive.

"That's good," he said, visibly relaxing. "So, what did your mom say when your sister decided to wear the hijab?"

"Oh, it was pretty funny," I recalled, a smile spreading across my face. "My mom asked her why she wanted to wear it, and my sister said to be closer to God. And my mom, ever the pragmatist, said, 'If you want to be closer to God, you just pray.'"

"Well, your mom is right," he said. There was something refreshing about his honesty and his ability to appreciate my family's quirks. "You know, I would love to meet her one day," he said.

My heart skipped a beat. Had he really just said that? We'd been talking for a month, sure, but this was only our second in-person date. Was he serious about meeting my parents? Or was this just how the older generation (Gen X) approached dating? I wasn't sure.

As the night went on, a warmth grew within me. The supposedly boring Banker had layers and maybe wasn't so boring after all.

"Do you want to come over to my place for drinks after dinner?" I offered, feeling comfortable enough with him to open up my personal space. It was a bold move, but something told me it was the right one.

"I would like that." He smiled, and I felt a flutter of anticipation in my stomach.

***

I sat on my sofa with a cup of tea, sharing my life story with him. "I used to live here with my ex-fiancé," I confessed, the words echoing in the quiet space.

He glanced around my humble abode. "It's nice," he commented, his eyes lingering on a framed photo of me from happier times. "But maybe it's time for you to find a new home?"

I nodded slowly, my gaze sweeping over the familiar surroundings. "I guess so," I murmured, memories swirling around me like the steam rising from my tea. "But I do like it here."

He gave me a nudge, a playful grin on his face. "You could move to Singapore..."

"Singapore is definitely an option," I mused. "Our headquarters is there, so there should be roles that I can do. And it's still close to home."

"That's important," he agreed, his expression turning serious. "It's really hard for me now being away from my son. And my parents are getting older."

I paused, taking a sip of my tea. "But after your divorce, do you actually want to get married again?" I asked, curious about his hopes for the future.

"Of course," he replied, his voice firm. "I want to have a family. It's really important for me."

I hesitated, the shadow of my canceled wedding looming over me. "Yeah, sometimes I'm still unsure if I'm ready to get married again. But I think I do."

He reached out and took my hand, his touch warm and reassuring. "It's okay," he said softly. "Take your time."

Our conversation flowed effortlessly, delving into the depths of our lives, our losses and our dreams. It wasn't a wild night of binge drinking; we didn't even open the second bottle of wine I had chilling in the fridge. We just drank tea, the silence punctuated by our soft laughter and shared confidence. It felt like the cozy, intimate moment we both needed. He felt comfortable and familiar; his wise words and insightful commentary felt soothing.

I knew the old me would have opened that bottle of wine, gotten drunk and ended up making out with him. But the new me wanted to take things slow. I wanted to get to know him without the rose-tinted glasses of alcohol.

"It's getting late," he said, glancing at his watch. "I should probably get going so you can go to bed."

I checked the time and was surprised to see it was almost 2 am. "Oh wow, yeah. I didn't realize it was that late already," I said, gathering our cups and taking them to the kitchen.

"Brunch tomorrow?" he asked, his eyes searching mine. "I would like to see you before I leave."

"Yes, brunch sounds good," I replied, a smile spreading across my face.

"When are you coming to Singapore again?" he inquired.

"Well, I actually have training to attend in two weeks!" I said. "Are you around?"

"Perfect! Yes, I should be back from Dubai by then—come stay with me," he offered.

"No, no. Work is paying for my hotel," I said, not wanting to rush things or impose myself on him. "Thank you, though."

"In case you change your mind," he said, "you're always welcome at my home."

"Thank you," I said, smiling at him, taking his hand and walking him to the door. I kissed him warmly on the cheek.

As I closed the door behind him, I leaned against it, feeling more hopeful than I had in a long time. His words echoed in my mind: *You're always welcome at my home.* It was a simple invitation, but it held so much promise. It was an invitation to explore our connection further.

A smile spread across my face, a genuine smile that reached my eyes. It was a smile of hope, a smile of anticipation, a smile of a woman who had dared to open her heart again.

***

"Why would you live in Sentosa, again?" I asked when the Banker told me where he lived in Singapore. It wasn't that I had anything against Sentosa, exactly. It was more like…well, Singapore already felt a bit like a man-made city/island/little country, you know? A bubble.

And Sentosa? Oh, Sentosa. Singapore's playground, its own little island off the coast with its beaches, Universal Studios, that massive aquarium—it took that whole manufactured vibe to the next level.

It was like someone had tried to create the "perfect" tropical island connected to the main island, but it all felt so manufactured. Every street, every grain of sand, every palm tree, all brought in and planted. It was like *The Truman Show*, but with more palm trees. Nothing felt organic, nothing felt real. It was a bubble *within* a bubble.

I mean, sure, Sentosa was super safe. I got that. It was probably the perfect place for families with young kids. But for someone like me, someone who craved a little bit of grit and authenticity? It was not my cup of tea.

I really didn't get why anyone, and especially him, would choose to live in such a bubble as Sentosa. Granted, it was the only place in Singapore where foreigners could own a piece of landed property, which made me a little suspicious. With those price tags in the tens of millions of dollars, it felt like a money laundering scheme for a lot of crazy rich Asians and wealthy foreigners.

"I wanted to be close to the sea," the Banker gently explained, his voice almost apologetic. "Also, I'm afraid of heights. So I can't live in one of those CBD high-rise buildings," he admitted.

"Oh," I thought to myself, surprised. Definitely not the reason I expected. "Fair enough."

"Seeing the water makes me calm," he said, a dreamy look crossing his face.

"I believe there's some research about that, right?" I wondered aloud, remembering something about the calming effects of water.

"Yes. It's called blue mind. Staring at water activates your parasympathetic nervous system, and it will calm the body," he confirmed.

Later, walking around the Banker's swanky neighborhood, I took in the sights around Sentosa Cove.

"Fancy yachts. People have too much money around here," I joked, thinking of all the things I could do with that kind of wealth.

"Tell me about it," he said as a yellow Lamborghini drove past us, its engine roaring like a caged beast. "And that's my supermarket." He pointed at a shop of Jason's Deli, a small gourmet supermarket tucked next to a wine shop. "That's where I got my $15 grapes. Everything is so expensive there!"

Okay, I guess despite his high-flying job, he still felt the pinch of living in Singapore. "Then why don't you just live somewhere cheaper?" I asked him again, curious about his choice of location.

"Well, work is paying for my rent," he conceded. "So I guess it's okay,"

"Ah, the perks of an expat package," I said, understanding his reasoning. But still..."Isn't the whole point of living abroad to, like, experience the culture and get out of your comfort zone?" I challenged him. "You're kind of living in a bubble here."

"I know," he smiled, acknowledging my point but not really engaging with it. "Come, let me show you my place." He invited me up.

The Banker's apartment was a sleek, modern, three-bedroom space spanning 130 square meters on the third floor of W Residence.

"How much is your rent, if I may ask?" I inquired, trying to be casual. "Six or seven thousand?"

"More," he replied, a little embarrassed. "Closer to 10."

"Well, I pay 1500 for my two-bedroom," I said. "You know, in Jakarta, you can get a huge house with a garden and a swimming pool for the kind of rent that you pay here."

His living room was spacious, connected to an open kitchen at the far end, but it felt surprisingly empty. It was like an apartment from a furniture catalog, all staged and pristine, but lacking the personal touches that make a place feel lived in. It felt like he was barely there. There were the basic necessities—a comfy grey modern sofa, a wooden dining table set, a TV cabinet and a speaker—but it was missing that extra layer of warmth. With all that space, he could definitely use some plants, art or maybe even a quirky throw pillow or two to make it cozier.

His bedroom was neat and organized, with a whole collection of suits hanging neatly in his walk-in wardrobe, like something out of a *GQ* magazine closet. As we walked through the hallway towards the back of the apartment past the open kitchen, he pointed to a door and said, "And this is my son's room."

Something warmed inside me as I saw the cute little room, with its small bed, a poster of a ship on the sea and pillows from the *Transformers*. It was like a glimpse into another world, a world filled with childhood innocence and wonder. He told me his son's name meant "the sea," and I could see even more now how much the Banker truly loved water.

I could sense his surge of optimism and pride looking at that room. There he was, a single father who had just moved across the continent for his job. It was the first time he was away from his son, but he had found a way to bring him along—not literally, but by recreating his son's world in this new space. He was clearly optimistic that his son would spend summers and school breaks with him in Singapore, and when he did, the Banker wanted to make sure his son felt completely at home. I may not have known this man that well yet, but one thing was for sure: He loved his son and would do absolutely anything for him. It was a beautiful thing to witness.

***

"Do you realize it's Idul Qurban this long weekend? You should stay and we can celebrate together," the Banker suggested, a playful grin spreading across his face.

"Oh my god, you're right! It's Qurban," I exclaimed, the memories of past celebrations coming back in a rush of fragrant spices and joyful gatherings. I'd been so consumed with my busy work week in Singapore, all day training and plenty of meetings, that the holiday had completely slipped my mind. The thought of experiencing this special occasion with someone new sent a flutter through my stomach.

"You can stay at my place, if you want," he offered casually, as if it were the most natural thing in the world.

"Thanks for the offer," I said finally, "but I'll just extend my stay at the hotel. I can get a corporate rate, so it's not too bad. Plus," I added with a playful wink, "We still need to figure out if we can survive a whole weekend together."

Idul Qurban, or Eid al-Adha as it's known in Arabic, is the second largest Muslim holiday. It's a time for reflection, celebration and of course, indulgence in some seriously delicious food. Think of it as the Muslim equivalent of Easter or Passover, but with a focus on sacrifice and sharing with those in need. The holiday commemorates the Prophet Ibrahim's (Abraham in the Bible) willingness to sacrifice his son as an act of obedience to God. It's a story that underscores the power of faith and devotion through the ultimate test of trust.

These days, families who could afford it would purchase an animal—usually a sheep, goat or cow—and have it ritually slaughtered. The meat would then be divided into three parts: one for the family, one for friends and neighbors and one for the poor and needy. It was a beautiful tradition that emphasized generosity, compassion and the importance of community.

"Honestly, I haven't celebrated Qurban properly in ages," I confessed. "My mom usually takes care of everything. She'd buy a goat in my and my siblings' names and arrange for it to be sacrificed back in my hometown, Medan."

I scrolled through my phone, searching for a photo.

"Look, here's my goat from last year," I said, showing him a picture of a skinny goat with a wooden placard that read "Mira" hanging around its neck.

"He looks scared," the Banker said, zooming in on the photo.

"Yeah, I guess he knew what was coming."

"How about we go for some Turkish food?" he suggested, his eyes lighting up. "They do amazing things with meat." He was clearly a proud ambassador of his country's cuisine, and I was more than happy to indulge him.

"I'm in," I'd said, my mouth already watering at the thought of succulent kebabs and aromatic spices.

As we set off to Arab Street for our impromptu Qurban feast, I couldn't help but reflect on my past relationships. Despite growing up in a Muslim family, I'd never really prioritized religion when it came to dating. For me, religion and faith were personal matters that you couldn't force on people. My ex-fiancé hadn't been Muslim, and while he'd been open to converting, he'd never fully grasped the nuances of the culture and traditions.

I'd forgotten what it was like to date someone of the same faith, so the connection with the Banker naturally hit differently. There was an unspoken understanding with the Banker, a shared cultural language that transcended words. As we walked through the bustling streets of Arab Street, the scent of spices and the sound of distant calls to prayer from the renowned Sultan mosque filling the air, I felt a sense of belonging, a connection that ran deeper than just a shared faith. It was the comfort of shared traditions, the ease of understanding, the feeling of coming home.

***

I woke up in the Banker's Sentosa apartment, disoriented and alone. The room was still dark, but the bedroom door was slightly open, a shard of light hinting at life beyond. Faint sounds drifted from the kitchen, a clatter of pans and the low hum of a familiar tune. I slipped out of bed, the cool morning air a stark contrast to the warmth of his duvet.

Padding towards the kitchen, I leaned against the doorframe, stifling a laugh. There he was, the typically composed Banker, spatula in hand like a rock star's microphone, belting out Ricky Martin's "Private Emotion." The man was serenading his scrambled eggs.

I couldn't help but giggle at his antics. I was right; there were so many layers to this person that were just starting to unfold before my eyes. I had seen his serious Type A banker side, his sad divorcée side, his gentle and proud dad side—now, I was seeing his goofy, playful side. It was endearing.

"Good morning," I said, trying to catch his attention and let him know I was awake.

He immediately turned when he heard me and started singing louder, *"It's a priiiiivate emotion..."* He brought the spatula closer to his mouth, singing at the top of his lungs. He was clearly happy and full of energy.

"You're up early!" I commented.

"I already did the groceries," he said. "And I'm making you a Turkish egg breakfast!"

"You went to your fancy supermarket?" I teased him, remembering our previous conversations about his gourmet neighborhood grocery store.

"Of course!" he said proudly, our playful banter already establishing its usual, comfortable rhythm between us.

"So, what is this Turkish breakfast that you're making?" I asked as I walked around the kitchen, eyeing the eggs and other ingredients on the kitchen counter.

"Menemen," he declared. "Scrambled eggs, tomatoes, herbs... a symphony of flavors!" He plated the dish with a flourish. The aroma was making my stomach rumble.

"Smells incredible," I admitted, taking a seat at his dining table.

"Sleep well?" he asked, settling down across from me.

"Pretty good, actually. Your bed was comfortable."

"Good, good," he said as he nodded, that calm, reassuring smile playing on his lips.

"And I felt calm," I said. "It was the first time we shared a bed together, and it felt okay." I smiled as I reflected on the night we had. "Usually, anxiety would kick in, and I would probably have left and been gone already by this hour," I said jokingly.

"You're home," he said simply—and something in his tone, in the way his eyes held mine, made those words feel profound.

Home. It was a stark contrast to the sterile hotel room I'd booked as an escape route, a mere three-minute walk away. That hotel room, a symbol of my anxieties, now felt far away.

"And I guess you were right, I didn't have to extend my hotel stay," I said. "It's a waste of a room now."

"I told you," he replied, smiling at my initial hesitation to stay over.

The night before, after that incredible Qurban dinner, we'd wandered through the balmy Singaporean night, drinks in hand and conversation flowing. It was one of those rare nights where everything clicked, where laughter came easily and silences were comfortable. When it came time to part ways, we debated where to go. The conclusion: We would first go to my hotel so I could grab my sleeping clothes and toiletries, but then we'd end up sleeping at his.

Yes, the hotel room was a waste of money, but it had served its purpose. It had been my safety net, a reassurance against a potentially disastrous night. But this...this was different. This was waking up to Ricky Martin and Turkish breakfast. This was easy banter and a surprising sense of belonging.

The Menemen was incredible, a burst of flavors I'd never experienced before. As we ate, the conversation flowed, punctuated by laughter and impromptu kitchen karaoke. After breakfast, I called my hotel to checkout. Then, we put on our trainers and headed for the beachwalk. It was during our morning walk along the Sentosa Cove, the salty breeze whipping through our hair, that I thought: *This is it.*

This was the kind of easy, comfortable connection I'd been searching for. He was kind, mature, successful, funny...and Muslim, a bonus that felt like a gift from the universe after the painful breakup I'd endured. It was almost laughable, the way a random Tinder swipe had led to this moment, this sunrise stroll with a man who felt like coming home.

Suddenly, I could see our future unfolding before me: A semi-long-distance relationship at first, navigating the Jakarta-Singapore divide; weekends stolen in each other's cities, exploring hidden cafés and sharing inside jokes; eventually, a Google job opportunity to relocate to Singapore, a chance to be closer, to build a life together; six months of independence, living on my own, savoring the city's vibrant energy; then a move into his Sentosa haven, conveniently close to the office before we officially tied the knot.

But I envisioned a different kind of wedding this time around—a simple, no-frills civil ceremony at City Hall. No grand parties, no destination wedding extravaganzas, no months of agonizing over seating charts and floral arrangements. Just a small gathering of our nearest and dearest (maybe 20 people, max) in an intimate, beautiful setting. It sounded like the perfect elopement.

Of course, there would still be family time. The Banker would meet my extended family regularly and face the inevitable chaos of family gatherings. And then—I surprised myself with the specificity of the vision—a baby girl. After about 18 months and a few post-breakup rebounds, I was finally feeling a shift. I was ready to care about someone again, to shed some of my selfishness, to have someone whose opinions I'd have to consider, someone to hold dear.

My heart knew, with a certainty that defied logic, that he was the one.

***

I gotta be honest with you: I've never been a "love at first sight" kind of person. For me, it's more like "the longer I know someone, the more I start to really like them." I just can't get behind the idea of falling head over heels for someone the second you lay eyes on them. It just seems a little too intense and unrealistic, you know? I'm skeptical of that initial intense burst of emotions and butterflies that some people experience when they first meet someone.

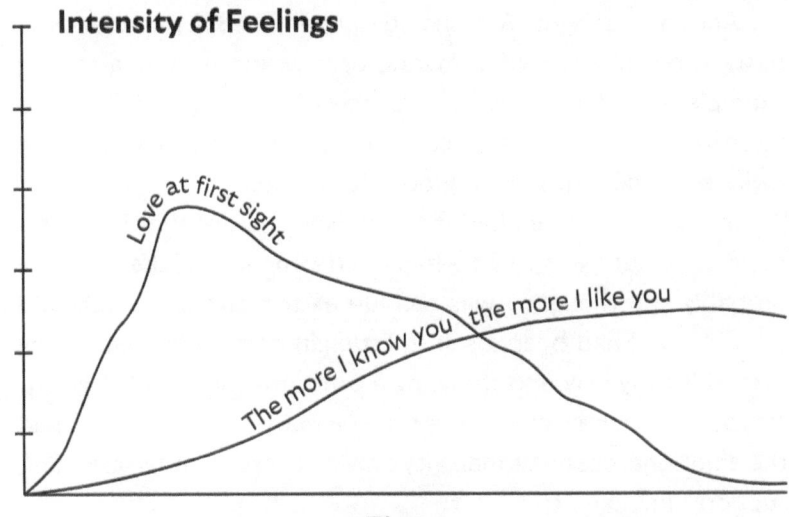

IMAGE 23: *The Love Intensity Chart Over Time*

Also, the other problem with love at first sight is that if you start high, you can only go downhill from there. Eventually, those butterflies will start to fade, even for the lucky ones who make it last a year or two—and then you start to wonder if there is something wrong with the other person. Though the truth is, there probably isn't; your hormones have just started to calm down, and now, you're faced with the same person but without the rose-tinted glasses.

My relationship with the Banker—now affectionately known as The One—fit comfortably into my ideal way of falling in love: slow and steadily increasing.

***

"As long as he loves his son and has a good relationship with him, it's okay if he's divorced," my mom, ever the pragmatist, said with her signature nonchalance. I was trying to get her approval to date a man who had been married before and had a child, and she, in her infinite wisdom, cut through my anxieties like a hot knife through butter. I guess I got my pragmatism from her.

And she was right. Why should I judge someone based on their past? After all, my own romantic past wasn't exactly a shining example of perfection, with my canceled wedding and all. It was more like a messy montage scene from a rom-com, complete with awkward encounters and regrettable decisions.

In my book, my ex had major personal issues that led to his departure, but I was sure he had a different side of the story. He probably still thought I was a cold-hearted bitch. And maybe I was. Maybe I had been a selfish little girl back then, demanding everything my way and throwing a tantrum when I didn't get it. Maybe I had put my own needs first. Or maybe I simply hadn't had the emotional capacity, maturity or willingness to understand and support him no matter what.

But hey, the past was in the past. That wasn't me anymore. I finally felt ready to be in a fully committed relationship, to meet my partner where they were and to be understanding. To put them first, above my own needs.

Over the next few months, as my relationship with the One grew steadily, I visited him in Singapore about once a month.

The island became our playground, a vibrant canvas for our budding romance. We weren't just two people getting to know each other; we were explorers charting the uncharted territories of this red dot city-state. He was new to Singapore, and I wasn't living there, so we both got to explore with the same level of excitement, like two kids in a candy store.

To satisfy his cravings for a taste of home, we embarked on a quest for the best Turkish food in town. He introduced me to what was to become one of my favorite desserts: Kunefe. The crispy pastry, soaked in sweet syrup and layered with gooey cheese, was a revelation. We'd savor each bite, our eyes meeting over the shared plate, a silent acknowledgement of the deliciousness we had discovered together.

Of course, we didn't neglect Singapore's local delicacies. We devoured plates of chicken rice—the best one, we decided, being at Far East Plaza. We slurped down steaming bowls of laksa, the spicy broth warming us from the inside out. Each meal was a culinary adventure, a chance to bond over shared tastes and discover new favorites.

But it wasn't just about the food. We spent our mornings cycling through the beaches of Sentosa, opting for the quieter side of the island, the far end of Tanjong Beach. With the sun on our faces and the wind in our hair, we'd pedal along the coastline, our laughter echoing in the salty air. Sometimes, he'd rent a buggy from his condo, and he'd let me take the wheel, the most driving I've ever done in my life. It was exhilarating, the freedom of the open road, even if it was just a small stretch of Sentosa.

In the afternoons, we'd find a cozy spot on the beach and sip on sunset drinks, the vibrant colors painting the sky a masterpiece. We'd talk about everything and nothing, our conversations flowing as easily as the waves lapping at the shore.

Evenings were for entertainment. We caught the latest blockbusters at The Projector, an independent cinema with a vintage vibe, where we'd share buckets of popcorn, our fingers brushing as we reached for the same kernels, a spark of electricity passing between us. Back at his apartment, we'd belt out our favorite tunes on his karaoke system, our voices blending together in a surprisingly harmonious duet. I bought a mini disco light, which elevated the whole experience.

There was a comfortable rhythm to our weekends—a blend of adventure and intimacy, of shared experiences and quiet moments. We were building a world together, one delicious meal, one scenic bike ride, one shared song at a time.

And as we started to spend more and more time together, traces of him started to show up on my social media. First, I started posting "hotdog legs" Insta stories from the W Residences' pool while tagging his condo, a subtle hint of my whereabouts. Then, slowly, more and more nondescript shots from his apartment started to show up on my Instagram story, like breadcrumbs leading back to him. Obviously, it was important that these appeared in my story and not my feed because, well, our relationship wasn't official, so he didn't deserve any permanent treatment just yet.

Then, one day, came the first feed post. His soft launch, you may say, on my feed: an elevator shot of us both as we were about to head to the pool, casually dressed, him in shorts and sunglasses. I took the photo cautiously, mainly showing myself, with him shown partially from the back. You couldn't see who it was, and that was done on purpose, but you could obviously see that I was with a guy. No need to tag him or anything, it wasn't time for that. I was just posting a story that showcased me with an unidentified male. That was the first sign of officially acknowledging him in my social media life, and that in itself was *huge!*

It's tricky, this whole social media acknowledgement when it comes to relationships. Some people may think that the steps all millennials take seem random, but oh no. Each one is a well-calculated move, like those in a synchronized swimming routine, carefully choreographed to convey a subtle message that correlates with the movement of our own hearts.

Timing	Social Media Format	Content	Intended Message
Fist date	NONE. It's just a first date for god's sake!		
Somewhere after date 3-5	Insta story	The photo of the hand with their drink at dinner date. Subtle hints	A hint to your network that you're out and about going on a date
When you start seeing each other exclusively	Insta feed	A beautiful photo of a place with your romantic person from the back	A hint that there's someone special in your life. But the identity is still a mystery!
When you're officially in a relationship	Insta feed	The couple photo "Warning: Proceeding directly to 'The Couple Profile Picture' may result in premature relationship demise	Showing the face of your boo but no tag so people can't stalk his Insta yet
When you go on trips together as a couple	Insta reel with collab tag	Full-on holiday video with a #couplegoalsvibe	I'm in a relationship and I'm in love!
When you breakup	You have two options: Delete your history or leave everything behind as a historical relic		

Disclaimer: *The progression through these stages may vary depending on the level of commitment phobia and Instagram follower count.*

IMAGE 24: *The Social Media Acknowledgement Chart*

***

That Thursday evening, I flew from Jakarta to Singapore, landing with a flutter of excitement. It wasn't just another visit; we were finally taking our first trip together—Cambodia! You know how it is, that first getaway is a *thing*. It's a relationship milestone, a real test drive to see if you can actually handle being in each other's space for more than a few hours. I'd taken a few days off from work, and we had reservations at this amazing resort a colleague had raved about. I'd even picked up some new swimsuits and sandals. But then, he dropped the bomb.

"Mira, I have some bad news," he said.

London. A sudden work trip. Some crucial meeting with the Global CEO on Monday, with prep meetings all weekend.

My brain stalled. "What?" I barely managed. "But...everything is booked."

He mumbled something about rescheduling, like it was just brunch plans and I just blinked at him.

"You're telling me this now?" My voice came out sharper than I intended.

He gave me the classic, "I wanted to tell you in person," like that somehow made it better. "And I wanted to see you tonight," he added, as if that was supposed to soften the blow.

Apparently, this urgent London trip kicked off on Saturday. Saturday! So I'd flown all the way from Jakarta for—what? One night?

I did the whole "understanding partner" act because sometimes you have to pretend you're not internally screaming. I told myself it was fine. Maybe the finance world, unlike Google, didn't believe in work-life balance. Maybe we'd rebook Cambodia. Eventually.

That night, lying next to him in bed, I wanted to say something—to let the frustration out, to make him understand—but I didn't. Maybe I was being dramatic. Maybe I should just be cool. So I swallowed it.

***

So, he jetted off to London, leaving me alone in his fancy Sentosa apartment. I'd canceled my own long weekend plans and decided to just work remotely from Singapore until my flight midweek. But waking up in that sleek, modern space without him was... weird. Suddenly, the fancy condo felt less like a romantic getaway pad and more like a gilded cage.

Even basic things became a hassle. Taxis were expensive, groceries at Jones the Grocer were highway robbery and there wasn't a hawker center in sight. I ended up meeting a friend in Arab Street just to get some decent, affordable food. It was then, over a plate of Maggie goreng, that I had a sudden thought. I texted my sister: "Is this what Mom went through with Dad?"

My parents had a huge age gap, 18 years. My mom married young, at 23, to my dad, a 41-year-old established engineer in the oil industry. He was constantly offshore—three months at sea, then two weeks home, then another two months away. It was the rhythm of my childhood. My dad wasn't a bad father, just one whose job kept him constantly away. My mom was the stay-at-home parent who basically raised us single-handedly until we were in primary school. I'd never really thought about what that kind of marriage must have been like for her until that moment, alone in the Banker's apartment.

I had a good job at Google, I traveled for work and I did cool stuff—but compared to his job, mine suddenly felt…insignificant. *Is this what being a "trophy wife" feels like?* I began to wonder. Was I the younger, less important partner, with a job that didn't even register on his radar? If we were to end up together, he could probably support us both without me working. Was that the expectation? That I'd just drop everything for his career?

Or maybe this is normal, I reasoned. Maybe I'd just never experienced a relationship like this before. I told myself I needed to be more understanding, like my mom, holding down the fort while my dad was away for months. I texted him: "Where are you now?"

No response.

He'd warned me he wasn't a big texter, but this felt different.

When 24 hours passed without a word, I started to get a little worried.

"Hi, are you okay? Just checking in," I texted again, trying to sound casual. Finally, a few hours later, a reply:

"Yes, in London. Quite busy here."

Busy. Right.

Maybe I *was* bothering him. I reminded myself he was practically at the cusp of being a Gen X and I was a millennial—

different texting styles, right? I tried to brush it off again, but a little seed of doubt had been planted.

***

The next month, we were back to our regular routine. I flew to Singapore on a Thursday so we could spend the weekend together, something that had become a pattern for us.

"What do you feel like doing tomorrow?" I asked as we discussed our Friday night plans, secretly hoping I could convince him to go out and see a DJ I liked who was coming to town.

"Can we just relax at home?" he replied, sounding worn out. "I've got a board meeting tomorrow afternoon."

I could hear the tension in his voice, so I offered, "How about I cook dinner tomorrow night? Something simple—maybe meatballs and couscous?"

"Hmm...that sounds good," he said, his voice softening just a bit. "Thank you."

"So, what time should I plan for dinner? Seven?" I asked, trying to nail down the plan.

"I think the meeting might run over, so maybe eight?" he suggested.

"Sure, sounds good," I said, trying to be flexible.

Then, almost apologetically, he asked, "Is it okay if I do some work tonight? I still have a lot to prepare for tomorrow."

"Of course, no problem," I assured him. "Actually, let me join you. I have a bit of work I can get done too."

I pulled my laptop out of my backpack and set up at the dining table with him. The atmosphere was quiet but tense—I could tell his mind was preoccupied with work. Wanting to lighten the mood, I nudged my laptop toward him and pointed at it.

"Hey, look! I added more stickers to my laptop. It's basically my personality in sticker form now," I said with a grin, gesturing at the bright, chaotic collage covering my MacBook. He glanced at it and then pointed at his plain, unassuming Windows laptop.

"I'm a banker," he said dryly, a hint of sarcasm creeping into his voice. "I'm not supposed to have a personality." I laughed, glad to see a small smile break through his stress. It wasn't much, but it felt like a little victory. Not long after, he pushed his laptop toward me with a frustrated sigh. "Can you help me with this training?"

"What training?" I asked, leaning over to take a look.

"Some compliance training. I have so much to do, and they're making me do this again!" he said, clearly irritated.

"Oh, one of *those*!" I said, rolling my eyes in sympathy. "I've had to do a bunch of those recently too. They're not hard—they just take forever and feel so pointless."

"Exactly," he said, his voice louder with shared frustration.

"And I'm sure being in a bank, you have even more of these to deal with," I added, trying to empathize.

"Too many," he groaned, shaking his head. "Help me?"

"Okay, sure. Let me see," I said, moving closer to his screen. I studied the training module, clicking through a few slides. "Okay, I think the answer is this," I said, pointing to the screen, "and then this one...and this one."

"Thank you," he said, his tone softer, though still tinged with stress.

I smiled. "Happy to help."

I stayed by his side, doing what I could to lighten his load, but I could tell something was weighing heavily on his mind, though he didn't say much about it. The tension lingered as we worked quietly side by side.

When we finally went to bed, I could tell his mind was elsewhere. He kept his worries close, and I tried to be patient, reminding myself that just being there might help—at least a little.

***

I woke to the sound of someone gasping for air. For a moment, I thought I was trapped in a nightmare. But as my eyes adjusted to the darkness, I remembered I was at the One's apartment—*he* was the one struggling to breathe. He was sitting upright in bed, his hand pressed against his chest, fighting for each shallow breath.

"Are you okay?" I asked, voice hushed and worried. I rested my hand gently on his shoulder, feeling the tension running through his body. "Breathe..." I whispered, taking in a long, steady inhale, hoping he would mirror me. "Slowly," I added, trying to guide him into a calmer rhythm.

"I'm okay...I'm okay," he repeated, though his voice shook in a way that told me he clearly wasn't.

I reached for the glass of water on the bedside table. "Here, take some water," I offered, and he took a few sips between unsteady breaths.

"It's okay, it was just a nightmare," he insisted, sounding like he was trying to convince himself as much as he was convincing me.

But I recognized that gasping, the sudden jolt awake, the frantic look in his eyes. I'd seen it countless times, in myself and in others. I suspected he was having a full-blown anxiety attack, and I was worried. My stomach clenched at the memory of my own episodes, how terrifying it felt to be trapped in my own body, convinced I was dying or losing my mind.

"Are you sure?" I pressed gently.

He gave a small shake of his head, as though brushing off his own fear. "I'm fine," he muttered, his breathing still uneven. "Let's just go back to sleep. I'm sorry I woke you up."

"No, it's okay," I told him, placing my hand over his and giving it a small squeeze. "I'm glad I'm here." The room was silent except for the slight hum of the air conditioning and his gradually slowing breaths. My own heart still pounded from the adrenaline spike, but I tried to keep my voice steady, offering what little comfort I could. "Do you need anything else? Another blanket? Should I get you something to eat?"

He just shook his head and exhaled shakily, as though any extra words would cost him the fragile composure he was clinging to. We settled back under the covers, but sleep felt distant for both of us. As I lay there, I couldn't stop my mind from wandering: *Was it the upcoming board meeting that triggered this attack? Something else at work? Something he wasn't telling me?* I knew all too well how mounting pressure could whittle away at your confidence until it erupted in the dead of night, turning into the kind of terror that felt impossible to escape.

Gradually, his breathing evened out, and he closed his eyes. I noticed his hand searching for mine under the sheets and when he found it, he gripped it tightly. The gesture made my heart ache with empathy. He was always so composed and poised in the daytime, yet here he was, vulnerable and shaken in the middle of the night.

I squeezed his hand in return, letting him know I wasn't going anywhere. In that moment, I felt a sense of purpose, a certainty that I was meant to be right there, helping him through this. For all his talk of board meetings and deadlines, maybe what he needed most was someone to remind him he wasn't alone in those early-morning hours when fear seemed to tower over everything else.

Eventually, he drifted back to sleep, his breaths growing deep and steady. I stayed awake a bit longer, listening to the sound of his breathing, feeling the weight of his hand in mine.

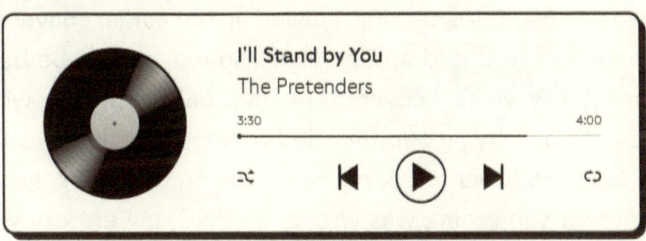

***

After his middle-of-the-night panic attack, I figured the One deserved a chill night in with my company and a nice home-cooked meal.

I was going full Martha Stewart, deciding to make the meatballs and couscous entirely from scratch. I hit up the bougie supermarket (because love makes you do crazy things, like spending $25 on organic, lean, ground beef), grabbed some garlic, onion, mint and all the fixings for the couscous: cucumber, tomatoes, the whole shebang.

He had told me he'd be done by 8 pm, so I planned my timeline carefully: I'd start preparing around 7 pm, mix all the ingredients, shape the meatballs and set the couscous aside—then wait for his text so I could time everything perfectly.

I mixed the ingredients into a well-blended paste, adding the last egg to bind the mixture before forming the meatballs and lining them up neatly on a plate. The couscous was prepped, with diced cucumber, tomatoes and chopped mint ready to be tossed together. At 7:30 pm, I checked the clock and smiled, confident that everything was on track. I then set the dining table: laying out placemats, polishing the wine glasses and ensuring that the bottle of wine was chilled in the fridge. Everything was ready.

I settled onto the sofa with a book, trying to distract myself while waiting. By 7:50, my anticipation bubbled. I was excited to show him my domestic side, that I cared enough to put in all this effort, to prove I could be the chill, supportive partner amidst his high-powered, Wall Street-esque life.

But when 8 pm rolled around, my phone remained silent. I checked again at 8:10, nothing. I pulled up our earlier conversation and confirmed he'd said around eight, so maybe he'd be back at 8:20 or 8:30 at worst. I covered the meatballs with cling wrap to keep them from drying out and tried to remain patient.

By 8:45, and then 9:05, my worry began to mount. I started to wonder if something was wrong. By 9:20, my anxiety was at its peak. I cracked open the bottle of wine and sent him another text, this time with a hint of frustration: "Hey, are you okay? Did your meeting run over? Can you let me know when you'll be home?" My fingers trembled as I hit send.

Now, I wasn't just anxious—I was also hangry. It was almost 10 pm, and my stomach reminded me that I hadn't eaten a proper meal because I was waiting for him. I gulped my first glass of wine, waiting desperately for a sign of life on my phone. Finally, at 10:20 pm—almost two-and-a-half hours past our planned time—a brief text appeared: "Sorry, the meeting went over. I'm on my way home now."

Two-and-a-half hours! And that was all he said? His meeting had run over by more than two hours, and he'd only managed a single sentence to explain it. Furiously, I texted back.

"Why didn't you text me two hours ago? The food's been ready since eight."

My message hung unanswered.

When he finally walked in, I reluctantly plated the meatballs neatly. He gave a casual nod.

"Hmm...smells good," he said, as if he hadn't noticed the tension in my earlier texts. That was the last straw.

"Why didn't you tell me two hours ago that you'd be this late?" I exploded. "I was waiting since eight, not knowing if something had happened to you! I could've gone out with friends if I'd known you'd be so delayed!"

"Sorry, I didn't know the meeting was going to run so long," he mumbled.

"It takes 10 seconds to send a text when you know your meeting is running over!" I pressed on. "You had two whole hours to let me know so I wasn't left hanging!" My voice wavered between anger and hurt as I tried to make him understand that I wasn't asking for much.

He offered another quiet, "Sorry."

I sighed, softening slightly. "I need to know what to expect," I said, trying to mask my disappointment as I gathered the couscous and moved everything to the dining table, hoping to salvage the evening. He sat down, took a bite of a meatball and said, "This is really tasty, but I'm not that hungry. They gave us some food at the meeting. Let's save it for tomorrow."

I stared at him in disbelief. After all the time and effort I'd poured into this meal, he casually dismissed it. I couldn't help but wonder: Was my effort to care for him so insignificant? Did my time and energy mean nothing to him? He'd once told me he wasn't much of a texter, but this went far beyond that excuse. I felt like I'd been left hanging, expected to drop everything for his stressful job, even though a simple courtesy—a brief update—was all I was asking for.

At that moment, as I sat there with half-finished food and a heavy heart, I questioned whether his priorities would ever align with mine. My anger mingled with hurt, leaving me to wonder if I was meant to continuously accommodate his unpredictable world.

***

Over the next few weeks, I began to notice that his distance wasn't just a one-off fluke—it was becoming our new normal.

He started coming home later and later. His apologies became as fleeting as his promises, replaced by a vague, "I'm busy," or "Work's just crazy right now." Our conversations dwindled into short, mechanical exchanges. I'd try to ask how his day went, and he'd brush it off with a tired smile, his eyes distant as if he were miles away even when he was physically present. The warmth that once filled our evenings was replaced by an uneasy silence and the constant hum of his phone, always buzzing with emails, reminders that his work was consuming him.

I found myself waiting by the door more often than not, clinging to the hope that one day, he'd set aside his responsibilities long enough for us to share a genuine moment together. I'd cook his favorite meals and arrange the table with extra care, hoping that the familiar comforts of home might coax him back into our world.

One Friday night, he promised he'd take me out to this new restaurant, the kind of place where you needed to book a table two months in advance. I spent hours agonizing over what to wear before finally settling on a cute dress and heels. I even splurged on a mani-pedi, because, you know, hope springs eternal.

He texted me at the last minute as I was already downstairs about to enter the taxi:

"Something came up at work. Rain check?"

Just like that. No explanation, no apology, just a curt "rain check," as if he was rescheduling a dentist appointment. I stared at my reflection in the mirror, my perfectly coordinated outfit suddenly feeling like a costume for a play I wasn't going to be in.

I was upset yet growing numb to his constant indifference—and for a moment, I considered retreating to his apartment, ordering takeaway and losing myself in Netflix as I sulked over his latest stunt. I'd become all too accustomed to sit pretty and simply wait for his next call or text. But that night, I reached a breaking point. I refused to be reduced to a decorative accessory in his life.

Enough was enough. I realized my life couldn't revolve around his whims and empty promises. With that thought sparking a newfound determination, I grabbed my phone and texted a few friends in Singapore to see who was out that evening. By sheer luck, my breakup BFF Mabuk and a couple of guys—AJ and Asri—were already out. I didn't hesitate; I decided to impose myself on their hangout and reclaim my night.

I called for a cab, leaving behind the oppressive silence of his fancy apartment and the heavy weight of waiting.

***

I sat by the Singapore River with Mabuk and the guys as I recounted everything that had happened with the One. Mabuk leaned over and said, "He sounds like dicksand."

I raised an eyebrow and asked, "Like what?!" while taking a swig of my beer.

"Dicksand—you know, like quicksand, but dick. Something you just can't escape from," he explained with a smirk.

"Did you just make that up?" I asked, incredulous.

"No, it's in Urban Dictionary! Just Google it," he replied.

I sighed. "Okay, fine. But yeah, he can be so shit sometimes, and I still don't know why I keep holding on."

"Maybe he's just not ready for a relationship," Mabuk probed.

"He got divorced years ago," I reasoned. "He said he wanted to have another family."

"Maybe he has someone else?" Mabuk suggested.

"Nah," I replied dismissively. "His work is insane. He barely has time for himself—he doesn't even have time for me, let alone another woman." I tried to justify his actions, though I wasn't entirely convinced.

"So, if he doesn't have time for you, then why are you with him?" Mabuk asked, his words cutting deep. I paused, considering his question.

"I don't know," I admitted. Then, I added, "I saw his anxiety attack. I saw his stress. And maybe I just want to be there for him. After my breakup, it was the first time I felt like I could really care for someone again. When he's around, it feels familiar and comfortable. So I want to make it work."

"See? Complete dicksand," Mabuk joked again.

"Hey!" I playfully hit his arm with my fist, laughing.

Soon, AJ chimed in. "We're heading over to Headquarters now. Are you coming with us?"

I hesitated, wondering whether a techno night at Headquarters was something I was up for, then said, "Hmm...nah, It's okay, you guys go ahead." I felt content from the night's banter. "I'm going to head back to Sentosa."

"Dicksand," Mabuk teased once more.

"Stop it!" I laughed, both at the irony and the truth of his remark.

Even after yet another last-minute cancellation and his disappearing act, I still wanted to be there when he eventually returned. He'd gone radio silent after our last chat, and I had no idea whether he was already home or still burning the midnight oil at the office. Was I *sinking*?

I got back to his apartment around midnight. Noticing his work shoes by the door—a subtle sign he'd returned—I went inside. In the bedroom, I found him passed out on the bed, still in his work shirt and pants. In that moment, all the hurt and disappointment I'd felt over his cancellation melted away, replaced by a quiet pity.

As I changed into my own pajamas, I slowly removed his socks, tucked him under the blanket and kissed his cheek goodnight. Turning off the light and settling into bed, I promised myself that we would talk in the morning.

***

"So...one day you might tell people, 'Oh, I met someone really special, but things didn't work out because he was bad at WhatsApp?'" the One joked, trying to sum up my frustration as I sat him down to talk about his terrible communication habits.

"I mean, if you put it that way," I replied, feeling a sting of defensiveness. He made me sound like some needy millennial, obsessed with constant attention and glued to my phone, craving an endless stream of messages. But that wasn't the point at all. I wasn't asking for hourly updates or clingy check-ins—I just wanted a little more effort when we weren't physically together. A simple message here and there to show I was on his mind. Is that too much to ask? I wasn't sure.

"Just because I don't say it doesn't mean I don't think about you," he added, as if that should put my mind at ease. It didn't.

"Is your work worth it?" I finally asked, my frustration bubbling over. "It's driving you crazy anyway. Was it always like this when you were in Turkey?"

"No, it wasn't," he sighed, the exhaustion evident in his voice. "But they're paying me close to a million dollars for it."

"Oh, wow," I murmured, only then grasping just how much he was earning. "That's...a lot of money." But the words rang hollow. What was the point of all that income if you were constantly on edge? "But you don't have a life. And you keep getting these anxiety attacks!" I blurted out.

"Well, I'm not supposed to have a life. I've sold my soul to the bank," he said, his voice dripping with sarcasm, masking what sounded like quiet defeat.

"But you're a VP," I pushed back. "You have people under you. Can't you set boundaries for your team? For yourself?"

"It never ends," he said flatly. "Even the CEO has to answer to the board and shareholders."

"So why are you doing it?" I asked quietly, genuinely trying to understand. "Is it just for the money? Or do you actually *care* about the work?"

"I don't know," he admitted after a pause. "Money, status, influence...maybe all of it."

There it was—his work wasn't just *part* of his life; it *was* his life. With no family waiting at home, no wife or kids to anchor him, his entire existence revolved around his job. He couldn't afford to stop, because if he did, there'd be nothing left to fill the void.

I couldn't imagine living like that. I couldn't imagine being a CEO, where your company becomes your identity. I even found myself wondering—did Sundar Pichai ever get anxious the night before a board meeting? Probably. It confirmed something I'd been sensing for a while: The higher you climb in the corporate world, the more you need something—or someone—to keep you grounded—a family, a partner, a life outside of KPIs and board meetings. Without that, work seeps into every corner of your waking and sleeping hours—until it swallows you whole.

Through him, I was watching someone crumble under the weight of it all, trapped because he'd built his entire identity around his job. There was no escape because there was nothing else waiting for him outside of it.

My life is 95 percent work and 5 percent my son, I remembered him telling me when we first got together.

Where did that leave me?

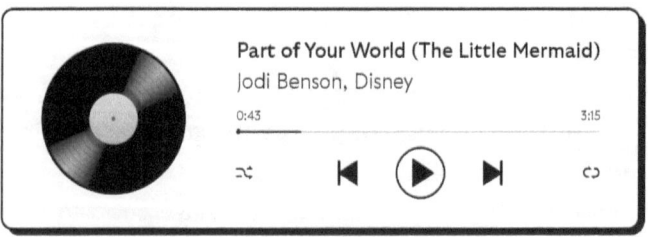

***

I thought long and hard about the life the One lived, and the more I reflected, the more it echoed my own over the past two years since the breakup. Work had consumed him, just as it had consumed me.

When your identity revolves entirely around work, even minor disruptions can feel catastrophic—because if work is everything, then anything going wrong feels like everything's falling apart.

That's when it hit me: We need to diversify our sources of happiness, like a financial portfolio. When one area falters—as it inevitably will—it shouldn't take down our entire sense of fulfillment.

But his life was wildly off balance—95 percent work, 5 percent his son. No wonder he had anxiety attacks before board meetings. No wonder he bailed on us so easily. I wasn't even on the chart.

For a while, I thought I could carve out space for myself in that tiny five percent, help bring some balance. But maybe he wasn't ready. Or maybe, after living this way for so long since the divorce, he'd simply forgotten how to live any other way.

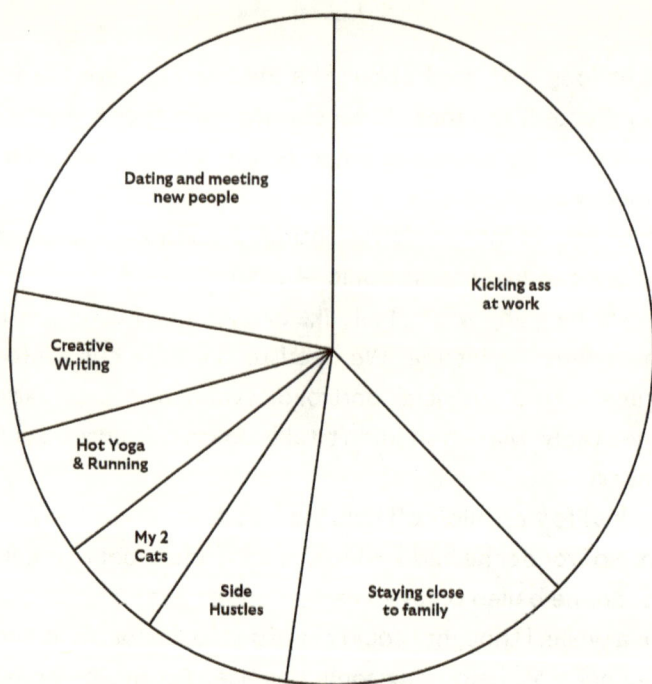

IMAGE 25: *The Diversification of Happiness Source Chart*

***

"I don't know," the Banker replied when I asked him when we were going to meet next. "I need to go to Hong Kong, then London and after that, I'll spend some time back home in Turkey for a while," he said.

I wanted to offer to join him on one of those trips to make it easier for us to see each other, but I didn't want to sound needy or stir up unnecessary drama, so I swallowed the thought and stayed silent. Instead, I simply exhaled a quiet sigh of disappointment.

"Oh," was all I managed to say.

"Sorry," he said over the phone—a word that, by now, had lost all meaning to me. It had been thrown around too many times, used as a flimsy band-aid to cancel countless plans.

"My birthday is in January," I told him, shifting the conversation. "I'm planning to do something in Jakarta." I hesitated before adding, "Can you please come? I'm giving you three months' notice now."

"I'll try," he said, his voice neutral, noncommittal.

I really wanted him to come, but I was also bracing myself for the inevitable—that he would bail at the last minute, just as he had so many times before.

"If you can't make it, please tell me well in advance," I said firmly. "I can't have you cancel on my birthday last minute."

"I'll try," he repeated.

And deep down, I already knew what that meant.

***

The next three months were an agonizing stretch in our relationship. I was often left in the dark, unsure of where in the world the Banker was. His texts became sparse, his replies slower and slower. If I didn't check in on him first, days could pass without a single message. Every time I raised my concerns, he brushed them off with the same excuse—*he wasn't great at texting*. But by that point, I refused to believe it.

It didn't take long for me to realize that my daily anxiety levels were directly tied to the time it took for him to reply. If more than two hours passed without a response, my nervous energy would begin to rise. After four hours, it became a spiral. By the end of the day, I was drowning in worst-case scenarios, consumed by a feeling of despair that I couldn't shake.

Two hours, as I confirmed with fellow millennial friends, seemed to be the tipping point—the universally agreed-upon window before our minds started spinning into overdrive, questioning everything. And yet, for him, two hours was nothing. For me, it was enough to feel like I was slowly losing my grip on whatever connection we still had left

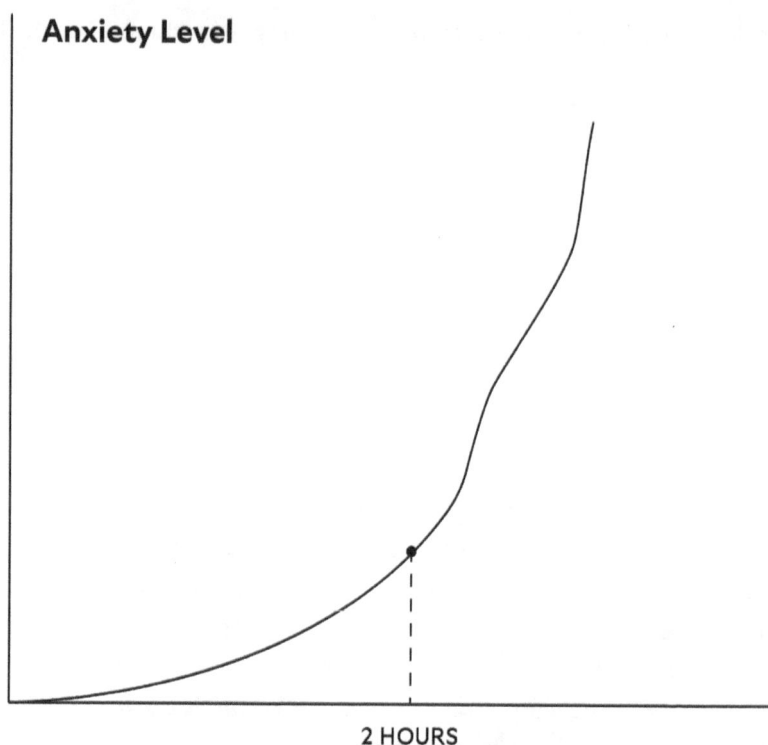

IMAGE 26: *The Anxiety Level & Time Taken to Respond to a Text Correlation Chart*

Why isn't he responding to me?
Is he with his son?
Is he with someone else?
How can I have a relationship with someone who takes two days to respond to me?

My thoughts spiraled, mushrooming into worst-case scenarios. I found myself deep in an obsessive loop, trying to make sense of his absence. I stalked his ex-wife's Instagram (don't ask how I managed to find it), scouring for clues about his whereabouts. I dissected his LinkedIn activity down to the smallest details. He was posting on LinkedIn, engaging with people there—so why wasn't he replying to me?

His constant disappearing act triggered the worst of my anxiety. It wasn't just about him—it struck something much deeper. It tapped into an old, familiar wound I'd carried for as long as I could remember. It activated my anxious attachment style, the fear of abandonment rooted in my relationship with my dad, who was always away, offshore for work. I never knew when I'd see him again. And even when he was home, I didn't know how to connect with him—or how to feel about his presence after so many absences. Layer that with a broken engagement, and my mind went into full defense mode. *Run. Leave before he does. Because one day, he will.*

The distance from the One made me feel like I was reliving my childhood all over again.

What I'd needed most back then was simple: to be held, to be reassured, to be told that things would be okay. I longed for an embrace, for words that could anchor me, for someone to say my feelings mattered. But that never came.

And before I had a chance to mend what was broken, my dad was gone. Cancer took him too soon. My sister had been luckier in that sense; she got more time with him. I didn't.

And my mother, though present, had never been one for emotional expressions. She loved me, I knew that, but she wasn't the type to say it or show it. So, I took care of my own emotions by shutting them down.

In my mind, there was no point in being emotional. No one was going to respond to it. Everyone was going to leave eventually. Just like my dad. Just like my ex. Even the people I loved the most would one day disappear.

So before they could do that to me, I convinced myself: *leave first.*

***

"Should I call it off?" I asked Mabuk, my voice hesitant, though deep down, I already knew the answer.

"Call what off?" he replied.

"My relationship with the Banker," I said.

"Oh, you mean with Dicksand. Was it ever a relationship?" he asked, forcing me to confront the reality of the one-sided situation I had entangled myself in over the past few months.

Later that night, I texted Mabuk again: "Why does it hurt to know that I will never, ever be number one?" I asked. "At least his ex will forever be his baby mama," I followed up, the frustration bubbling up inside me. "And me? What am I to him? I don't even know," I concluded.

"Well, you chose to get involved with someone who's divorced," Mabuk replied, blunt as ever.

"Yeah, but I thought someone who'd gone through a divorce would have learned a thing or two about relationships," I shot back.

"I've met plenty of divorced people who still make the same relationship mistakes over and over again. Not everyone learns from their past."

I sighed; he was right. Loving a pre-loved partner was a strange thing.

Why did it hurt to know that, at *best*, I was number four in the One's life—behind his son, himself and his ex? Yet, despite all of this, I craved him every single day. It was painful, but I convinced myself it would all be worth it. Maybe this wasn't love. Maybe I was just in love with the *idea* of love. But then, *why did it hurt so much?*

As much as I dreaded being alone again, I also started to wonder if I could endure this forever.

***

"I'm coming for your birthday," his text read one day.

I stared at my phone, rereading the words, my heart skipping a beat. *He's coming.*

"You are?" I replied, surprised, yet undeniably happy. A rush of excitement coursed through me, but I forced myself to stay cautious. "But please don't cancel on me last minute," I added quickly, trying not to sound too hopeful.

"I won't," he assured me.

I wanted to believe him. *I needed* to believe him.

"I'm hosting a 20-person sit-down dinner at home," I explained. "I can't have you disappear last minute." This wasn't just any casual meet-up—this was my birthday, my carefully planned night with my closest friends and I wasn't about to let it be another one of his vague commitments that never materialized.

"I'll be there," he said.

"My mom will also be there, just so you know," I told him.

"I'm looking forward to meeting her," he replied.

That was it. The moment I read those words, I felt giddy, so giddy—like a child about to unwrap the biggest present on Christmas morning. He was coming! And not just coming—he was *meeting my mom.*

All the doubts I had from months of inconsistent communication, all the frustration from his last-minute cancellations, the long silences, the endless waiting—I shoved them aside. None of it seemed to matter now because he was coming.

***

That night, on my thirty-first birthday, I felt happier than I had in a long time. Twenty of my closest friends and colleagues from Jakarta filled my mom's Bellagio apartment in Mega Kuningan with their laughter and chatter

I enlisted my favorite local caterer, Als, to prepare the food and asked friends to bring bottles of champagne to match my chosen theme: fried chicken and champagne. A little unconventional, perhaps, but undeniably fun.

By 7 pm, two-thirds of my guests had already arrived and the apartment was buzzing with energy, yet amid the sea of familiar faces, I found myself anxiously waiting for one in particular—the

One. I knew he was already in Jakarta, so it was only a matter of time before he showed up.

"You really like this guy, huh? I've never seen you like this," Teguh remarked, noticing me glance at the door every other minute.

"I do. And he is going to meet my mom tonight!" I replied.

Finally, a little past 7 pm, the doorbell rang again. My heart skipped. I walked over and opened the door, and there he was. Dressed in a sharp two-piece suit with a crisp white shirt—effortlessly adhering to the night's "overdressed" theme—he looked as composed and dashing as ever.

"Happy birthday M," he said, leaning in to kiss my cheek.

"I'm glad you made it," I replied, feeling a rush of relief at seeing him again after weeks apart. "I was worried you'd disappear at the last minute."

"I wouldn't do that," he reassured me with a small smile.

Throughout the night, I kept stealing glances at my mom, watching her expressions, trying to gauge what she thought of the One. For all my rebellious middle-child tendencies, for all the ways I had defied her expectations throughout my life, when it came to the man I was with, I wanted her approval. *Needed* it.

The One, to his credit, chatted easily with my friends. His presence at this dinner, meeting my closest circle, was more than just a social occasion—it was a statement. A quiet confirmation that we were together, officially.

As the last dessert was served and people began to move about the apartment, I noticed my mom and the Banker in a quiet conversation at the corner of the dining room. Curious, I made my way over.

"Mama....," I said softly as I approached.

"He's a good guy," my mom said bluntly, in the way only she could.

"Yeah, but he's old. And he still doesn't know how to text," I teased, glancing at the Banker.

"Don't say that! He's still young!" my mom retorted, immediately coming to his defense.

"Thank you," the One said, siding with her. "She was telling me all about her trip to Turkey," he added.

"Beautiful country!" my mom exclaimed, giving an approving thumbs-up.

"You should come next time," he said, his eyes locking onto mine with an unspoken invitation.

"Sure, I'd love to," I replied.

"If you ladies will excuse me for a moment, I need to find the restroom," he said.

"First door on the left." I pointed down the hallway.

As he walked away, I turned to my mom, seizing the moment. "So…what do you think?" I asked, my voice laced with both excitement and trepidation.

"I like him. He's a good man. And he really loves his son," she said.

But…

I heard it before she even said it.

"But what?" I prompted.

"If you want to be with him, you'll have to be the one to give in. You'll need to be patient," she said, her tone measured.

"Oh…," I murmured, turning over her words in my head. *But can't he meet me halfway?* I wondered silently.

"He's set in his ways," she continued. "You won't be able to change him." She paused, then added, "Just like your dad."

I swallowed, letting her words sink in. My mom—ever the intuitive, ever the psychic—had seen something, had read something in him that I had perhaps been too caught up to notice. Or maybe I had noticed but had chosen to ignore. Either way, her words lingered, carving out a space in my mind that I wasn't quite ready to confront. Not yet.

***

After my birthday weekend, I felt optimistic—almost giddy—picturing the One inviting me to join his next trip home to Turkey, introducing me to his family as an exchange of sorts. It seemed like the natural progression, the next milestone.

But my optimism evaporated the moment he left Jakarta. Almost instantly, he slipped into his usual disappearing act—the same old "Sorry, I'm not good at texting" routine. His messages became sporadic, vague and frustratingly cryptic whenever I reached out. I never knew when he would reply, or when we would see each other again.

"I have a lot of trips coming up," he said. That was his excuse.

I wanted to tell him, *I can fly anywhere to meet you*, but I held back, again. Besides, why did it have to be me making all the effort? The longer I went without knowing when we would see each other again, the more my insecurities gnawed at me.

At one point, a simple text—just asking where he was—went unanswered for days.

Is he ghosting me?

Am I actually being ghosted...by a Gen Xer?

For fuck's sake.

I thought ghosting was something *my* generation did. But apparently, technology had made it an equal-opportunity act, spanning generations.

As his messages grew more sporadic, a quiet realization settled in one morning—a thought I'd been avoiding for weeks. Maybe I'd been seeing things—not just him, but us—through rose-colored glasses. Like that scene in *500 Days of Summer*, where the split-screen shows expectation versus reality, and the truth hits like a punch to the gut.

Has the past few months been an illusion?

Had I been so desperate to make this work that I ignored every glaring red flag?

Maybe he was never that into me?

Maybe I had wanted it so badly, I convinced myself it was real.

And how could I be so foolish—again? After everything I'd been through, how had I allowed myself to end up in such a vulnerable place? To be ghosted, like some forgettable fling?

From the start, he'd told me his life was 95 percent work, 5 percent his son—and that's exactly how it felt. I was getting the leftovers: fleeting attention—crumbs. I was an afterthought in a life where I never really belonged.

Maybe I'd been in denial. Maybe I'd wanted it so badly, I looked away from the truth staring me in the face.

My mother's voice echoed in my mind. She'd warned me: "If you want to be with him, you'll have to be the patient one. You'll have to give in."

But what more could I possibly give?

Before he disappeared again, I knew I had to take back control. I couldn't keep waiting for someone to leave me.

So the next time I got a hold of him, I was already sure of what I needed to do. This time, I'd be the one to walk away.

***

"I moved to Hong Kong," the Banker said one day, in a rare message actually initiated by him.

I stared at my screen. What? A whole cross-country move—and he hadn't mentioned a single word? Not once?

"Wait, what?" I replied, disbelief crashing over me.

"I'm going to be the CEO of a new digital bank that I'm setting up," he said.

My heart clenched. *I don't fucking care about your job!* I wanted to scream. Instead, I typed, "What about us?"

Three dots appeared. Disappeared. Reappeared. I held my breath.

"I'm sorry," he finally said. "You deserve to be happy."

WTF.

Is he breaking up with me?

No. No. I was supposed to be the one breaking up with him!

And "You deserve to be happy?" That vague, patronizing line people use to make themselves look noble as they walk away. As if they're doing *you* a favor by leaving.

I'd been patient for so long, clinging to the hope that one day I'd carve out even one percent of space in his life. But now, after a life-changing move I wasn't even informed about, I finally saw the truth: even that one percent had been a fantasy.

I didn't know if he was just a selfish prick, or if—despite his professional brilliance—he was simply clueless when it came to love. Just because you're smart enough to be a CEO doesn't mean you're emotionally capable of a relationship. *That* I was learning the hard way.

"Well, now that you're a CEO, maybe you can finally make more time for yourself," I said, bitterness seeping through.

"Hmm…probably the opposite," he admitted. "I'll likely have even less time." There was something in his tone—fatigue, maybe even regret.

"Then what's the point?" I asked, exasperated.

"There's no point, M."

I swallowed hard, pushing back the lump rising in my throat. "I hope you have a good life," I said, sarcasm barely masking the ache beneath.

"I'm sorry," he said.

And that was it.

No fight. No real conversation. Just a breakup over text. And a move.

An ending I should've seen coming long before—but now, it was unmistakably, irreversibly real.

***

That night, as I lay in bed sobbing, feeling like my chest was caving in, I did what I knew best. I redownloaded Tinder and started swiping.

Mindlessly, I flicked through hundreds of profiles. There were men in Jakarta, in Singapore, in Hong Kong. All the places that reminded me of the One.

I wasn't looking to meet anyone. I wasn't even searching for a connection. I just needed something—*anything*—to numb the blow of what had just happened. Before I had the chance to walk away, the Banker had ended things over text, like I was nothing. It left me feeling discarded, betrayed, *worthless*.

So, I swiped.

Not for love. Not even for lust. Just to feel something: a cheap hit of validation, a quick dopamine rush to drown out the ache in my chest.

Match.

Match.

Match.

Seven out of 10 right swipes turned green. I should have felt exhilarated and should have ridden the high of instant approval. But instead, each match sent a sickening twist through my stomach. Each name, each face, felt like a dull blade pressing into my ribs. I wasn't excited—I was disgusted.

Had I really been rejected so brutally that I now craved the shallow validation of complete strangers? Was this what I had been reduced to?

I paused, my finger hovering over the screen.

What the fuck am I doing?

Is this my new reality? Again?

I hated it. I hated every profile I matched with. I hated the way I was playing this game I had once perfected.

I wanted a happy ending, but maybe happy endings were just a fairy tale. And fairy tales weren't real.

What was real, though, were my feelings. The feelings I had for him were real.

The warm, familiar glow when he made one of his inside jokes, a humor only he understood. The tiny flutter in my stomach when he woke up smiling, singing under his breath. The ache in my chest every time we were apart. The frustration of trying to understand him. The heartbreak, the anger, the rejection. All of it was *real*.

After everything, after years of guarding my heart behind an iron wall, I was truly feeling again.

I wasn't numb. I wasn't detached. This pain, as unbearable as it was, meant something—my heart was still beating, and I was capable of love again. I had thought the Banker was *the One*. I had wished for him to be *the One*. But no—he was simply the one who truly made me *feel* again.

***

In hindsight, I saw a painfully familiar pattern with the One: I had become the good girl again—the one who stayed quiet, who swallowed her feelings, who made herself small to keep the peace.

As a child, I had longed for my father's attention, his love, his presence. And just like with the One, I told myself it was fine. I rationalized it, convinced myself I didn't need more than the scraps I was given.

To be clear, my father wasn't a bad man—far from it. He was brilliant, kind and humble but absent, not because he didn't love me but because his offshore oil and gas work kept him away. I never cried. Never begged him to come home more often. Never told him I missed him. What would be the point? He was just busy. He was just working. So I taught myself to be okay with less. I convinced myself it was enough.

And decades later, there was the One—canceling our Cambodia trip a day before departure. I told him it was fine. The One who disappeared for days without replying. *He must be busy*, I told myself. The One who never said when he'd be back from work. *I should find ways to entertain myself while I wait*, I reasoned.

I never let on how hurt I was. I never cried. Because good girls don't cry. And good girls, I hoped, don't get left behind.

Maybe the One never meant to hurt me, just like my father never meant to be emotionally absent. But their circumstances— and the choices they made within them—*did* hurt me, whether they intended to or not. For the first time since my canceled wedding, I had opened my heart again. I let him in. I saw a future with him. I admired him. I loved him. And I was willing to bend, to shrink, to sacrifice parts of myself just to make it work. But in doing so, I lost myself. I let him hurt me—and never told him how deeply it cut. I denied my own feelings to keep him close.

But that was never a foundation for real love. And that's when I finally understood: the ending was necessary. Letting him go wasn't just about walking away from him. It was about breaking free from the old attachment patterns that had defined me for far too long.

***

"Mira, it's your turn now," Tia said, passing me the mic after finishing a dramatic rendition of a Celine Dion classic.

The moment Andara heard about my breakup with the One, she wasted no time. She summoned our closest friends in Jakarta for an *emergency* karaoke session, a ritual for heartbreaks, setbacks and anything that called for loud, off-key singing and copious amounts of soju. The crew was set: Andara, Tia, Natasha and Jaka. The venue? A dimly lit, speakeasy-style Korean karaoke bar tucked away in Senopati.

The room pulsed with neon hues, the mirrored disco ball scattering specks of light across my face. I gripped the mic, unsure of what to sing. Another breakup. Another round of emotions I wasn't quite sure how to process yet.

"Don't worry, Mira, you'll get over this," Tia reassured me, her voice light but firm. "You've been through worse."

"I knew it wasn't going to work out from the beginning with the daddy," Jaka said bluntly, earning a chorus of laughter from the group.

I sighed, flipping through the song selection. And then, my fingers stopped.

"Okay, I know what to sing," I said, my voice barely above a whisper.

An old Indonesian band I had loved in high school stared back at me from the screen. I wiped away a stray tear before turning to take the mic, hoping no one had noticed. The opening chords rang out, a familiar melody that wrapped around me like an old friend. As the beat kicked in, I stood up, nodding my head, tapping my foot to the rhythm. And as the first verse started, I lifted the mic to my lips:

Losing you it's not the end of the world
But it's true that it definitely hurts

Chapter 8

THE PRAGMATIC ROMANTIC

For a while, I tried to move on from the One, even venturing into the chaos of dating yet again. That's how I ended up with a high school friend—a familiar face who seemed like a safe choice. Spoiler alert: he wasn't. It turned out he was already in some sort of "open relationship." Or at least that's what he claimed. Let's just call him *Mistake 2.0* because he's not worth more than a passing mention.

Shortly after that, I got my test results back from the doctor following some suspicious symptoms. They were positive for herpes. Yep, that happened. Cue months of awkward conversations with therapists, hours of Googling everything under the sun and excruciating disclosures with potential dates. There's nothing quite like saying, "Hey, before we go further, there's something you should know..." to test your emotional stamina. It was, as they say, a character-building experience.

Somewhere in the midst of that whirlwind, I made a big move to Singapore for a new role at Google. It was the reset button I so desperately needed. A fresh start, a new city and the hope of finally getting my personal life back on track. For a moment, it felt like everything might just fall into place.

Like so many others, I entered 2020 with high hopes. Big dreams, even. I wanted that to be the year I finally got into a proper, long-term relationship. I wanted another promotion at work. I wanted everything to feel like it was coming together. After seven chapters of love, lust, mistakes and heartbreak, I was convinced I'd learned everything I needed to learn. I was ready. Ready to fall in love again. But then, like everything else in the world, 2020 was canceled. And so was my romantic life.

At first, I clung to hope. Like everyone else, I thought, *surely, this won't last long.* Maybe by Q3, things would start to turn around. We'd flatten the curve, go back to normal and get our lives back on track.

But as the months dragged on and the pandemic tightened its grip on the world, that hope began to fade. Normal felt like a distant memory, and every headline, every press conference, every day spent staring at the same four walls of my apartment made it clear: This wasn't ending anytime soon.

With each additional day in lockdown, the isolation pressed down on me harder. The silence in my apartment felt louder. The texts from friends became less frequent. Dating apps felt like a cruel joke because even if I matched with someone, what was I supposed to do? Schedule a Zoom dinner date? Go for a socially-distanced walk where we awkwardly shout small talk through masks?

And as the days turned into weeks, and the weeks into months I found myself grappling with a fear I couldn't shake: *What if this is it? What if I end up alone...FOREVER?*

That's also when the ridiculous fantasies started. I imagined my ex-fiancé stranded in some far-off place, like Bali, his visa expired, no flights out and definitely no flights back. I pictured him scrambling for a way home, but no one answering his calls for help. Or better yet, I'd imagine him stuck in quarantine, miserable, with no Wi-Fi and nothing but instant noodles to eat.

The worst part? These fantasies actually made me feel better for a fleeting moment. I'd catch myself smirking at the absurdity of it all, but then a wave of guilt would wash over me. *Seriously, Mira?* There was already enough negativity going on in the world—why was I still holding onto all this bitterness over something that happened four years ago?

I couldn't deny it anymore: I still hated my ex-fiancé. And I hated that I hated him. I hated that the world was at a standstill, and I had nothing to distract me from this all-consuming negativity.

I started asking myself hard questions:

Why am I so angry?

Why do I still care?

What does hating him even accomplish?

The answers weren't coming to me, but the more I sat with those feelings, the more I realized how deeply I'd buried my pain.

It wasn't just about the breakup; it was about all the things we left unsaid. After everything, we'd just stopped talking. We never had a real conversation about what went wrong, never screamed at each other, never grieved the loss of what we had together. Except for that one awkward phone call where we agreed to cancel the wedding, we'd avoided dealing with it altogether.

In lockdown, those emotions bubbled up again. And one thing was clear: I couldn't keep carrying this weight around anymore. It was time to stop wishing bad things for him and start figuring out how to let him go for good.

Hindsight is 20/20. And it took me until the year 2020 to realize the pattern that had been there all along. Looking back, I always felt better when I stopped running from my feelings. Every single time. Like when I chose to return to Bali, a place filled with painful memories, just so I could overwrite them with new ones. Or when I faced my demons during that intense out-of-body shrooms experience. Or when I showed up for my sister's wedding, still mourning the loss of my own. Or when I embraced the sadness of a relationship not meant to last with the One. Each of those moments terrified me, but facing the fear head-on always helped me heal, little by little.

And yet, for every time I leaned into my feelings, there were countless times I did the opposite—swiping mindlessly on dating apps for that low-grade dopamine hit, drowning my sorrows in alcohol, staying late at the office or avoiding any family gathering—it all felt like relief in the moment, but it never lasted. Instead, I'd wake up the next day feeling worse. I'd regret the impulsive decisions I made in those moments of avoidance. They made me feel like an angrier, lonelier, sadder version of myself. Since the wedding cancellation, I'd worked to face more and avoid less. That's where I found freedom and healing. Now, with all the time in the world to reflect, I was able to see it clearly: There was still one thing, one *person*, I hadn't yet dared to face at all: my ex.

Even if the timing wasn't perfect, even if it had to be done through WhatsApp in the middle of a bloody global pandemic, it had to happen. I had to reach out to him. I didn't know how he'd respond or if it would even make a difference, but I knew one thing: It was time to pour it all out. Let *him* hear it all. What followed was, without a doubt, the longest text message I had ever written in my life.

I didn't hold back. I told him how much his actions had hurt me. His decision to leave five weeks before our wedding and his subsequent silence—refusing to talk to me after his departure from the life we built together for years—flipped my life upside down and sent me deep into a pit of depression and crippling anxiety. I told him how it felt to wake up every morning after he left, consumed by sadness, humiliation and this unbearable sense of failure. How I'd spent weeks—no, months—wondering what I had done wrong, what I could have done differently, why *I* wasn't enough to make him stay.

I told him how much it hurt that he never apologized. Not once. How he never acknowledged the mess he left behind for me to clean up. I carried that weight alone, and it festered inside me growing into this bitterness that I didn't even realize was still there until now.

I needed him to hear me. I needed him to understand that his actions and silence were like a grenade that exploded in the middle of my life, leaving me to pick up the shattered pieces by myself.

And so I wrote. And rewrote. And deleted. And rewrote again. Every word felt like peeling back another layer of pain I had buried deep down. It was raw and unfiltered and vulnerable in a way that terrified me. But I didn't stop. For the first time, I let myself put all those emotions into words, every single one of them.

By the time I finished, my hands were shaking, and my chest felt like it might collapse. The text stared back at me, this huge, unfiltered confession that I wasn't sure he would even read. The reply came almost immediately.

"I'm sorry," it read.

I burst into tears. Not the delicate, cinematic kind of tears you'd see in a rom-com—no, this was messy, ugly, full-body sobbing. Four years. Four *fucking* years I had been holding onto all these emotions. Four years of anger, pain, bitterness and questions without answers.

His apology, simple and overdue, hit me hard. It wasn't elaborate. It wasn't full of explanations or excuses. Just two words: "I'm sorry." And though it came four years too late, I couldn't bring myself to care anymore because this emotional outpouring wasn't about him. It had never been about him. It was about me validating my own pain. I needed to expose my wounds to the light of day so they could heal, because concealing them was beginning to eat me alive.

For years, I told myself I'd moved on. I convinced myself that I was fine, that I didn't need closure, that I didn't care anymore. But my tears told a different story. They weren't just tears of release, but of relief. Relief that I had finally let myself share these feelings honestly with him. Relief that I no longer had to carry my resentment or keep trying to answer all of my what-ifs. I didn't care who came out better four years after the breakup; I just needed him to understand the depths of the pain that he left me with.

I realized how much I had underestimated the power of facing my pain head-on. I wasn't crying for him, or for the apology, or even for what we had lost. I was crying for myself, for the girl who'd been stuck in that pain for so long and for the woman who had found the courage to set herself free.

***

A week later, out of nowhere, Jaka sent me a screenshot on Instagram. Classic Jaka—no context, no warning, just vibes and chaos.

I opened it and blinked. It was him. My ex.

My ex and I unfollowed and blocked each other on social media four years ago, so I had no idea where he was or what he was up to.

In the photo, he was in a traditional Balinese outfit, standing next to a Balinese girl, it seemed. It looked like a wedding. *Wait a minute, it's his wedding!* In the middle of a pandemic, no less.

"Did you know?" Jaka asked, curiosity practically oozing through the text.

I stood there for a while, looking at the photo. They were posed in front of a pool filled with flower petals, the whole scene bathed in that over-the-top, tropical romance vibe. It was picturesque, sure, but not my style at all. I refrained from judging the overtly romantic setup of their wedding (okay, maybe I rolled my eyes just a little).

I braced myself for the tsunami of emotions I always thought would come if this moment ever arrived. I had imagined it more than once: the sharp sting in my chest, the flood of old memories. But...nothing.

There was no collapse. No ache. No bitterness. Just quiet. And then—unexpectedly—my eyes welled up. Not in the chest-heaving, heartbreak kind of way. These tears were gentle. Unrushed. They slid down my cheeks like warm rain after a long drought.

I reached up to wipe them, surprised by how soft they felt. Not heavy. Not angry. Just...tender. I wasn't crying because he got married. I was crying because I didn't care as much as I thought I would.

I cried because this moment, the one I had dreaded for years, had finally arrived, and instead of shattering me, it passed through me like a breeze. The liberation was profound. I had survived the worst of it long ago. And now, all that was left was the quiet release of a fear I no longer needed to carry.

I studied the photo again, taking in the image of him standing there in that ornate outfit, his long, hippie hair tied back in a loose knot. He looked like a completely different person—foreign, almost theatrical. I didn't recognize him anymore. He wasn't the man I had once cried over in the dark. He wasn't the man I had imagined building a life with.

He had changed. And so had I.

The version of us I used to hold onto—the shared future I once ached for—no longer fit who I was now. That vision had faded, like an old photograph left out in the sun.

And in that moment, I felt something I didn't expect: gratitude.

Gratitude that I'd told him how I felt just last week. That I had finally spoken the words I'd kept inside for too long. Saying it all out loud—messy, honest, unscripted—had lifted a weight off me. It made this moment feel lighter, like I could breathe through it.

"No, I didn't know." I finally replied to Jaka.

His reply came quickly: "How do you feel about this?"

I paused, checking in with myself. My heart felt still. No tightness in my chest, no lump in my throat. Just clarity.

"To be honest...I feel fine. Actually, I'm surprised by how okay I feel. I thought this day would wreck me. But it didn't. I'm genuinely fine."

Seconds later, Jaka responded with his usual blunt humor: "I'm glad you didn't end up marrying him! Look at his hair now! He's turned into such a cliché—a brokenhearted white guy in Ubud who becomes a hippie and marries a local Balinese girl."

I laughed—an actual, full-bodied laugh that came from somewhere real. "Yeah," I said aloud, to no one in particular. "Who would've thought, right?"

Life really does have a twisted sense of humor. The moments we once feared might break us often pass with barely a bruise. And sometimes, they don't shatter us at all. They set us free.

***

There's a strange kind of beauty in hitting rock bottom. Beneath the crushing weight of it all, there's this tiny, almost terrifying opportunity—a chance to hit reset. When my love life fell apart—the canceled wedding, the future I'd planned suddenly dissolving—it wasn't a gentle landing. It was like a vase, maybe one I'd cherished, slipping through my fingers and shattering on the floor. Hundreds of sharp, jagged pieces of me, scattered everywhere.

And god, the fall hurt. The pain, as blinding as it was, *was* the harsh, unwanted light forcing me to actually see the fragments scattered across the floor of my life.

At first, you just want to find them all, shove them under the rug and pretend it never happened. It's tempting, isn't it? To just sweep up the mess, toss it out and buy a brand new, shiny vase and pretend to be whole. But I knew if I did that, I'd miss the point. I wouldn't understand *why* the vase fell in the first place. Why *my life* fell apart.

So, I began the slow, painstaking process of gathering the pieces one by one. I looked at each shard, *really* looked at them. I turned each piece over in my hands. *Does this still fit? Does this still feel like...me?* In trying to rebuild, I was forced to re-examine every single part of my life, my beliefs, my expectations.

Some pieces just didn't align anymore. The repair isn't perfect, maybe a little asymmetrical, with visible lines where the breaks had been kintsugi'd[10] back together with newfound understanding. Old dreams, old habits, old ways of seeing relationships—they felt foreign, like they belonged to a different vase altogether. And that's okay, too.

That canceled wedding was my shattering point. And diving back into the world, especially the weird, sometimes wonderful, sometimes soul-crushing world of dating apps, became part of my reconstruction. I half-jokingly started calling it my *Swipe Therapy*, like retail therapy when you're feeling down, but instead of buying shoes I didn't need, I *was* endlessly swiping. Honestly, at first, maybe it was just about distraction, a low-stakes way to feel... something other than heartbroken. It'd be a quick hit of validation from a match notification, a momentary escape scrolling through profiles or maybe just a reason to put on actual clothes and leave the apartment for a date with a stranger. It felt vaguely proactive, like doing something tangible when my whole life felt stalled.

---

[10] Kintsugi is basically the ultimate glow-up for your broken stuff: the Japanese art of fixing cracked pottery with gold, making its "flaws" part of its fabulous new story instead of trying to hide them

But "therapy" turned out to be surprisingly accurate, just not necessarily in the quick-fix way I first imagined. It wasn't about finding "The One" to magically heal me. Instead, the process itself, the act of putting myself back out there, interaction by interaction, became therapeutic. This *Swipe Therapy* evolved into a real-time laboratory for figuring myself out. Every swipe, every awkward coffee date, every fleeting connection (or cringey disconnect) was a chance to examine those broken pieces I was slowly gathering. It was a chance to see how they felt out in the real world, to test their edges against someone else's.

Some people were mirrors, reflecting back flaws I needed to own or strengths I'd forgotten. Others showed me entirely new facets of myself I hadn't known existed. Still others taught me, simply, what I didn't want, which turned out to be just as crucial.

Through it all, I had to consciously let go of old beliefs about love and partnership and break patterns that just weren't serving me anymore. It honestly felt like clearing out space, preparing the ground in my own heart for something genuine, whenever it might decide to arrive.

It even made me rethink the whole narrative around dating apps. I started to see how much pressure we—*my generation, maybe?*—put on them. We expect our future partner to be everything: lover, best friend, life coach, therapist, all rolled into one hot, perfect package. An impossible ask for any human, right? Then we hand that impossible checklist over to an algorithm and expect magic. No wonder we get so frustrated and burned out.

What if we set a different expectation on dating apps? What if we lowered the stakes? Maybe it wasn't about finding Mr. Right immediately, but about learning from Mr. Right Now, or Mr. Rebound, or even Mr. Mistake-I-Won't-Repeat. What if every swipe outside the comfort zone, every interaction, wasn't a failure if it didn't lead to forever, because they all serve as...insight? A chance to experiment, to learn, to discover who I was becoming in real-time? Maybe the whole point of dating apps isn't always to find "The One." Maybe it's about finding yourself.

Breakups, of any kind, are brutal. I wouldn't wish that kind of pain on anyone. But standing where I am now, with some distance and a whole lot of perspective, I genuinely believe it all happened for a reason. The biggest lesson? Letting go of the expectation that I'd ever be the exact same person again. I wouldn't be.

I know love will find me whenever I'm truly ready. And as for that messy, painful, transformative chance to rediscover and rebuild myself after my breakup? I am, surprisingly, incredibly grateful.

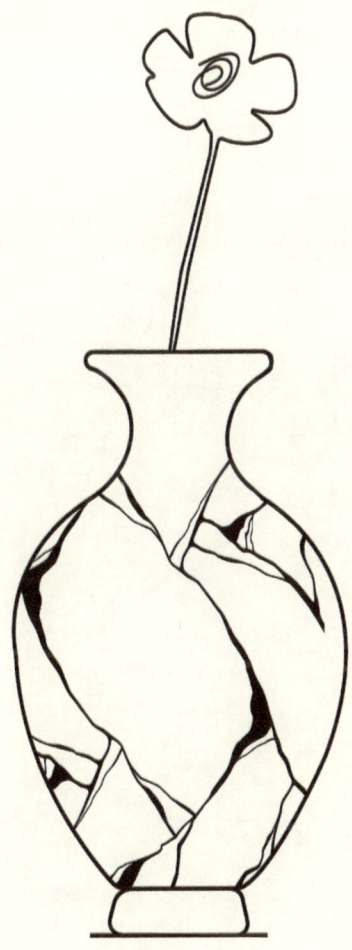

APPENDIX

Guide: How to Survive a Breakup Up In Your 30s

This book was never meant to be written as a self-help book. But after navigating what felt like my own monumental breakup disaster, I picked up a few things. Maybe, just maybe, some of the messy lessons I learned crawling out of the wreckage can help if you're going through something similar right now. (Seriously, I feel you. Hang in there!)

Breakups suck at any age; we know this. But having your world implode right around the big 3-0, when you thought you had the blueprint sorted (great career by late 20s, married by 30, maybe a kid or two by 35—sound familiar?) and suddenly you're single again…just in time for the existential dread of a new decade to kick in? Yeah. That sucks a little extra. Especially when your friends are getting engaged or having babies left and right.

Time does eventually take the edge off a broken heart. And since I somehow managed to navigate my recovery without completely losing my mind (the jury's still out on this one), here are my hard-won tips for surviving a breakup…in your 30s.

1. CLING TO YOUR JOB LIKE A LIFE RAFT

Honestly, the *last* thing you need when your heart is in pieces is to also be broke and adrift. Your job—even if it's not your passion, even if your boss is annoying—is your anchor right now. It's 40-plus hours a week where you *have* to focus on something other than the Dark Pit. It provides structure, a routine and maybe even a tiny sliver of purpose. (Thanks, corporate overlords?)

Plus, pro tip from me and countless heartbroken friends: You might actually get *better* at your job post-breakup. All that energy you poured into your ex? Channel it into that next big project; nail that presentation. Getting those work wins provides a much-needed confidence boost when everything else feels shaky. So, seriously, unless your job is genuinely toxic, resist the urge to rage-quit right now. Don't do it!

2. ASSEMBLE YOUR BREAKUP RESPONSE TEAM (AKA YOUR BREAKUP BFFS)

You need your people. Specifically, find that friend (or friends) who *gets it*. Ideally, someone who's weathered a similar storm and won't judge your 2 am sobbing calls and is available for emergency wine/ice cream/venting sessions 24/7. Bonus points if you have BFFs in different time zones! Because sometimes the urge to dial the 1-800-CRYING hotline strikes at 3 am your time. Having a bestie on the other side of the world who's just starting their day? Genius.

3. SET UP YOUR EMO-GENCY FUND

We all know saving for a rainy day is important. Well, consider this your emotional downpour fund. High emotions + impulsive decisions = potential financial disaster. The EMO-gency fund is your safety net.

Here's how it works: Put aside some disposable income specifically for emotional first aid. Rule No.1: You can spend it on *whatever the fuck you want* to soothe your soul (within reason, maybe). Rule No. 2: You can *only* spend what's in the EMO-gency fund. This prevents you from making huge, regrettable financial decisions while you're vulnerable. Know thyself—if you're an emotional spender, maybe pad it a bit more.

Been eyeing those Chloé boots? Go for it (if it's in the fund!). A spontaneous trip to find yourself in Bali? Do it! Two boxes of fancy macaroons because you deserve them? Absolutely. Permission granted, guilt-free (within budget!).

EMO-gency item	Description	Amount
Therapy	Talk therapy with a professional to help you process the breakup	10 x $100
Healing retreat	Two weeks all-inclusive lux healing retreat to Bali. Because if you're going to cry your heart out with strangers, you want to do it in style	$3,500 + flight ticket
Yolo trip(s)	A few solo or girls trip to party and have fun	3 x $2,000
Retail therapy	A guilt-free emotional shopping splurge budget that allows you to buy whatever your heart desires	$5,000
Total		$15,500 (yes, breakup ain't cheap 😉)

IMAGE 27: *EMO-gency Budget Sample*
(amount may differ based on where you live)

4. GO ON A SWIPE THERAPY & GET A REBOUND

Okay, let's talk dating...or rather, *rebounding*. Remember that *Swipe Therapy* I mentioned? This is where it can really come into play, but handle with care.

If you feel up to it (and only if!), dip your toe back in. Get on the apps. Swipe a little. Chat with someone cute. Go on a low-pressure date. It's about reminding yourself that you're desirable, that other people exist and frankly, just practicing how to interact with potential romantic interests again. It's a confidence booster. Take it *slow*. If you don't feel like meeting anyone, don't, but be honest with them.

Now, rebounds. Controversial, but often critical. Depending on the breakup's severity, you might need different kinds—someone to talk to (mental), someone to make you feel attractive (emotional), someone for...well, you know (physical). The point is *not* to find your next life partner right now.

Crucial PSA: Do. Not. Fall. For. The. Rebound. Why? Because your judgment is shot to hell right now. You're hurting, maybe lonely and it's easy to mistake temporary relief for true connection. Someone just "okay" can seem like a knight in shining armor when you're in the depths. Don't trust those feelings (yet)! You need stability, not more drama. Rebounds are Mr./Ms Right Now, designed to give you a little boost (some validation, maybe some fun) to help climb out of the darkest pit.

5. MASTURBATE

If you haven't already, now is the time to explore the fine art of self-pleasure. Invest in a good vibrator (or several!). Feeling down, anxious or just need a quick mood lift? Masturbation delivers endorphins on demand, zero potential for *BoyDrama* or awkward morning-afters. Bliss. Plus, let's add a feminist angle: taking charge of your own pleasure? Damn empowering.

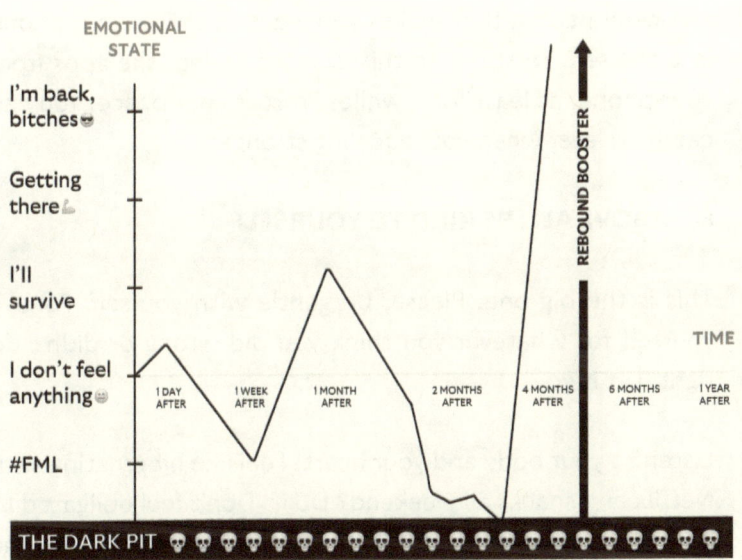

IMAGE 28: *Rebound Booster*

6. MOVE YOUR BODY, MOVE THE SADNESS

Find a sport or activity you enjoy (or can tolerate)—yoga, running, boxing, spin class, pole dance, whatever—and *commit*. Build it into your routine. Make it your go-to response when the sadness hits. Feeling overwhelmed? Hit the gym/mat/trail. Saw an old photo that stung? Sweat it out. Would-have-been anniversary? Channel that energy into smashing your personal best. Like orgasms, exercise releases those lovely endorphins, nature's own antidepressants. Your mind (and maybe your butt) will thank you.

7. LOG OFF SOCIAL MEDIA

Scrolling through Instagram when you're heartbroken is a self-inflicted torture. The endless parade of engagements, weddings, adorable babies and perfect couple vacations. It's comparison culture on steroids, designed to make you feel like the world's biggest failure/loneliest person. It will induce a visceral nausea that makes you want to throw your phone into the sea. Trust me on this: *Log Off*. Delete the apps from your phone, at least for a while. Protect your peace. You can catch up later when you're feeling stronger.

8. ABOVE ALL: BE KIND TO YOURSELF

This is the big one. Please, be gentle with yourself. Forgive yourself for whatever you think you did wrong or didn't do right. Let it go.

Listen to your body and your heart. Feel like hibernating with Netflix and snacks all weekend? Do it. Don't feel obligated to be "on" for anyone. Your real friends will understand. Feel the urge to go out dancing until dawn to shake it off? Do that too.

There's no "right" way to heal, and it's definitely not linear. Some days will be better than others. Just keep putting one foot in front of the other, be patient and know that this chapter *will* eventually end. You'll look back one day and see it for what it was: a painful, messy but ultimately survivable part of your story. You've got this.

ACKNOWLEDGEMENTS

When my wedding was canceled, I never set out to write a memoir. I wrote simply because I loved journaling, because I needed to express my feelings and because it was therapeutic. Then, one day, my sister heard my stories and said, "Your life sounds like chick lit." It was then that the idea for this book came to life. The journey of writing it became a therapeutic process all over again—a chance to look back at all the broken pieces and make sense of them.

So my first and most heartfelt thank you goes to my sister. Thank you for inspiring me to write this book, for getting engaged not long after my breakup (and forcing me to confront my own wedding fears!), for being my non-judgmental confidant and for always being the wiser one.

To my mother, thank you for trusting me with all my crazy decisions and for supporting me in your own way. Most importantly, you reminded me there's no point in worrying about what other people think of our life choices.

To my number one breakup BFF and my 1-800-CRYING hotline, Mabuk, thank you for always picking up the phone. And to my whole Morabito crew, my Amsterdam and Jakarta BFFs—Ibti, Gerald, Linda, Lieke, Marieke, Ela, Casper, Paulo, Tati, Natasha,

Bergas, Amir, Rama, Akina, Tia, Nurul, Teguh, and Mario—thank you for your unwavering support and for dancing with me through my sorrows.

To the dancefloors and the DJs who provided a space to move through my pain, my deepest gratitude, in particular to Optimo (forever my favorite!) and the queen, Nicole Moudaber.

To all the swipes, men and rebounds I met along the way (whether featured in this book or not), thank you! Thank you! Thank you! Every encounter was a lesson, a piece of the puzzle that ultimately helped me find myself. And to my ex—yes, THE ex—thank you for the times we had together, and for, ironically, giving me the best material for this book.

To the therapists and mental health providers who helped me heal, thank you for illuminating my patterns, embracing my quirks and helping me process my traumas.

To my incredible managers, colleagues and the wonder women at Google—Veronica, Fibri, Firda, and Sapna—you are a force of nature. Thank you for inspiring me to seek balance in my life. This book was written in the quiet hours after long days of tackling campaigns and planning decks. And thank you, Google, for making work a place of constant inspiration and for paying my bills so I could build my "EMOgency" fund when I needed it most.

To Feli and Amanda, thank you for believing in my creative vision from the very beginning and for being my trusted sounding board. And to my creative collaborators—Gemma, Firda, Alfonso, Antti, Sedat, Beng, Priscilla and Astrid—who helped make it a reality.

To my publisher, Legacy Launch Pad: Anna, Kaitlin, Jennifer, Serena, Kate, and Ryan. Thank you for being my biggest cheerleaders and for making the entire process not just manageable, but truly fun! And to the lovely folks at Brand Builders Group: Isla, Ben, Emily and Larissa. Thank you for your constant strategic support and for helping me crystallize the answer to "what do I want to do with this book after it's out?"

To God, in the name of Allah, for always being so kind to me, and for unfailingly showing me the light.

And last but not least, to the one who always believes in me even when I don't believe in myself, my forever Halloween partner in crime, the best father to our son Daniel, and the love of my life: Theo. Thank you for entering my life when I was finally ready. And don't you worry—the sequel is all yours.

ABOUT THE AUTHOR

Mira Sumanti is a global marketing executive, creative storyteller and pragmatic romantic whose international adventures greatly inform her writing. Originally from Indonesia, Mira spent over a decade living between Europe and Asia, working for companies like Adidas and Google (and with global icons like Justin Bieber and Snoop Dogg). When she's not leading creative teams or launching marketing campaigns, Mira can be found throwing Halloween parties, curating lifestyle content or planning her next Bali escape. *Swipe Therapy* is her debut book.

For more information about Mira Sumanti,
scan the QR code below

ABOUT THE PUBLISHER

Legacy Launch Pad is a boutique publishing company that works with entrepreneurs from all over the world.

For more information about Legacy Launch Pad Publishing, go to: www.legacylaunchpadpub.com.

www.ingramcontent.com/pod-product-compliance
Lightning Source LLC
LaVergne TN
LVHW092014090526
838202LV00031B/2642/J